TH
BEHIND
IN THE YEAR'S MOST
SENSATIONAL MURDER TRIAL

On the night of May 1, 1990, a single shot
shattered the peaceful town of Derry, New
Hampshire and catapulted it into the spotlight
of worldwide attention. Twenty-four-year-old
Gregory Smart lay dead, a bullet from a .38
revolver in his head. A year later, his twenty-
three-year-old bride of one year stood trial for
his murder in a sensational courtroom drama
of lust, hate and seduction that mesmerized the
nation.

Here is the scandalous story behind the headlines. Written by Stephen Sawicki, the *only* national reporter to cover the case from arrest to
conviction, he has interviewed friends, neighbors, former classmates and family members
of both killer and victim to write THE SHOCK-
ING TRUE STORY OF PAMELA SMART—THE
SCHOOLTEACHER WHO GAVE LESSONS IN
LOVE . . . AND MURDER.

Teach Me to Kill

STEPHEN SAWICKI

AVON BOOKS ◈ NEW YORK

TEACH ME TO KILL is an original publication of Avon Books. This work has never before appeared in book form.

AVON BOOKS
A division of
The Hearst Corporation
1350 Avenue of the Americas
New York, New York 10019

First Avon Books Printing: November 1991

AVON TRADEMARK REG. U.S. PAT. OFF. AND IN OTHER COUNTRIES, MARCA REGISTRADA, HECHO EN U.S.A.

Printed in the U.S.A.

RA   10 9 8 7 6 5 4 3 2

Teach Me to Kill

Acknowledgments

I owe many unpayable debts to the people who allowed me into their lives to share what they know about the murder of Gregory Smart. More people than anyone will ever know—families, extended families, friends, teachers, even entire communities—suffered greatly because of this tragedy. My apologies to any of them if my presence or questions in any way deepened their sorrow. Many others sacrificed much of their personal lives to see that justice was done. I thank them for taking even more time away from their jobs, family, and friends to assist me with this book.

Some sources spoke or provided information on the condition that they not be named. I have, of course, respected their wishes and hope they know how deeply I value their assistance and in some cases their friendship.

Many people consented to both lengthy and brief interviews for this book, all of which helped shed light on the case and the personalities involved.

My appreciation to: Paul Maggiotto and Diane Nicolosi of the New Hampshire attorney general's office; Paul Twomey and Mark Sisti, attorneys for Pamela Smart; Dr. Roger Fossum, New Hampshire chief medical examiner; Edda Cantor, superintendent, New Hampshire State Prison for Women, Goffstown, New Hampshire.

Also: William and Judith Smart, Elaine Flynn, Diane and Vance Lattime, Patricia Randall, Cecelia Pierce, Cecelia and Allen Eaton, Danny Blake, Tom and Heidi Parilla, Steven Payment, Ted Chappell, Terri Schnell, Brian Washburn, Sonia and Chris Simon, Dave Bosse, Rich LaFond, Yvon Pellerin, Paul Reis, Steve Schaffer, Joseph O'Leary, James Weiss, Barbara Kinsman, Leonard Barron, Harvey and Mary Jane Woodside, Judy Liessner, Paul Dacier, and Art Hughes, among others.

From the Derry police department: Chief Edward B. Garone, Capt. Loring Jackson, Sgt. Barry Charewicz, Sgt. Vincent Byron, Dan Pelletier, Michael Surette, Michael Raymond, and Gerald Scaccia.

My appreciation also to Pamela Smart, who agreed to be interviewed by telephone from the New Hampshire State Prison for Women in Goffstown on December 21, 1990 with the understanding that the material not appear prior to her trial.

Linda and John Wojas, the parents of Pamela Smart, were interviewed for several hours in the course of working on an article that appeared in *People* magazine.

Thanks also to the staffs of the Derry, New Hampshire, public library; Boston public library; Lawrence, Massachusetts, public library; Lane Memorial Library, Hampton, New Hampshire; Brown Library, Seabrook, New Hampshire; Pollard Memorial Library, Lowell, Massachusetts; Haverhill, Massachusetts, public library; and the Dimond Library at the University of New Hampshire in Durham.

From the time that Gregory Smart was found murdered through the conviction of his wife nearly eleven months later, the media covering the case has at times been harshly, and often unjustly, criticized. Few of the reporters that I met while working on this book have been anything other than professional. I am indebted to many of them for their kindness, insights, and in several cases, friendship.

Thanks to: Christopher Dorobek, *Foster's Daily Democrat*; Pendleton Beach and Diane Rietman, Nashua *Telegraph*; Linda Bean, The *Lawrence Eagle-Tribune*; Bill Spencer, formerly of WMUR-Channel 9; Ric Waldman, *New Hampshire Seacoast Sunday*; and freelance correspondent Tami Plyler.

Special thanks to Kevin J. Rieke, Valencia, California, for his research into the death of James William Flynn.

This book originated as a story for *People* magazine. Thank you for your kind words, friendship, and encouragement, to: John Saar, assistant managing editor; Sue Brown, Boston correspondent; and Dirk Mathison, San Francisco bureau chief.

Thanks also to my agent, Mitchell Hamilburg, and my editor, Thomas J. Colgan.

Finally, my love always to my father Peter Sawicki, Leslie Graham, James Young, Keith LaBott, Beth Albert, and Mark Palmer. And, of course, Mary Alice Welsh.

Author's Note

For readability, a number of conversations in this book have been reconstructed from statements made by key participants. A variety of people and materials were tapped for this information, but author interviews and court testimony were the primary sources.

A number of other conversations, including courtroom dialogue and the secretly recorded conversations between Pamela Smart and Cecelia Pierce, are derived from television line-feed tape recordings of Smart's trial at the Rockingham County Superior Court in Exeter, New Hampshire, in March 1991. The transcriptions are mine.

In the Smart trial, as in most court cases, the testimony of various witnesses was at odds. Weighing the different sides, I have provided those scenarios I regard as the most likely.

Raymond Fowler was the fourth teenager in the car the night that Greg Smart was killed. As of this writing, he is charged with accomplice to first-degree murder, conspiracy to commit first-degree murder, attempted first-degree murder, and tampering with evidence. He has pleaded not guilty to all charges, and his trial is scheduled to begin in late 1991. Plea bargaining appears to be a strong possibility.

On a lesser note, Pamela and Gregory Smart each had a unique way of spelling their nickname. Pamela signed hers "Pame," which she pronounces as "Pam," and Gregory wrote "Gregg." To spare the reader, I have used the more traditional spellings—Pam and Greg—throughout this book.

Lastly, many innocent people, including juveniles, unwittingly were swept into the events that surrounded Gregory Smart's murder. To protect the privacy of certain individuals, I have changed their names in this book. Jenny Charles, Sal Parks, Tommy Sells, Johnny Mylo, Louise Coleman, and Robby Fields are fictitious names.

Prologue

In southern New Hampshire there is a road that some call Death Highway.

It begins at the sea in the resort community of Hampton Beach. There it is known as Route 51. But after a few miles westward, it becomes Route 101. And if you follow that mostly two-lane roadway from end to end you will have traversed Rockingham County.

Despite the nickname, it is a pretty road, gently rising and flattening and snaking by marshes and woods and streams. In the spring, the roadside grows lush and wild; in the autumn it blazes with yellow and scarlet.

It connects two worlds, taking you away from life on the ocean, with the neon arcades and cheap souvenir shops and stifling tourist traffic, through quiet towns and by peaceful homes on into Hillsborough County and the edge of the state's largest city, Manchester.

It is also a fearsome road, one that over the years has claimed numerous lives in the carnage of unending traffic accidents, and thus its moniker. Most drivers follow the advice of the roadside signs and keep their headlights on day and night—to alert oncoming traffic—like one continuous funeral procession.

So many have died, in fact, that local communities have taken to hammering in white crosses along the highway to commemorate the dead and to send a message to state officials about widening it.

At night, it is perhaps the eeriest road in America. Lighted only by the moon and your headlights, the crosses appear luminously out of the darkness and the fog as you push on for your destination.

One spring evening in 1990, four teenage boys drove that road in an old Chevrolet Impala belonging to one of their grandmothers. They lived in working-class Seabrook, on

1

the ocean, and put a couple dozen miles of pavement behind them before they got off at the exit that led to Derry.

And there they went to the part of town where a young man, Gregory Smart, lived. They had never even met him. Yet two of the youths crept into his house and waited. When Smart came home from work, they killed him.

Eleven months later, through most of the blustery month of March 1991, an unusually large number of people got to know the road those boys had traveled. Numerous journalists, attorneys, and the just plain curious all made their way onto at least a strip of it.

For not far from that road in the town of Exeter, a trial was taking place. A jury had been selected to decide the fate of one Pamela Ann Smart, the victim's twenty-three-year-old wife.

Millions of words had been churned out about the case. The trial would include everything reporters could have hoped for—love and hate, sex, violence, even the skulduggery of secretly recorded conversations.

Certainly there were legal points to be won and lost, testimony to be weighed, issues to be analyzed.

But at the core of it all, the trial was about control. The crux of the matter was whether Pam Smart, driven by demons of her own, used love and lust to convince a sixteen-year-old named Billy Flynn, and in turn his friends, to commit a brutal crime.

Actually, the central question laid before those seven women and five men was not complicated at all: Did Pamela Smart point the boys down that road to murder her husband?

Chapter 1

Derry, New Hampshire, is a bedroom community. Every weekday morning by seven o'clock, hundreds of the town's residents are in their cars, swarming down Interstate 93 for Boston and the high-tech firms on that city's outskirts. Or they are off for nearby Nashua. Or Manchester. Or the gritty cities of Lawrence and Haverhill in Massachusetts' Merrimack Valley. Or the seacoast.

Most of the people who live in Derry are employed somewhere else, but no one minds very much. After all, work was usually not the main reason they came to southern New Hampshire. They came to get away. And except for the sacrifice of time and the test of their patience during their daily commutes, escape they did.

More often than not, they came from Massachusetts. Both white and blue collar, they left behind excessive taxes, a real estate market that was bursting through the roof, and the fear born of drugs and crime. More than anything, they simply came to get some quiet and to enjoy the fresh air and open space of New Hampshire.

Derry, like the other towns near the Massachusetts–New Hampshire border, had a lot to offer within its thirty-five-square-mile boundary: decent schools, a sense of security, and store clerks who smiled. It was Main Street come to life. And nothing exemplified it better than the pride that the citizenry exhibited in 1961 when native son Alan Shepard became the first American to be rocketed into outer space. After that, Derry started calling itself Spacetown, U.S.A.

So it only made sense that when the newcomers started pouring into Derry they kept pouring in. In 1960, a few years before the interstate opened nearby, fewer than seven thousand people called Derry home. Over the next thirty years—the eighties the busiest period—that number would quadruple.

With the new faces came apartment complexes and condominiums and a new feel to the town. Hood Commons, a shopping center, opened over on Crystal Avenue. And Broadway, the strip that constituted downtown Derry, lost its prominence as the heart of town.

Much of Derry remained rural, but the small-town flavor, like the numerous family farms that once were prevalent, was virtually gone. Many of the newcomers lacked a true stake in Derry, gone as they were from early morning until after nightfall. They came home after work, shut their doors, and did not open them again until the next day's push down the interstate started all over.

As the population grew so did the crime rate. It only made sense that the days of unlocked doors were past. "We get a lot of people who moved up here seeking the geographical solution to their problems," explained one Derry policeman. "But they just brought them with them."

Break-ins were not unusual. Drug busts. Child abuse. An assault here and there. Perhaps a biker gang every now and then that needed to be put back in its place. But all in all the lid was on. At least folks in Derry were not killing each other as they were, for instance, in Boston. Who was not glad these days to be leaving Beantown for New Hampshire when the workday was over? Every morning the Boston newspapers were blaring about street gang wars and innocent bystanders who ended up either in the hospital or the morgue. Every new story updated the city's worst-ever homicide rate.

Then, in January 1990, came the revelations about the notorious Charles Stuart, who grabbed national headlines when he apparently murdered his pregnant wife in a tough Boston neighborhood and blamed it on a black man. All this before he jumped off a bridge to his death.

At least the residents of Derry did not have to contend with that sort of madness.

It was well into 1990, after all, and Derry's homicide body count was holding fast at zero. And with the blossoming of the lovely New Hampshire spring, no one was expecting any changes anytime soon.

Tuesday, May 1 had arrived with some clouds and drizzle.

By afternoon, though, the sun had broken through and the temperatures pushed up to the high sixties. It was pleasant enough for a round of golf at the public Hoodkroft Country Club, a minute from downtown Derry. Or a bicycle ride along the town's gently graded backroads. Or a nice jog.

For the Derry police it had been business as usual all day. The DWI traffic accident of mid afternoon faded into the juvenile shoplifter around dinnertime, which in turn faded into a routine arrest of a twenty-one year old wanted on some bench warrants. A false alarm sounded. A car accident. A handful of traffic stops with warnings issued rather than summonses.

About a mile from the police department, down and behind Hood Commons, the residents of Summerhill Condominiums were settling in for the night. Those who lived in the clusters of beige town houses, built on what was once the sprawling Hood dairy farm, were often educated young professionals, many with one or two kids.

Despite the closeness of the dwellings, most neighbors were not on a first-name basis. Friendships tended to be forged when couples had children the same age. For the rest it was hello, hello at the garage, then off to work.

Clouds hid the stars. As ten o'clock passed, the residents had put their children to bed and were now finally sitting down themselves to catch up on their spouse's day or simply to click off their minds in front of the television.

It was around 10:10 when the silver 1987 Honda CRX wheeled into the complex and the cul-de-sac idyllically named Misty Morning Drive. HALEN read the green on white New Hampshire vanity plate—a tribute to the heavy metal rock and roll band Van Halen. Underneath, as on all plates around the state, was the motto "Live Free or Die."

The car rolled into the garage. Pam Smart stepped out and made her way along the walk, past her husband Greg's 1989 Toyota pickup that was parked out front, to the end unit that the couple rented.

Oddly, the front light was off. Pam climbed the few wooden steps to the porch and opened the storm door. She inserted her key into the front door, pushed it open, flicked on the light, and took a single step inside.

Her scream that next instant was wordless and shrill and resonant enough to be heard in most of the surrounding units. Neighbors stiffened. A birthday party halted in the middle of "Happy Birthday." A number of parents immediately bolted for their own children's rooms, fearing it was their kids.

"Help! My husband! My husband!" Pam shrieked as she hurried to the adjacent unit. She rang the doorbell and began banging on the door. Her screams were chilling. "My husband's hurt! He's on the floor! I don't know what's wrong with him!"

In unit 4D, Kimberly Mercer, who worked as a contracts administrator, and her fiancé, Paul Dacier, a lawyer, had been upstairs in their bedroom chatting. Kim's nine-year-old daughter from her first marriage had just gone to bed. Then they heard Pam's screams and the pounding on the door.

"Oh my god, Paul, she needs help!" said Kim. "Something's wrong!"

They ran downstairs. Kim started for the door, but Dacier told her no. Not knowing what awful scene was unfolding outside, just that this hysterical woman seemed to be trying to come through the door, Dacier leaned against it to keep it shut and told Kim to call 911.

Mercer did so. "I need a policeman at 4D, Misty Morning Drive!" she shouted into the phone.

"OK. What's going on over there, ma'am?" asked the Derry police dispatcher, Sergeant Vernon Thomas.

"*4D, Misty Morning Drive!*"

"Where are you, ma'am?"

"Summerhill Condominiums!"

"Where are you? What number?"

"*4D*! As in David!"

"OK, calm down. Can you tell me what's going on there? Do you know?"

"There's a woman screaming outside!"

"OK. We'll send someone over."

"Please! It's an emergency!"

Pam, meanwhile, gave up on 4D and broke for the next one down, 4C. Again she started banging and screaming. Judy and Chris Liessner were just about to go to bed when they heard the commotion.

"I went downstairs and I saw this young girl outside, banging on the door, and I really didn't even know who she was," recalled Judy, who is in her mid twenties and who works as a software engineer. "She just was carrying on and crying, so I opened the door and pulled her in because she was looking behind her like someone was following her. I pulled her in and I shut the door behind her.''

"Dial 911!" Pam said. "My husband's on the floor! I don't know what's wrong!"

Judy rushed to call the police while her husband tended to Pam.

"What is going on there?" asked dispatcher Thomas when the call came through.

"There's someone passed out," said Judy. "I don't know. A girl is hysterical in here. She just ran over. Her husband is passed out in 4E."

"OK, we've got units on the way. Do you know why he's passed out there, ma'am? Do you have any—"

"Help is on the way!" Judy shouted to Pam. "Do you know why he's passed out?" She turned back to the phone. "No, we don't know."

Not much of what happened that night would ever become completely clear to Judy. For one, she could not figure out why Pam kept refusing Chris Liessner's offers to go and help her husband. More nonsensical, even a year later, were the words Pam had uttered shortly after she came into their foyer: "Why do they keep doing this?"

In the bedlam of the moment it little mattered what she was talking about. By now, a half-dozen neighbors were out on their stoops to see what was happening. Art Hughes, a station manager for an air delivery service in Manchester, had been watching *thirtysomething* when he heard Pam's screams.

He rushed over from his building off to the left, ran between the structures, and looked for the woman he had heard. He saw no one. He went to the front of Pam's building where he heard Pam's shrieks once again, only this time she was coming out of 4C onto the stoop.

Art felt certain that her husband had been beating her.

"What's wrong?" Hughes yelled. "What's the problem?"

"My husband's on the floor!"

"What's wrong with him?" Hughes shouted back. "Where is he?"

Pam pointed toward her unit and Hughes, in his bedtime T-shirt and sweatpants, frantically ran out in front of unit

4E, looking madly into parked cars and all over the parking lot and lawn.

"Where the fuck is he?" he shouted in despair.

"Inside!" Pam yelled from the Liessners' stoop. "He's inside!"

Hughes bolted up the steps and went to open the storm door when he heard Pam again.

"Don't go in there!" she said. "There may still be somebody in there!"

At this, Hughes' wife also started yelling. "Arty! Don't go in. Be careful!"

Hughes crouched slightly, pulled back the storm door, and pushed open the front door. He didn't realize that another neighbor, Harvey Woodside, was right behind.

The foyer light was on, but the rest of the place was in darkness. As the door opened the first thing they saw, ten feet away, was a brass candlestick, the light playing off it. Then a shod foot. The door fully opened, and the two men surged forward—over the floor mat depicting two cartoon ducks and past a maroon portfolio left carelessly near the entrance—and beheld the facedown body of a man.

The pair froze and stared. The man was dressed in gray pants and a gray sports coat. Looking like a discarded, broken toy, most of his body was on the blue wall-to-wall carpet of the dining area. His legs were splayed, his right arm contorted. Resting on his left cheek, his exposed skin had taken on a nauseating blotchy purple-grayish cast. And a small amount of blood stained the carpet beneath his nose.

Only the man's feet and ankles were on the tiled floor of the foyer. His left foot was twisted against the stairwell wall and pressed against the fallen candlestick. His right foot lay flat, pointing toward them.

Hughes and Woodside instinctively backed off. This was beyond anything they could do.

Outside, Derry patrolman Gerald Scaccia, twenty-seven years old and a four-year veteran, pulled into the complex with his cruiser lights flashing and his siren screaming. He glanced over and saw Pam on her knees on the stoop in front of the Liessners' unit, sobbing and moaning. Woodside's wife, Mary Jane, directed him to 4E.

The patrolman hurried in, Mary Jane in tow, and felt the fallen man's wrist for a pulse. Nothing. Yet his own heart was pounding so hard that Scaccia was picking up his own pulse, making him uncertain of the man's condition.

Mary Jane, then a medical assistant at a hospital, offered to perform CPR, so Scaccia set to rolling the man onto his back.

Suddenly, he saw the bloody hole on the top left side of the man's head.

He stopped. Seconds later, the paramedics confirmed Scaccia's diagnosis: dead.

More police cruisers arrived. Scaccia's backup, Officer John Twiss, hurried in. With their sergeant guarding the door, Scaccia and Twiss took out their guns, Glock 9 mm semiautomatics, and began to search the condo, figuring that whoever did this might still be around.

They moved through the first floor. Beyond the dead man was a combined living room and dining area that took up most of the space. A small kitchen. A bathroom. A couple closets. Contemporary furniture. Nice.

But someone had obviously ransacked the place. A pile of stuffing from what seemed to be a pillow was on the floor. Compact disks were strewn about. The VCR, still hooked up, was upside down on the carpet. A pair of stereo speakers and a small television were by the back door.

Upstairs, the master bedroom was a mess as well. Clothes had been tossed around. Drawers had been pulled out and left overturned. A second bedroom seemed untouched. On the bathroom sink was an empty jewelry box.

Twiss poked his head into the attic and came back down. No signs of life anywhere.

That is, until Scaccia opened the basement door to search there. He started down and stopped suddenly when something near his feet moved.

He looked. There, in the shadows, quietly sitting behind the door, was a tan, shaggy little dog. Cowering.

Outside, all was confusion. More neighbors gathered. More police cars. Yellow crime scene tape was stretched around the house.

At Pam's request, a neighbor called Greg's parents, Bill and Judy Smart, who lived in another condominium complex right around the corner. The panicked caller said that their son was "very, very sick" and that they should come quickly. So the Smarts threw on something over their pajamas, and with their twenty-one-year-old son, Dean, at the wheel of his Camaro speeded to Misty Morning Drive.

When they got there they rushed to 4E, where they were met by Sergeant John Toki, his visage hardened, his body unmoving in front of the entrance. The Smarts tried to brush past, but Toki said no one without authorization could enter. No one.

"What's going on!" shouted Bill Smart. "What's the matter? What's wrong with my son?"

Pam came over to join the Smarts, and Greg's mother pelted her with questions.

"What's wrong with him?" demanded Judy Smart. "What's wrong with him?"

"I don't know," replied Pam.

"Where were you?"

"I was at the school," Pam said. "There was a meeting."

The family was frenzied. Bill Smart, a smallish, middle-aged man with a head of snow-white hair and moustache, tried to bull his way in, but Toki held him back. Judy kicked at the cop, crying and shouting.

"What the hell is wrong with him!" Dean finally pleaded. "For god's sake, if he's sick, someone go in and please help him!"

At this, an official from one of the response teams came down the porch stairs. "We can't help him," he said. "He's already dead."

Seconds later, the door opened and someone stepped out. Bill Smart, standing near the top of the steps, could see the candlestick and then his son—feet to head. From the base of the steps, his wife and youngest son also caught a glimpse of Greg's body.

Judy became hysterical, and the paramedics helped her to the ambulance. As Greg's mother was tended to, Pam seemed dumbstruck, but not screaming or coming visibly unhinged in the least.

"Oh, that poor thing," Mary Jane Woodside whispered to her husband as Pam stood there, looking very alone and forlorn, as the paramedics looked after Judy Smart. "Everybody's giving all the attention to the parents and nobody's even doing anything for her. She looks like she's in total shock."

That night various neighbors went to Pam, the twenty-two-year-old looking like a waif, hugged her, and tried to provide a modicum of comfort. Pam mentioned to one that she suspected trouble when she found the front light out even though Greg's truck was there. She puzzled another when she started talking about Greg and muttered, out of the blue, "He's been so messed up lately."

The family was told that Greg had suffered a head wound; almost everyone assumed the candlestick had done the job.

The police ushered Judy and Pam over to the Liessners' to get them settled down and away from the crime scene. They sat on the couch, both obviously shattered.

Judy's grief could not be contained; her mind and body rebelled at the thought that the second of her three sons was dead. It was all too incomprehensible. She asked the police for a paper bag as she expected to be sick.

Pam was not weeping uncontrollably but seemed unmistakably sad. "What will I do with the rest of my life?" she murmured. No one thought twice when Pam shifted her attention away from the loss of Greg to her worries about her Shih-Tzu and whether he was all right.

Her concern may have seemed a bit misplaced, but everyone wrote it off to shock. It was as if she could not face the awful truth that her husband was dead two doors over so she focused on other things. It was as if shock were protecting her, keeping her sane.

Pam would remain that way much of that long night, even after the dog—named Halen, also after the rock band—was finally brought to her, even after going back with Greg's parents to their condo for a vigil.

No one doubted that Pam was upset. Brian Washburn, one of Greg's closest friends, later recalled getting the telephone call about Greg's death, going over to Greg's parents' place, and seeing Pam seated on the living room floor. "She started crying and I just kneeled down and we hugged," he said. "And she just asked, 'Why?' She said, 'Why would someone do this?' "

Still, surrounded by stunned and desolate family and friends, Pam at times seemed out of sync emotionally. "I walk into the house and Pam starts crying," remembered Tom Parilla, Greg's best man at his wedding just a year earlier. "And I start crying. Then all the sudden she just stops crying."

A minute later, Pam would bewilder Parilla as she nonchalantly moved on to other topics, such as her frustration at not having her contact lens solution, which was inside 4E, Misty Morning Drive, with her dead husband.

Whoever Gregory Smart had been, his problems were officially over at 11:19 when Gene Nigro, an investigator for the New Hampshire Medical Examiner's office, pronounced him dead. It was around that time, though, that a number of other people were just learning that they had a new problem in their own lives—finding out who had done this.

The Derry detectives got to the crime scene and reported to their supervisor, Captain Loring Jackson, to begin the spadework of the investigation.

Jackson, dark haired and heavyset, wore a permanent look of having failed to get enough sleep the night before. Only now, the truth was that he had not. His Rotary Club had met first thing in the morning that day and he had been up since five. When the call came from the station he was home relaxing before turning in for the night.

When Jackson heard it was a homicide, he took a minute or two and was out the door, into his unmarked LTD Crown Victoria, sweeping the maroon beast over the back roads for Summerhill Condominiums.

Jackson, forty-eight years old, had been a cop since 1966, and had grown less and less fond of calls like this. He had been in Derry now for eighteen years and was just a couple more away from nailing down his pension.

The captain had grown up in the suburbs west of Boston, where with his buddies he raised his own brand of hell and set some still unbroken speeding records on the area's usually tranquil streets.

After high school, Jackson kicked around for a few years, went to school with an idea of going into commercial art, but then family life called. He was driving an ambulance, carting around cardiac arrests and head-on colliders, in Natick, Massachusetts, when a friend suggested he apply for a job at the local police department. Jackson had laughed. Imagine that.

Twenty-four years later, after jobs as a cop in Natick and Newport, New Hampshire, he was here in Derry. The job had been hard on Jackson's family and there had been countless apologies to his wife and his four kids, now all grown.

Jackson was looking forward to a normal life, one where he could spend more time on his artwork, painting landscapes and portraits and hand carving decorative ducks. Something with normal hours. Something where half his time did not revolve around lowlifes.

Still, police work had its moments. Jackson's world-weary look gave way to merriment when a bust he and his men were making had a touch of surprise, cops in deliverymen's outfits, for example. Or when a good hunch paid off big time.

There was a camaraderie to police work that he liked, too. And while it was not the same now that he was a captain, Jackson liked the opportunity occasionally to be out of the office and in the field with his small band of detectives.

At 4E, Misty Morning Drive, Jackson dealt out the assignments for the evening: Dan Pelletier would videotape the interior and exterior of the condo. Michael Surette and Barry Charewicz would team up to take the stills and to jot down what they saw. Sergeant Vincent Byron, meanwhile, would do the initial search of the area.

Byron checked around the neighborhood for a while then moved further out. Behind the condos was an unmown grassy hill that gradually stretched up toward the Derry Meadows Professional Park, and, behind that, the shopping plaza. The field was a shortcut that kids sometimes took on their way to the stores or the nearby McDonald's. It seemed like a possible getaway route.

Byron pulled into the professional buildings' parking lot, when suddenly his headlights glimmered off an object. He got out of the car and walked over. There, on a strip of mowed lawn, about one hundred yards back from the Smarts' condo and just beyond the hill, Byron found a long carving knife jabbed into the ground. It had come, he would soon learn, from the Smarts' kitchen. Nearby were a couple pieces of paper towel, a white plastic jewelry box, and two pieces of a cardboard jewelry box.

It was around one o'clock in the morning when Cynthia White and Diane Nicolosi of the state attorney general's office arrived at the condos.

Their job was to oversee the investigation—standard policy that dated back to when New Hampshire was vastly more rural. Having the AG's office in control brought some uniformity to homicide probes. It also prevented the police chief of some fiefdom, who maybe had never even seen a corpse before, from claiming that this was *his* town, and he was going to solve this crime *his* way.

The population boom in southern New Hampshire, however, had changed things. Many police departments were regularly conducting investigations into practically every conceivable crime, and it was not always easy for them to subordinate themselves to one or two prosecutors—usually only a few years out of law school at that—when the most heinous of crimes had occurred in their town.

No one had to like it, but they did have to do it. And for the most part, the AG's office did let the police take care of the daily ins and outs of any given investigation, making demands only when they saw holes that needed to be filled as the trial neared.

Still, it did not go over easy when two women prosecutors, officially called assistant attorneys general, stepped out of the car that morning and said they wanted the state police, with whom they had worked before, and not the Derry police, to process the crime scene.

Jackson and his men grumbled. But then again, no one had to like it.

To get the process going, Detectives Pelletier and Charewicz were sent to the Smarts' condo to ask Pam to sign the standard papers allowing investigators to search her home and Greg's truck.

They found her in the living room, with a doleful expression and her head in her hands, amid the many mourners. With her mother, Pam joined the detectives in the relative quiet of the kitchen, where they chatted briefly.

Pelletier showed Pam the consent-search forms and explained that she had the right not to sign them. Linda Wojas, who worked as a legal secretary, told her daughter that these would save the police having to get search warrants.

As far as Pam was concerned this was not a matter that needed much thought. Of course she would sign.

"I'll do anything I can to help," she said.

Pamela Smart was indeed willing to be of assistance. So much so that it bothered her that Pelletier and Charewicz had only come by to get the consent forms signed and then were leaving. She told some friends and her mother that she did not understand why they did not want to ask her any questions. They, in turn, relayed to the cops that she was anxious to talk.

It was around 2:30 A.M. when the New Hampshire State Police Major Crimes Unit began the arduous task of combing through the apartment, taking more photographs, jotting down everything they saw, gathering evidence, and dusting for fingerprints.

The Derry police, meanwhile, could start some interviews. So Pelletier and Charewicz went back to the home of Greg Smart's parents. Pam came downstairs to meet them with a few of her friends, who in turn drove her to the Derry police department to be interviewed in a quieter setting.

Leaving her friends, Pam went into the interview room and gave the detectives her statement, verbally then in writing.

She worked as media center director for School Administrative Unit 21, the body that manages a number of school districts on the New Hampshire seacoast, Pam explained. Her building was across the parking lot from Winnacunnet High School in Hampton. That evening she had been at a schoolboard meeting because several of the issues being voted on related to her job.

Her husband, who had flexible hours at Metropolitan Life Insurance in Nashua and who worked mornings and at night, had left at 9 A.M. that day. And although she herself usually worked from eight to four, Pam said she had gone in a few hours later, leaving at quarter to ten, because of her night meeting.

When that meeting was over, she drove the forty-five-minute trip back to Derry and discovered Greg sprawled on the floor.

She remembered seeing her husband, a brass candlestick, and what she mistakenly thought was a blue pillow against his head. Having watched television shows like *Rescue 911*, she decided against touching the body and instead began screaming for help.

She wondered aloud why none of the neighbors reported hearing Halen barking as the dog most certainly would have if strangers had entered the house.

As for the condo itself, it was possible, she told the detectives, that Greg may have returned to a darkened house that night as the couple did not usually leave a light on. She and Greg may also have accidentally left the French doors unlocked after having a cookout on the back deck just a couple days earlier, she said.

If the couple was careless in making sure the place was locked, they certainly were not when it came to cleaning. The condo had been immaculate when she left it Tuesday morning, Pam said, having just been thoroughly vacuumed and dusted that weekend.

Pelletier asked most of the questions that night. Barry Charewicz was exhausted and kept nodding off. When the hour-long interview was over, Pelletier was bothered. He could not quite place it but something about the widow was irksome. She had only known her husband was dead for a few hours, yet she was calmer than he would expect. Pam never lost her composure, never fell apart, never cried. Pelletier thought she seemed anxious more than sad. Throughout the interview she had seemed on edge, her eyes shifting nervously all around the room.

Well, the detective said to himself, everyone suffers loss in his own way.

When the sun came up on May 2, it was only the skies that had begun to clear. Now, reporters and photographers and the Manchester television people were arriving, wanting to know all about a crime that did not completely make sense to the investigators themselves.

That morning, state police colonel Mark Myrdek led a half-dozen policemen in a line search of the area where the knife and jewelry boxes had turned up. They were looking for anything that might somehow tie in, anything at all.

But nothing considered of any worth cropped up among the discarded soda cans and candy wrappers. The cops only stopped the line twice for Myrdek to take a closer look at possible evidence. One item was a cigarette. Myrdek ruled it unimportant and disposed of it.

The other was a latex glove. It was slightly dirty and wet from the gentle rain of the early morning. Myrdek looked over at a nearby dumpster, considered the medical offices located in the professional park, and figured the glove had blown over from there.

Trash, he said.

* * *

For everyone—Pam and the police—May first and second seemed like one long day, with sleep coming in snatches, if at all.

For Jackson, countless details needed to be tended to, as after any homicide. He sent his detectives home at 3:30 for a few hours sleep and stayed on himself to work with the state police.

For Pamela, widowhood brought duties as well, from making arrangements with the funeral home to selecting a casket to deciding what clothes her husband should wear.

Jackson was at the crime scene late that morning when two cars with Pam, her family, and friends pulled in. They had come to get some personal items, but Jackson said no one would be allowed inside until late in the afternoon.

As might be expected, Pam was curious about how the investigation was going and whether the police had any ideas about what had happened to Greg.

The captain talked to her for a bit, then sat her down in his car for some follow-up questions.

Jackson was division commander, a supervisor, so he seldom allowed himself to wade too deeply into an investigation. Still, he tried to touch base with the players in the bigger cases, so he at least had a feel for the people he was reading about in the reports.

He started with asking Pam how she was holding up and then moved to more personal matters. Don't be insulted, he said, but these questions have to be asked. Was Greg having an affair? Were you? Did you have money problems? Drug problems?

Point by point, Pam said no.

Like Pelletier, Jackson wondered why this young woman did not cry more. "Her husband hadn't been dead for twenty-four hours yet," he said, "and generally if you've got a victim and you start talking about their husband they'll break down. There were a couple tears, but she did not seem overly remorseful."

At the time, though, that bothered Jackson less than the widow's reaction when he made the routine suggestion that she please not talk to the media. As a courtesy, she was being filled in on the investigation, but to release any details now could be harmful later, he said.

"She got very defensive about the press," Jackson remembered. "She said, 'Don't talk bad about them, I'm one of them too.' That struck me as odd."

After all, Pam was not quite "one of them." She had majored in communications at Florida State University, from which she had graduated a couple of years earlier, and had dreamed of following in the footsteps of Barbara Walters. Instead, she had taken the media center position in Hampton, married Greg, and settled down.

In her job she wrote press releases and ran around to the schools, taking pictures and writing newsletter features about kids designing toothpick bridges and the like. She also purchased media equipment and now and then held workshops for the students in how to use it.

Jackson was taken aback but quickly wrote her reaction off. "My thought was that this woman is showing grief in a little bit of a strange way," he said. "But people do."

Late that afternoon the state police finished their work on the crime scene and Jackson allowed Pam, Greg's father, and Pam's mother inside to choose the clothes for Greg's funeral as well as pick up some odds and ends.

A towel was placed over the large bloodstain where Greg's head had been so the family would be spared. When Pam came in she stunned the cops by walking right on top of it. Not much later she lit into Jackson because he had come in from the rear doors and accidentally closed them on the drapes. Then she started complaining about the black fingerprint dust on her sofa.

"Who's going to clean this up?" she demanded.

Bewildered, the cops said nothing.

Upstairs in the master bedroom she started picking Greg's clothes. Over the years Jackson had been there, Derry had had twelve to fifteen homicides, and as a result he had seen his share of grief-stricken families. Usually they lingered when going through their loved ones' belongings as they tried to select just the right items for the deceased to wear, a favorite tie, perhaps, or a shirt that brought back memories.

Pam hardly hesitated. "It was open the drawer and grab a shirt," remembered Jackson. "First one on the top. It was like, OK, give me some underwear, give me some socks, give me a shirt. Which struck me as somewhat strange. The other cops on the scene were picking up on it too. After she left you'd look at each other and you'd kind of raise an eyebrow.''

Bill Smart looked at what Pam was selecting. He remembered stopping her because nothing matched. He said he would select the clothes. That done, they went to leave. Then Pam stepped outside and broke down.

The crime scene investigation had finally been completed. The cops had canvassed most of the neighborhood. And very little was perfectly clear.

Only one neighbor remembered anything being out of the ordinary the night before. Paul Dacier in 4D had noticed Gregory Smart coming home at around nine and then heard a ''pitter patter'' of what he thought were feet scuffling across the floor as well as two thuds separated by a few minutes. Both sounded like the door slamming.

Only slightly more enlightening was the crime scene itself. A good bet was that whoever did this had come in through either the French doors in back or the bulkhead that led to the cellar. Both were unlocked and seemed not to have been forced open.

Most likely the escape was through the back. A glass-topped table was slightly imbedded in the wall near the rear doors, as if someone had slammed into it while fleeing.

That morning the chief medical examiner, Dr. Roger Fossum, performed the autopsy and ruled that Gregory Smart had been shot once in the head. The bullet, which was medium caliber, had entered from the top of his skull, slightly left of center, and ricocheted within. Smart surely died instantly.

Yet the autopsy only revealed the cause of death, not the way he died. That was another mystery.

Fossum noted that the wound was not clean but torn, a telltale sign that the gun had been extremely close, maybe even touching Smart's head when it was fired.

But other characteristics of such a shooting were missing: No substantial gunpowder residue could be found on Smart's scalp. And lead fragments were recovered from the skin near the wound. That meant the bullet probably had started fragmenting *before* it struck Smart's skull. And, of less significance, no blood from the bullet's impact had splattered on the wall—or anywhere for that matter—near the body.

Nothing was certain, but the best explanation was that something—even an object as soft as a pillow or a towel—had been placed between the gun barrel and Gregory Smart's head. But what? And why? Was it an attempt to muffle the sound? Or was it something even more sinister?

Equally baffling was the blue towel—Pam had told police she thought she saw a blue pillow—that had been found slightly under Smart's head and covering most of the wound on top. It apparently came from the upstairs bathroom. And it made the investigators wonder: Had the killer had a change of heart and tried to help the victim after shooting him? Or was the murderer a neatness freak of some kind, someone who either consciously or unconsciously wanted to avoid bloodying the carpet?

A white paper towel, again inexplicably, had been on the floor just to the right of the body. One had been found under Smart's legs as well.

The condo itself clearly looked as if it had been burglarized. The things near the door appeared to have been set there for quick removal, and it seemed as if Smart's arrival had interrupted matters.

The place had also been torn apart. But upstairs it was neater. Things did not seem to have been strewn about as haphazardly, so there was talk that perhaps two people—one being more fastidious than the other—had been present.

And missing was a black pillow from one of two sets of color-coordinated pink, blue, and black pillows on one of the couches. It only followed that the criminals had emptied the stuffing and used the pillowcase to carry whatever they stole.

Something, though, was just not right about the scene. When Greg Smart's body had been removed about 4:30 that morning, the state police found a three-diamond gold ring that had been beneath him as well as his keys and wallet, which had been between his legs. If he had had any cash, it was gone now, but his credit cards remained.

Indeed, it looked as if Smart had interrupted a burglary and paid for it with his life.

Yet that theory had its problems. For one, it made little sense to rob a high-density condo at night, especially since most of the people who lived there were gone during the day but were usually home in the evening. The gun also seemed out of place, considering that most small-time thieves do not pack firearms. And one would think that a professional robber would want the credit cards and the diamond ring. After all, those items could be quickly turned over for cash. But they had been left.

Someone had said that Greg gambled now and then. He and his parents and friends had often gone to Atlantic City to take in the casinos and the nightlife. Maybe Greg had crossed the wrong people somewhere along the line.

Drug involvement was also a possibility. Certainly some of the neighbors were convinced that a drug deal had gone sour and that Smart had paid the price. After all, they reasoned, a number of loud parties had taken place at unit 4E in the past year, and all kinds of people—long-haired and strangely dressed—were always over. A neighbor had even gone to the condo association to complain about the noise.

For the police, narcotics were as good a guess as any. So when a marijuana cigarette had been discovered during the search of Greg's pickup truck, the state police had brought in two German shepherds, Magnum and Wolf, to sniff around the condo and the neighborhood for narcotics or any other evidence the police may have missed. The dogs found nothing.

Murder always plays well with the media in the Granite State, largely because it happens more seldom there than in Massachusetts and Boston in particular. Derry is also located such that it is saturated by regular coverage not only from its own twice-weekly newspaper but also the dailies out of Manchester, Nashua, and Lawrence, Massachusetts. The state's ABC affiliate, WMUR-Channel 9 in Manchester, also kept regular tabs on happenings in Derry.

So when a twenty-four-year-old life insurance salesman took a slug in the head in his rented upscale condominium, news editors all around knew they had a good one. The morning after, the local reporters descended on Derry, chasing down anyone who knew anything about the killing or the victim. WMUR's Bill Spencer even did a live report from in front of the condo at noon.

Rumors about Greg's involvement in the drug trade were rampant, but were proving difficult to pin down. One of the anchors at channel 9 said on the air that narcotics could have been the motive for the shooting, but most of the media played it safer. Some papers quoted the police as saying this did not appear to be a haphazard attack or a burglary gone awry, but most simply reported that it was too early to say.

Why Smart was killed was a mystery, but the pathos was obvious. Married six days shy of a year, he had been an up-and-comer, co-winner of the regional rookie salesman-of-the-year award at MetLife, seemingly without enemies. "Shooting victim called all-around American boy," read the headline in the *Lawrence Eagle-Tribune*.

Deeper layers of melancholy were to be discovered as well. There was, for one, the aspect of the newlywed wife having found the body. And the reporters also learned about the special relationship Greg had with his father, with whom he worked at MetLife.

"He would give you the shirt off his back," co-worker Bruce Dube told the *Union Leader* out of Manchester. "That's why this is so confusing. He wouldn't hurt anyone."

Paul Breault, the manager at Greg's office, told the Nashua *Telegraph*: "Gregory was always ready to help anybody. He had an excellent sense of humor and was always laughing. He did his best to make everyone smile. He was very much in love with his wife and was very close to his father."

The *Derry News* got hold of the widow's parents. "Pamela Smart's father, John Wojas, of Windham, said his daughter was sad, but bearing up well. 'She keeps asking who will hug me and tell me they love me,' he said. 'She's holding up OK, but now she's brokenhearted.' "

Out on the New Hampshire seacoast, the story earned only a few inches in *Foster's Daily Democrat*. This, after all, was not a story that mattered to people who lived so far from Derry. The only reason it got reported at all was that the victim happened to be married to someone who worked in the school system in Hampton.

"George Smart," was how the paper identified the dead man, "the husband of media center director Pamela Smart."

Greg Smart had been dead about a day and a half, and Bill Spencer, thirty at the time, had just come into work. The son of a former Miss America contestant and a Lincoln Continental salesman, Spencer had the ideal genetic makeup for a television reporter. A native of Detroit, he had started his career with stations in Texas, first in Midland and then in Odessa. He had been one of the first reporters on the scene when little Jessica McClure fell into a well and the rescue efforts mesmerized the nation.

Now, in New Hampshire at channel 9, Spencer had won a reputation as an aggressive reporter. At times, though, his hot pursuit of even the most basic stories irritated local police departments. Particularly bothersome was Spencer's penchant for shouting questions and shoving microphones in suspects' faces when they were being transported in handcuffs to or from court. To many, Spencer was playing big-city reporter in a venue that called for a gentler approach.

Today for Spencer it was back to the Gregory Smart murder. Having done his basic reporting the day before, he was planning to make an attempt to interview the widow. All things considered, her grief would undoubtedly be severe. This was not a mission Spencer was savoring.

Just before he got to his seat, someone called to him. "Hey, guess what, Bill, Pamela Smart's on the phone," he said.

"Yeah, right," Spencer said with a laugh. "Wouldn't that be great."

"I'm serious."

Figuring he was the target of a newsroom prank, Spencer thought he would play along. He picked up the phone and said hello, but rather than the laughter he expected, Spencer heard a small and quick female voice.

"Hello, Bill?" he heard. "This is Pam Smart."

She was calling, she said, because of all the talk that Greg's killing was drug related. She wanted Spencer to know that that was preposterous. She told him that the police were not telling the public what had really happened inside the condo that night. She would like to talk.

That afternoon, not long before Pam was to leave for Greg's wake, she met with Spencer outside her parents' house in Windham. She said she thought it would be inappropriate to be formally interviewed on camera, so soon after Greg's death, but she did allow the cameraman to get some footage of her without sound.

As is standard practice, the police were releasing no details about the crime scene, in order to prevent the killer from covering his trail later. Now, here was the widow, about to go to a wake, perfectly made up, wearing a fuchsia dress (the color, she would later say, that Greg liked best on her), and telling a TV reporter that she was certain Greg had interrupted a burglary. Drugs, she said, had nothing to do with it.

The house had been ransacked, she said, the stereo speakers placed by the door, and her jewelry was missing.

"I just want the truth to be known," Pam told Spencer.

Greg Smart's wake was broken up into two parts, one in the afternoon and the other in the evening. As friends entered the Peabody Funeral Home in Londonderry for the afternoon session, they were startled to see Greg's father in the hallway arguing feverishly with Pam's parents.

"This is my son," Bill Smart was saying emphatically, "and I want the casket open!"

"But Pam wants it closed," said Linda Wojas. "Pam won't go in there if it's open!"

This had not been the first clash between the two willful families since Greg's death. The parents had already exchanged words over what Greg would wear, the site of the wake, and in which town Greg would be buried. Bill Smart and Pam had also disagreed about the gray metal casket Pam had selected.

Then, at the funeral home, Pam had announced that she wanted a closed casket during the wake. Bill Smart, grief stricken and angry because he felt the Wojases were trying to run the show, and simply wanting what he wanted, said no. The coffin would be open, he had said. Pam did not go to war over the issue. She said she would just stay out of the viewing room and they could shut the coffin when she came in.

Now, just as the wake was beginning, the families were back at it. That is, until almost everyone around could hear Bill Smart's voice starting to boom.

"John, you were in that room with me and we agreed on this casket being open," he said to Pam's father. "And it's going to *stay* open!"

Bill Smart turned to Pam's mother before stepping outside to calm down. "Don't close that casket!"

So it went, with Pam out in the hallway greeting the visitors—again crying one minute and collected the next—and the Smart family openly venting their anguish, at times not budging from before the coffin for as long as a half hour, while friends were forced to wait to pay their respects.

Dozens of mourners, young and old, made their way in, embracing Pam and the family, offering their condolences and pouring out their grief. (Pam would later joke with friends that she was glad when the wake was over because everybody had been hugging her and she spent half the time with people's armpits in her face.)

"You guys think of a good saying for the headstone," Pam would say every now and then to friends. "See if you guys can think of something so that Greg will be remembered."

The dead man would not soon be forgotten. The numerous people who passed along their sympathies, in person and from a distance, seemed to guarantee that. Dozens of flower arrangements, even one from the Trump Plaza in Atlantic City, where Greg and his dad had loved to gamble, were overflowing the room.

A sign in the funeral parlor that day also told mourners that a memorial fund had been established in Greg's name. The cause was not medical research or any of the usual charities one would expect. This one was to buy equipment for a mass media course that was to start the following fall at Winnacunnet High School. The class, in fact, had been approved at the school board meeting the very night Greg was murdered.

Its teacher, of course, was to be Pamela.

"I'll know that Greg is a part of my day, every day," she said to a reporter a few days later. "He'll touch the lives of every person who goes through that course in some way. It'll be like a piece of him being there. For me it was important to find something positive out of this tragedy."

Greg was now just a memory. Once he had been the life of every party, his light-brown tresses dangling to his shoulders. True, he had cut his hair and gotten into the insurance business, but everyone still remembered Greg's restless energy and his happy-go-lucky life-style.

These were the darkest days for the young man's friends, many of whom, like Greg, were carefree, heavy metal aficionados. None of them could settle this in their minds. They could understand a traffic accident, maybe if Greg was driving after having had too much to drink. But this?

Why would anyone want to kill Greg? They were certain that drugs had had nothing to do with it.

The only answer that seemed to make sense was that maybe Greg had gotten in a little too deep during one of his forays to Atlantic City. Maybe he owed a lot of money to the wrong people. Maybe this was a professional hit.

One of the few moments that anyone could bring themselves to smile at the wake was when one of Greg's buddies arrived having overlooked zipping his pants. He wandered around as sad faced as anyone, but with a length of his shirt hanging out of his fly.

It was that afternoon, too, that three students and a guidance counselor from Winnacunnet High School, across the way from Pam's office in Hampton, showed up. The counselor, Barbara Kinsman, had heard about the tragedy and knowing that these students—Cecelia Pierce, Billy Flynn, and Vance Lattime, Jr., whom everybody called JR—had become friendly with Pam at school, took it upon herself to bring them to the wake to pay their respects.

They were kids, as stereotypical as could be found anywhere: Billy, who at sixteen had brooding eyes and shaggy dark hair that hung down his neck; Cecelia, who was fifteen, overweight, and clingy; and Vance, seventeen, quiet, inscrutable, and bespectacled.

Pam had gotten to know the kids the previous autumn through a freshman orientation program that Kinsman ran called Project Self-Esteem. A year earlier Pam had written a newsletter story about the three-day drug- and alcohol-awareness program and thought she would like to get involved. When she did, she met Cecelia, Billy, and JR, all of them sophomores.

Pam was closest to Cecelia and Billy, having recently worked for a few months with them on a high school videotape competition. Cecelia was also Pam's student intern in the media center. Vance, meanwhile, was one of Billy's closest friends. He knew Pam more as an acquaintance.

And so they came, looking as awkward and out of place as anyone on such an occasion. Pam seemed genuinely surprised and pleased to see them, thanking them profusely for coming.

"Come here," she called to a friend. "These are the kids that worked on my video. Come meet them."

The teenagers chatted with the widow for a bit, and Billy

and JR each kneeled before the casket. And then, after ten or fifteen minutes, departed.

Pam stayed true to her word and never entered the viewing room while the coffin was open. It struck some as strange, but then again, Greg's death must have been an awful blow. Who could blame the widow if she chose to remember Greg from happier times?

When the viewing was over, the casket was shut and Pam stepped into the room. "They closed it up and she walked down shaking," remembered Pam's best friend, Sonia Simon. "She just leaned over, put her hands on the casket, and was saying a prayer. Then she kneeled down and was saying another prayer and she just like totally leaned over the casket. I thought it was going to fall over she was crying so hard. She was shaking. I swear she was going to shake the casket off the stands. And she was screaming, 'Why?'

"She was there fifteen or twenty minutes. They had to pull her away. The guy at the funeral home was there first because he was standing right there in the room with her. He helped her up. Her parents, we all went over and hugged her and practically carried her out of the room."

That evening, the wake went much as it had in the afternoon. Only by now, Greg's family had begun placing items in the casket with him: a family picture of the Smarts with Greg during his long-haired days, a snapshot of his little niece, photos of relatives, a baseball hat.

Bill Smart slipped his own sapphire ring onto Greg's pinky. Judy put an earring that she had worn at his wedding in Greg's suitcoat pocket. A small bouquet from his niece was laid inside as well.

And in Greg's hands, the Smarts placed a memento from one of the happiest days in the young man's life—a wedding picture of Greg and his bride.

Like every night since Greg's death, no one got much sleep afterward. Sonia Simon, who had been friends with Pam since their high school cheerleading days, took the rest of the week off from work, left her husband to fend for himself, and stayed with Pam at her parents' house for three days. She even slept in the same bed as her friend.

"I remember sleeping there at night with her in her old bedroom," Simon recalled. "I would hear her cry in her sleep. I don't think we got more than four hours sleep in three days. She just tossed, turned, cried, had nightmares, and envisioned him on the floor. It was so weird. Being twenty-two years old, Pam was a widow.''

At Greg's parents' condo in Derry, meanwhile, Greg's mother was not faring much better. Following the wake and after everyone had left the family gathering and gone to bed, Judy Smart could not sleep. The trauma of Greg's death had caused her to be hospitalized the day before. Just that morning the psychiatrist had broken it to her that Greg had not been killed by the blow from candlestick but had been shot.

It was well after midnight, and the thought came to Judy that she should go to Greg's condo, to the last place where he had been alive. She rose from bed and padded down the stairs when her eldest son, Ricky, and his wife, who had been camped out on the couch, stopped her.

"I'm just going for a walk," Judy insisted.

"No, you're not," Ricky said. "Not by yourself."

So the three of them set off on a walk that inevitably led to 4E, Misty Morning Drive. The crime scene had been released, so they entered and went upstairs. Judy ran her fingers over a few of Greg's possessions, stared at his pictures, and stretched out on his bed. It was a comfort.

All of a sudden, they heard a noise downstairs. They stood there, half believing that Greg's killer had returned.

Judy reached into her pajama pocket and brandished a knife.

"Mom!" said Ricky. "Where did you get that?"

"Don't you worry," said his mother quietly, almost as if she had become another person. "If there's somebody down there, we're gonna take care of them."

The sound, however, proved to be just an inexplicable noise in the night. Everyone breathed easier. Settling the score with Greg's killer would have to wait.

Friday afternoon was the funeral. More than two hundred people filed into Saint Thomas Aquinas Church in Derry. Across the street was a crowd of reporters, photographers, and the crew from channel 9. The Derry police, meanwhile, photographed everyone coming and going, looking for anyone who might prove suspicious.

The Mass got off to a disquieting start when a huge wreath of roses, from Pam to Greg with a banner across it that read "I Love You, Honey," crashed facedown in front of the altar. Some remember its toppling all on its own, while others say an altar girl hit it. But everyone's heart was breaking for the widow.

The casket was covered with a white shroud emblazoned with a gold cross. Father Thomas Bresnahan gave the blessing and proceeded.

"This gathering was not scheduled in any of our date books," he told the mourners. "Most of us had other plans. Yet we find ourselves here despite those other plans. The fundamental question of all of us here is why. Why? Why is someone who loved life as much as Greg did, who had accomplished so much in a short period of time, being taken from us?

"Incidents such as this force us to reflect on our lives. There are always those questions as to why this had to happen. Greg's life was cut short, but we do not mourn his destiny. We grieve what we have lost—a husband, son, brother, grandchild, or co-worker and friend.

"Greg has no more tears, suffering or pain. . . . His influence will live on with us. He would have been celebrating his anniversary on Monday. For Pamela it will now be a time to honor his memory."

Few of those in attendance would remember much of the Mass, so wrapped up were they in their private grief and thoughts. But Bill Smart said he has at least one distinct memory. "Tears are coming down from my eyes, Judy's eyes, everybody's crying," he said. "And Pam turns to me and of course I leaned forward. I thought something was wrong. And she said to me, 'Did you ask for a full Mass?' I said, 'No.' I'm not Catholic. I don't know a full Mass from a half Mass. And she said, 'I *told* him to make it short.'"

When it finally did end, Pam, at one point kept upright by her parents and older sister, Beth, appeared devastated as she carried a single rose and left the church.

Still, before her limousine pulled away for the cemetery, Pam had the presence of mind to notice the television crew across the street. She rolled down her window, caught the attention of Steve Payment, one of the pallbearers, and, pointing, commanded him to go over and talk to them.

"I'd just like to say, Greg was the kindest person I ever knew," Payment told Bill Spencer through his tears. "He was a real good friend of mine and he didn't deserve this."

The hearse ferried Smart's remains to the Forest Hills Cemetery in east Derry. There, a sea of friends and relatives circled the grave as the final prayers were intoned.

When they were through, Pam turned to her in-laws. "Why don't we each take a rose and walk up together?" she said.

One by one, they did, and after Pam had placed hers on the flower-covered coffin, she turned to Greg's parents. There they hugged, all differences of the past few days behind them, unified by their loss.

Afterward, the Smarts and the Wojases had separate get-togethers at their respective homes. Many of the younger people, both Greg's and Pam's friends, went to the house in Windham to be with the widow.

It was, as might be expected, a gloomy gathering, with many of them, just in their twenties, shell-shocked but trying to smile now and then. Not far below the surface there was anger as well. Most obviously it was rage at the still-unexplained loss of Greg. Pam, too, was irritated with the police investigators because no one had told her the autopsy results; she had learned that Greg was shot while listening to her car radio. And nobody was very happy with the media, which struck them as downright callous for camping out across from the church and in some cases even coming to the cemetery.

Still, one of the first things the mourners did once inside was to turn on the television. Everyone gathered around for the local news to see if there had been any break in the case. Pam found a seat right in front.

"State police are analyzing fingerprints taken from the home," channel 9 reporter Jack Heath said, finishing his part of the story. "Sources say it's possible that more than one suspect was involved in this killing. Officials have ruled Pamela Smart out as a suspect, and police say the couple has a clean background check."

Chapter 2

Since girlhood, Pamela Smart has signed her name "Pame," which she pronounces "Pam." The unique spelling, of course, is nonsensical, but no matter. Pam has seldom missed an opportunity to draw notice.

Certainly she attracted plenty of attention in March 1991, when her face was seen in newspapers, magazines, and television news programs all over the United States and much of the world. She is the "teacher" who seduced her teenage lover into killing her husband.

Time and again, reporters would describe Pam as "attractive." In its vagueness, it is perhaps the perfect word for her appearance. After all, Smart has a look that one sees in countless young women in malls and nightclubs. Made up to perfection, with hair fluffed out in front and curled down to her shoulders, sometimes frosted, Smart would hardly stand out in a crowd.

What's more, little is compelling in Pam's features. Thin lipped, with a slightly upturned nose, she is almost nondescript. One writer compared her skin to porcelain, and someone else said that her visage was "like a cameo." In many ways, it was all the same. What people remembered was a mannequin-like quality.

Even Pam's physique, baby-fat round in high school and trimmed down in recent years, was not unlike that which is seen in a department store statue.

Newsmen and others who knew nothing about Pam, other than her physical traits and the fact that her tears failed to flow in court, would come to call her the "Ice Princess."

It is a less than apt nickname. Friends—and enemies, in fact—speak of a complex, confusing woman whose feelings run deep. The problem, though, may very well be that Pam Smart's emotions run even deeper than her own awareness of them. "I think underneath there is a real hurting person," said one woman who worked with her. "A lot of people look at her and say 'Look at all the things she had going for herself,' and yet underneath, who *knows* what's underneath there?"

Smart was born in Miami, Florida, on August 16, 1967, a fact that in itself, according to Pam, explains her ego-centricity. "I'm definitely the typical Leo," she said. "You know, walk in, have to be the center of everything. Everywhere I go I'm always attracting attention for some reason or another. I'm loud, very outgoing, and stuff."

She was the second of three children born to John and Linda Wojas. Her sister, Beth, is six years older than Pam and brother, John, whom the family has always called Jay, is three years younger.

The Wojases married when Linda was just eighteen and John twenty. John had a job with a printing company, and Linda was a stenographer. They struggled, but the couple scraped their way up and ultimately out of blue-collar Lowell, Massachusetts, where they'd both been born.

After a stay in Georgia while John was in the service, the Wojases moved to Miami. John had lived there during high school before he returned to Lowell and got married. He would come to work his way up from some of the lowest level jobs around the airport to the high-prestige position of flying commercial jets for Delta Air Lines.

In the process, he and his family were elevated into an upper middle-class existence, giving the Wojas children many luxuries that the parents had lacked as kids. "They had the dance lessons, the piano lessons, gymnastics; they traveled; they've been all over the world," said John Wojas. "And they never had to hurt for anything."

The family lived in a ranch-style home in Miami's Pinecrest-Palmetto section, a dozen miles away from the racially combustible center of town. Despite the comfortable surroundings of their own neighborhood, the Wojas children attended the integrated public schools, learned their share of Spanish, and by all accounts got along fine.

Even as a youngster, Pam was an organizer, a leader, and the focal point of whatever was going on. "She even organized all those black kids and had a big dance routine at the end of the year one year," John Wojas recalled. "Fifth grade students! She had 'em all up there dancing."

By 1980, when Pam was still in junior high, Miami's

crime rate was burgeoning and the Wojases thought it would be better to raise their kids elsewhere. Said John Wojas: "When they started burning the place down, when they had the riots in Miami, I says, 'I'm getting my family the hell out of here. I don't need this aggravation.' "

The family had often spent their summers in New Hampshire, and with Beth already in college, they decided to make the move north to a seemingly more wholesome place.

They settled on Windham, a tiny community of eight thousand people, just south of Derry. Their house was located in a part of town known as "the Estates." Yet the Wojas' eight-room ranch, on less than an acre, valued today at about $150,000, is hardly grandiose. If anything, it was convenient, being close to Interstate 93 and an easy drive for John to Boston's Logan Airport.

In the summer or on weekends the family could escape to Lake Winnisquam in central New Hampshire, where since 1976 they had owned a Cape Cod—style house on what is known as Mohawk Island. Today the place would sell for about $240,000.

Pam's parents have been together for more than thirty years. Her mother was the more active in Pam's young life, and friends from high school almost unanimously recall the friendliness bestowed on them by Linda Wojas when they visited or slept over.

Pam's father, though, was away at work much of the time, and when he was home Pam and he were often in conflict. As an adult, Pam would astound friends and acquaintances with her open criticism and hostility toward John Wojas. "She didn't really have a close relationship with her dad," allowed Sonia Simon. "But then again he really wasn't home much. I think she thought he was kind of cheap."

Other friends got a similar impression. When Pam was in college she and some pals were driving to Walt Disney World and realized that Pam's tires were obviously not up to the lengthy trip. She called her father long distance, collect, for advice on buying new ones, but he refused to accept the charges.

For himself, John Wojas says he always believed that his children should learn the lessons of hard work. As a result, Pam held jobs since she was thirteen, be it at a bakery or a Dairy Queen. "I always insisted that my children work," said John. ''They've always worked, whether they were baggage boys, waitresses, all that kind of stuff, because I had to work for everything I have today. I always felt that's part of their education.''

Adds Linda Wojas, ''All our kids have been overachievers. That's what we instilled. You work hard and then you reap your harvest.

''We grew up with nothing. Both my husband and I are from big families. You didn't have a quarter to go to Girl Scouts. You didn't even ask. You didn't even have pets because you had all you could do to your feed your family. That's how everybody was in our neighborhood. But at least we were both in homes and not tenements.''

Pam learned that lesson well as she was never one to idle away the hours. Yet those who knew her as a teenager say that Pam seemed to lack a childishness at home. Her room, they say, was usually immaculate, decorated primly, and lacking the usual teenage fare of rock and roll and movie star posters. And her clothes, they say, would be color-coordinated in her closet.

Pam, however, was never demure. Unlike many children who are uprooted and left to find a place in a new school, for example, Pam used her sense of humor to adapt at Windham Center School, where she attended eighth grade, and at Pinkerton Academy, her high school.

Pinkerton is in Derry, about a mile from the Summerhill Condominiums, where Greg and Pam Smart would live as newlyweds. One hundred and seventy-five years old, Pinkerton possesses a bucolic New England splendor, the centerpiece its red brick tower building. A young Robert Frost was once employed there as an English teacher.

Technically a private institution, Pinkerton serves as the public high school, grades nine through twelve, for students from five towns, with Derry being the largest. Pinkerton educates a variety of kids, overwhelmingly white, from the children of chief executive officers to farmers' sons and daughters.

More than two thousand students attended the school in any given year during the early 1980s, and Pamela Ann Wojas promptly found a place among the most popular.

She was class president her sophomore year, for example, no small accomplishment since Derry students so heavily outnumbered the rest. Few kids from the smaller towns, particularly as underclassmen, could ever muster enough votes across the student body.

Pam was also one of the few sophomore girls to win a spot on the basketball cheerleading squad, a rarity at such a large school. What Pam had going for her was an enthusiasm that she could summon instantly and an ability to perform gymnasticlike moves. She would remain a fixture before the crowds as a cheerleader for both the football and basketball teams throughout her years at the school.

What friends from high school remember most, though, were her attention-getting ploys, which could be hilarious. One time, at the annual Shrine Game between New Hampshire and Vermont high school football all-stars, Pam was nowhere to be found. Suddenly, her fellow cheerleaders saw her ride into view on the back of a mechanized camel, the mascot of another school. All the while she was laughing and screaming that she did not know how to stop the monster.

Another time, while running for junior class office, Pam and the other candidates were asked random questions at an assembly to give the students a feel for their views. Most took the exercise seriously. When Pam's turn came, she was asked where she expected to be in five years. "Probably Pinkerton," she muttered sarcastically, and brought down the house.

There was an unmistakable caring side to Pam. Her mother likes to talk about how she volunteered to read to elderly nuns. And a friend and neighbor from high school remembers how she came over, on her own, and spent time with his mother, who was dying of cancer.

She also had a starkly contrasting side, a hurtful aspect to her personality that came out in her cutting remarks designed to bring people down a notch, presumably to make herself look better. "I think she was an insecure person," said one old friend. "I don't think she thought that she was better than everybody else, but she wanted people to think that she was."

Or, as a college classmate told the *Boston Globe*: "Pam's a real enigma. She's a very bright, tough, and competitive woman, but there always seemed to be real strong anger simmering inside her."

At Pinkerton Academy, she was also intensely possessive of the boys she liked, whether they cared much for her or

not. Classmates from high school smile when they recall
the time that one of Pam's crushes at Pinkerton showed a
new girl around the school. As soon as the boy left, Pam
hurried over to her and said in no uncertain terms: "He's
mine! Stay away from him!"

Beneath her senior photo in the 1985 edition of Pinkerton's yearbook, *The Critic*, Pam wrote that her pursuit was
"to dance the night away with David Lee Roth," who was
the manic lead singer for Van Halen. The quote itself is a
reference to one of the group's biggest hits, "Dance the
Night Away."

Pam, often called "Wojo" by her friends, was enthralled
by heavy metal—a common enough predilection for a high
school student—and Van Halen was her favorite.

Senior year, during the Pinkerton Horror Picture Show,
an evening of student skits and performances, Pam and
Sonia Simon, whose last name was then Fortin, and a few
friends dressed up like Van Halen—with Pam of course
playing the starring role of David Lee Roth—and lip-
synched the song "Unchained."

Pam and Sonia would play Van Halen tapes continually.
Pam particularly liked the album *Fair Warning*. "It was
like a ritual," recalled Sonia. "We would learn every word
on every album, know the chronological order of every song
on every album, and name it when it came up."

Pam did more in high school, however, than listen to
rock and roll. To look at the listing of her accomplishments
and activities in the yearbook, one would think her the all-
American girl: cheerleading, school government, Winter
Carnival, Spanish tutor, honor roll, Students Against Drunk
and Drugged Driving.

Pam was undeniably busy at Pinkerton, but in many ways
it was more image than substance. She was clearly intelligent, had an excellent memory, and did well academically.
She understood how the system worked and took advantage
of that knowledge. Or as Pam's father put it: "Pam was the
kind of kid that could get good grades and excel without
putting in all that effort. You know the kind of kid you
always hated in school? Pam would get the A with one-
quarter of the effort."

What seemed to be lacking was a respect for her teachers
and other authority figures. Truth be told, she often under-
mined them to draw attention to herself. Pam was always

the student who would steer the classroom discussion away from whatever the teacher had planned to talk about toward whatever *Pam* wanted, such as something she had seen on television the night before. And if the teacher allowed it to go on, an entire class period would be wasted. "I'd be going on and on," Pam recalled, "and next thing you know—ding!—the bell would ring. And I'd say, 'Yes! One more day of nothingness.'"

Although certainly an active member of student government during her years at Pinkerton, Pam did not run again after her junior year. Among other things, school officials had serious questions about Pam's possibly rigging an election in her own favor, skimming money from class funds, and drinking alcohol on school grounds. No dismissive action was ever taken—there was only partial proof—but Pam's mother was contacted and Pam did agree to bow out of student government if the matter was kept quiet and out of her student file.

In addition to *The Critic*, Pinkerton also had a video yearbook, which showed Pam and her classmates in the middle of all kinds of work and play. At one point, Pam is asked on camera what song she thinks would best sum up senior year at Pinkerton: "I would have to go with 'Unchained,'" she said, referring to the Van Halen tune. "Because that's a song about letting loose and everything. And senior year is the time to go out of control and just go crazy, have a good time."

By her senior year, that good-time image was closer to the real Pam than the one seen on paper. A ribald individual around her friends, she had also developed a reputation for promiscuity, which she did little to defuse.

A number of the boys, for instance, took to calling her Seka, after the hardcore pornographic movie star. Pam herself would include that nickname in the blurb under her photo in the yearbook. "Seka-n-Reis-Cup," she wrote, alluding to her relationship with then-boyfriend Paul Reis, one of the captains of the football team.

The nickname Seka grew out of the lurid stories about himself and Pam with which Paul Reis would regale his buddies over lunch. When Pam happened to be there, she had no objections. "Pam would love it," said Steve Schaffer, a friend of Pam's from junior high and high school. "She'd laugh at it, too. She thought it was funny."

Reis, who went by the nickname Sausage, was an all-star offensive lineman and one of the most popular kids in school. If a party was hopping, Paul Reis no doubt was there. And if girlfriend Pam was not around, so be it. "It was a serious relationship in her eyes," said Reis. "But on nights we weren't together, well if something happened, it happened."

How much was locker room talk and how much was reality, only Pam knows, but it did not help that some kids around school took to calling her Wham-bam-thank-you Pam.

Six years after graduation from Pinkerton, when Pam's face would be recognized in virtually every home in New Hampshire, ex-boyfriend Reis, today a construction worker, told a reporter from the supermarket tabloid *Globe* that in high school he almost married Pam because they thought she was pregnant. "She was a wild, wild girl," Reis was quoted as saying. "We were doing everything your parents tell you not to do."

They dated from September to May of their senior year, said Reis, a take-it-as-it-comes, husky guy, before he unceremoniously broke it off in the school parking lot. "I just got sick of her," he recalled. "That's terrible, but that's how I was in high school."

Pam knew lots of people in high school, including kids outside of her clique, even the "druggies" and "scum," as she put it. Her closest friends were Sonia and two other girls, who together called themselves the Little Dolls, or LDs, a twist on the 1980 Tatum O'Neal, Kristy McNichol film *Little Darlings*.

They would see each other very seldom as adults, but in those days probably no one was closer to Pam than Sonia. They became friends as sophomores at cheerleading tryouts. As their friendship blossomed, Pam tended to have the stronger, more opinionated, personality. Sonia looked up to her and followed Pam's lead.

The two spent many an afternoon after school, usually engaged in some activity revolving around food, eating Funny Bones or Italian subs or McDonald's hamburgers, sharing secrets about boys and their plans for the future. They were so inseparable that friends took to calling them Frick and Frack, and often people thought they were sisters.

Sonia, a brunette with a warm smile and an inclination

to get misty eyed at anything short of greeting-card sentiments, today is an accountant. She is married to Chris Simon, a truck driver whom she started dating when they were both in high school.

Sonia remembered that the Pam of her high school days only cared about three or four boys. When a relationship developed, Pam would throw everything into it. And if it failed, she would be devastated, as she was about her breakup with Paul Reis.

"She never really was the type to dump a guy," remembered Sonia. "She was always dumped. And she would fall hard. It would tear her apart. She really got attached to that one person. It was like a necessity in her life. And it wasn't always easy for her to pick up and go on."

Pam had never been completely happy in New Hampshire and longed to get back to her native state and the warm weather. "I'm a sun bunny," is how she once put it. So in the summer of 1985, she spent a semester at the University of Florida in Gainesville, where her sister attended law school. Then she transferred to Florida State University in Tallahassee, which had a media performance program in the communications department—that would prepare her for her dream of being a television reporter.

Christmas vacation found Pam back in chilly New Hampshire, catching up with Sonia and the rest of her friends and stepping out to parties. It was like old times. The flame of the old friendships still burned.

Yet change was underway. Pam had been away at college, unlike most of her high school buddies. Sonia, meanwhile, had moved in with Chris Simon, her husband to be, and was no longer always available when Pam beckoned. And a girl named Terri Schnell, who had never fit in with the cheerleaders and the popular kids in Pam's circle of friends at Pinkerton, was now one of the gang.

Terri had known Sonia since grade school in Derry. But for most of high school, she was an outsider. She liked heavy metal and a good party as much as anyone, but she was gangly, a bit awkward, and did not have a "go team" bone in her body.

So Terri found her friends elsewhere. One Saturday night in the summer of 1983, she and a girlfriend were in a Burger King in Londonderry, one town west of Derry. Terri had a key chain with a trinket on it that looked vaguely phallic. Another customer, a guy who looked like he was a year or two older than she, with light-brown locks down to his shoulders, looked over and grinned.

"What's that?" he asked. "A dildo?"

It was the kind of remark that makes a girl get her order to go, but Terri couldn't help but smile. This kid had such a silly, infectious laugh. Next thing Terri knew, she and her girlfriend were off to a party with him—his name, it turned out, was Greg Smart—and one of his buddies.

Almost every weekend after that, Terri could be found hanging out with Smart, who had recently graduated from high school, and his crowd from Londonderry. They became the best of friends, with Greg dubbing her Giraffe, because of her height, and Terri calling him Greggles. They would talk for hours about anything and everything. Smart was the only person that Terri ever let read her diaries. And on Sundays, Greg would come over to the Schnells' house and Terri would make him breakfast.

Still, they were content to keep the relationship on a just-friends basis. Smart, after all, showed no real propensity for staying with any one woman. "Greg was basically a stud," said Schnell. "He didn't want a girlfriend. He just wanted to have some fun."

Toward the spring of 1985, meanwhile, Terri found herself growing closer to Pam and Sonia. They had run into each other at a mall while getting Madonna tickets and some of their differences seemed to fade. Senior year, after all, was quickly falling away, and before long it was as if Terri had always been part of the crowd.

So it was in December of that year that Terri told everyone about a New Year's Eve party Greg was throwing at his parents' house in Londonderry, a place his family owned before moving to Derry.

Greg's bashes, inevitably thrown when his parents were out of town, were legendary among his friends as the utmost in bacchanalian delights. "Unbelievable parties," said Tom Parilla. "Tons of people. Parties where girls would be dancing on the overhang over the doorway, with the music blaring."

Alcohol would flow. Cocaine and pot would be passed around. And Greg, baby faced and long haired, would go to work seducing the ladies.

Stories, some perhaps apocryphal, abound of Greg's sexual encounters. He and some of his friends would actually hold contests to see who could seduce the most women. Ted Chappell, a drummer in a local heavy metal band who goes by the nickname Terror, told of one party at the Smart house when Greg scored with three women in the course of a night, none knowing about the others. Terri Schnell recollected an evening when it was four. And another pal laughed about the time he and Greg had sex with a pair of cousins in a Cadillac. The friend said he still hears echoes of Greg in the backseat with his date, his high, patently silly laugh bursting forth as he exchanged merry glances with his buddy in the front.

Heaven only knew what a party at Greg Smart's would bring; but Pam, Terri, Sonia, and a few others from the Pinkerton crowd were looking forward to finding out as they made their way through the snow and up the driveway to greet 1986.

Unlike at the usual high school parties, Pam and her friends were now on new turf. Most of the thirty to forty people there that night were from Londonderry. And although adolescent rivalries had largely been laid to rest, everyone was aware that Londonderry High School had long been Pinkerton Academy's archenemy.

Nonetheless, it was a party that lived up to Greg Smart's standards. Boone's Farm and beer were in good supply. Coke was circulating. Motley Crue and Van Halen were roaring from the stereo speakers. And Greg, as always, was the party's lifeblood, jumping around in a black party hat.

Terri had introduced Pam and Greg at a party a little earlier that month, but this was the first time they hit it off. What caught Pam's eye was his hair. Greg reminded her of rock star Jon Bon Jovi.

What's more, he had a lot of the characteristics of Paul Reis. Greg was less burly and had never been a high school sports hero. But they were both renowned wild and crazy guys, the egotistical hub of their respective circles of friends, and proud of their exploits with the opposite sex.

Smart made his requisite move on Pam that night, along with those on several other ladies, but he was less than enthusiastic about Pam becoming a permanent fixture. They went out, sledding and to the movies, over the next couple weeks, and then Pam returned to college, head over heels for Greg.

Smart, however, could take her or leave her and had no plans for changing his life-style. They exchanged letters and calls. And Pam did use her father's airline connections to come home for free to see Greg around Valentine's Day and over spring break. But Smart, who at this time was working in construction, was busy with another woman as well.

"There was this person that he had been dating," said Pam, "and he said basically that he didn't want to break up with her and he didn't want to break up with me. He wanted to go out with both of us. So I said, 'Well, it's either her or me.' And he said, 'OK, I'll see you later.' And I was saying to myself, 'That wasn't such a good plan.'"

That summer, though, their relationship took a turn. In June, Pam and Greg and some of Greg's buddies went to Vermont for a few days, to celebrate one of his friends' eighteenth birthday, and to take advantage of the state's drinking-age laws. Something sparked between Pam and Greg, and for the rest of the summer they were together.

Pam was totally infatuated. But Linda Wojas was less enthused. When Pam's mother first laid eyes on Greg she too noticed his hair. And while the daughter thought it was gorgeous, Linda had a different perception. "When I first met him I had my reservations," allowed Linda Wojas. "This kid walked in my door and he had long hair and I didn't like it. He looked like a girl. He almost looked pretty."

The mother had hoped the relationship would pass, but for the first time in his life Greg Smart was enamored. By the time Pam headed back to Tallahassee for her sophomore year, he was headlong into his most serious relationship. The phone bills, for instance, started climbing into the hundreds of dollars. Pam would send him little gifts, T-shirts and other forget me nots. She started flying home more often. And that fall, Greg and a friend even traveled down to Florida to see Pam and to check out the lay of the land.

Early that next year, Greg surprised everyone when he said he was relocating to Florida to be with Pam. "None of us ever expected him to do something like that,'' said Terri Schnell.

"During the week she was down there,'' said Brian Washburn. "She'd come up on the weekends. Greg would have her on the weekends and during the week he could do whatever he wanted. We were like, What are you, stupid?''

Pam's parents also took notice and wondered aloud whether their daughter's grades would be affected when Greg headed south in early 1987.

The Smarts went to Florida with him and helped find Greg a furnished place in what was apparently an old motel that had been converted into apartments. They paid the first month's rent and the deposit, and then went out and got him necessities like silverware and pots and pans, dishes, and bedding. When it was time to head north, separation anxiety set in. "On the way home I was crying,'' said Bill Smart, "and Judy was crying, too, because we had to leave him there.''

Greg lived in the apartment and Pam had a dorm room, but they were together as much as possible. They liked to take in heavy metal concerts when bands like Motley Crue were in the area or spend their evenings in the local clubs. On weekends they would often go away, to Tampa or Daytona or Orlando. And if friends came for a visit they might head out to Disney World or Busch Gardens.

Once, Greg's buddy Brian Washburn came to Tallahassee for a visit and they all wound up at a huge outdoor party, complete with a bonfire and band, with nearly four hundred other revelers, most of them Florida State students. Suddenly, the police descended and rounded up everyone who was too young to be drinking and put them on a bus to the police station.

Greg was of legal drinking age, but Pam, Brian, and nearly two hundred others were brought in to be charged. "They let Pam and one of her friends go because they went to college there,'' remembered Washburn. "So I'm sitting there with like a hundred other people. They had these two tables up in front with everybody's license laid out on it. They were taking one license at a time and writing out a report for a court date.

"There's nothing I could do. Greg and Pam and her friend, meanwhile, are standing at the side of the room. Greg looks around, walks up to the table, grabs my license, puts it in his jacket pocket, and walks back to Pam. He stands there for a second, looks at me, winks, and goes, 'Let's go.' We all got up and left."

But the fun times were not as often as one might expect: Greg had found work as a landscaper and whatever manual labor jobs he could pick up. Pam, instilled with her father's work ethic, went further than simply throwing herself into classes. She worked for the Florida Department of Commerce as a part-time clerk, first with the Bureau of Economic Analysis and later with the Motion Picture and Film Bureau, for four dollars an hour. And she plugged away as a news intern for WCTV-Channel 6, the CBS affiliate in Tallahassee.

Typically, the internship was unpaid, but it gave her a feel for the world of television news. Like most interns, Pam wrote a bit for the voiceovers, helped out in production, and did a little reporting. She liked the work, though it was not what she had imagined.

"Being a reporter isn't as glamorous as it looks when you're in college," she said. "I would see people with beepers getting called in when there's a fire at two in the morning, and the pay is low, and—I don't know—sometimes nobody wants you around, and nobody wants to talk to you.

"Everything was pressure. Nothing happens all day long and then something blows up at quarter till six and everyone's running around like chickens with their heads cut off.

"I liked some aspects of the craziness, but I wondered if I wanted to do that for the rest of my life."

On Thursday nights, meanwhile, she was a disk jockey for the school radio station, WVSS. Pam hosted a two-hour show that she herself conceived, *Metal Madness*. She called herself the Maiden of Metal, a moniker that evoked a much different image than that of someone as petite as Pam. "People were very shocked to see me," she would later tell a newspaper reporter.

Pam got involved with the radio station to build her credentials, but at the same time being a deejay was fun. Greg would assist, chasing down records, while Pam issued her listeners doses of Van Halen, Aerosmith, and Stryper. And if friends were visiting, they could help, too—reading the weather on the air, for instance.

She also created a job for herself as the station's promotions director. She helped stage a number of shows, including one concert that ballyhooed safe sex. Pam also wrangled backstage passes to a number of concerts. One time she and Greg even had their picture taken with Eddie Van Halen of Pam's most beloved band, which Pam ultimately would come to carry on her photo keychain.

Their relationship, meanwhile, had evolved into something far more serious than any of Greg's friends anticipated. Greg and Pam eventually got an apartment together, a two-bedroom place, along with a woman that Pam knew from one of her jobs with the state.

Greg's parents were aware of the living arrangement, but Pam felt that her mother and father would be better off knowing nothing about it, a deceit that would spare her from an inevitable battle over her life-style.

Said Tom Parilla: "Every time her parents came down, Greg would move all his stuff out and go live with another kid until they left."

"Greg thought it was stupid," added Brian Washburn. "He'd say, 'What are they gonna do when they go in the bedroom and find my underwear?' "

Before long, Pam and Greg were talking about marriage and even stopped at a jewelry store to look at engagement rings. Then, after pulling together what he could from his meager pay, Greg bought Pam the diamond solitaire she had said she liked. Pam remembered the January night in 1988 when they got engaged.

"Every single person who's ever near me tells me that I smell like a baby because I'm always showering myself in baby powder. I'm the only person that I know that wears deodorant before going to bed. I always had perfume on and, I don't know, I just hate everything that stinks.

"So every time I take a shower I use powder. So one day I came home and I don't know what happened but I was totally aggravated. I had had the worst day and I was crying and complaining about something. And Greg kept saying, 'Why don't you take a shower and you'll feel better.' And I'm like, 'Why? I don't want to take a shower.'

"So finally I took a shower and he had put the ring underneath my powderpuff. I came out of the shower and I was using the powderpuff and I saw this box in there. I was like, 'What?'

"I opened it up and said, 'Oh, my god.' I started crying

and he wasn't even saying Will you marry me or something. And I'm like, 'Well, *say* it.' And he's like, 'I'm not going to say it.' So I started saying, 'Get down on your *knee*' and he's going, 'No-o-o-o, I'm not getting down on my knee.' Finally I said, 'Yes, I'll marry you,' even though he never really asked me. He never said, 'Will you marry me?' ''

Pam then called her mother to tell her the good news. Linda Wojas was happy, Pam remembered, but only after the daughter answered a few key questions. ''My mom was like, 'Are you pregnant? Are you still graduating from school?' I said, 'Gee, don't rejoice too much.' ''

The time in Florida was a period of subtle changes for the couple. Pam was as driven as ever, but she seemed to have loosened up a bit. In high school, she had a style of dressing that was neat, vaguely preppy. Now away from her parents, she let her hair, lightened by the Florida sun, grow longer, and when she got off the plane in Boston for a weekend visit, friends noticed that she had a trendier look, wearing, for example, spandex.

Greg, meanwhile, was on his own for the first time and showed hints of maturing. Marriage, once unheard of, was on his mind, and he started to understand that the nice home and boat and other possessions his father had acquired would not come easily at $3.35 an hour.

So he listened when the old man, in Florida for a conference of Metropolitan Life's top regional salesmen, suggested that Greg consider the insurance business. It might not sound sexy, Bill Smart said, but the right kind of person could make good money and pretty much set his own schedule.

With Pam's encouragement, Greg started studying for the exam so he could sell insurance in Florida. He eventually passed it. Then one day he cut his hair so he could start work as a trainee with MetLife.

''I almost had a heart attack,'' Pam remembered. ''I was sitting out at this café with my friend and Greg comes over and sits down next to me. I just looked over and then looked away and just kept talking. I didn't even know it was him. I turned back around. I could almost die. I couldn't believe how short it was.''

Almost imperceptibly, their life was changing, slowly taking on the shape of the married life that awaited them. Pam was still uncertain whether anyone would hire her as a television reporter, but it looked as if Greg's future was in insurance. Like a lot of young couples, meanwhile, they talked about getting a dog, a sort of precursor to children.

Their budgets, though, had prevented them from purchasing one. Finally, Greg had saved enough money, close to four hundred dollars, and decided that he would buy Pam the kind of dog she was always talking about, a Yorkshire terrier, as a graduation present.

The day he went to get it, he had been gone for a while. Then Pam's phone rang. It was Greg. Something had come up on the way to the Yorkshire terrier.

"Pam," he said sheepishly, "would you be really mad if I got a Shih-Tzu?" It was the same kind of dog that Greg's family owned.

"A Shih-Tzu?" she said. "What do you want *that* for?"

"Well, there's this one here and it's the cutest thing I've ever seen."

They went back and forth a bit. Pam hesitated, thought about it, then finally gave in. "OK," she said. "Surprise me."

That day Greg came home with a tan ball of fur that he could practically hold in one hand. The puppy was so young that he could hardly even walk. Pam's heart melted. It was the nicest present Greg had ever given her. She liked him so much that she named him after another of her favorite things in life—the band Van Halen. Halen became the dog's name.

Not everything, however, was always pleasant about the relationship. Pam and Greg, in fact, had personalities that were destined to clash. Each liked to be the center of attention. Each had a strong ego. Neither was a follower.

Pam liked to be in control, and Greg had no problem challenging her from time to time, lowering her a peg or two. Sometimes he would tweak her, pronouncing her name as she spelled it—"Pame," so that it rhymed with "tame."

Greg knew the buttons to push to make Pam burn, and from time to time took pleasure in hitting them. Once, early in their relationship, he let her out of his car miles from home in a snowstorm, laughing out loud at the very idea of her having to trudge home by herself.

Other times, he was more subtle. Pam would obviously be fixing for an argument about one thing or another and Greg would ignore her. Instead of trading insults he would simply say, "whatever," and get on with what he was doing. Pam had no comeback and it drove her to distraction. Or as Greg's friend Brian Washburn put it: "That pissed her off big time."

And then there were occasions when Greg simply went too far. One instance was when Tom Parilla and his fiancée were visiting Pam and Greg in Florida. One night, the two couples were in a bar where the waitresses wore tight T-shirts and hot-pink shorts. Greg and Parilla had spent the better part of the evening making suggestive comments about the attributes of one particular waitress as well as every other attractive woman that walked in. It only got worse when the beers started going for a nickel each.

All night long Pam and Greg had been sniping at each other, with Pam growing increasingly angry about Greg's lewd remarks. And when Pam was outraged, her comments too could be less than commendable.

Finally, the exchanges reached critical mass. Greg took a mouthful of beer, turned to Pam, and squirted a stream of brew into her face. A direct hit. A bouncer rushed over, seized Greg by his jacket, and hauled him out, while a flabbergasted Pam wiped away the suds.

A little later, when things had calmed down, Parilla went and talked to the bouncer in an attempt to salvage the evening. He assured him that it was all a misunderstanding and that if he let his buddy return it wouldn't happen again. Parilla gave his solemn word. Reluctantly, the guy said OK, and Parilla telephoned Greg at his apartment and told him to please come back, that all was forgiven.

"So he came back," Parilla remembered, "and Pam said something. She was being wise to him again. And frigging, 'Ppppffft.' He does it again. 'Fuck you,' he says. And the bouncer's like, 'You're outta here buddy,' and frigging took him away."

Pam Smart was tired of school and she wanted to get out of FSU as soon as possible. She hated working so hard, in and out of the classroom. She had regularly been taking extra credits on top of her normal class load and even took summer courses. Within three years Pam had completed all the credits she needed and graduated cum laude.

Toward the end of her time in Florida, meanwhile, WCTV helped her pull together a resume tape, and Pam began the maddening quest for an entry-level reporting job. She sent her tapes to stations all over, but nothing was turning up.

Greg, meanwhile, decided to go back to New Hampshire. Being new on the job, work at MetLife in Florida was a struggle and Greg thought he would do better if he went to work where his dad could help pave the way. Both he and Pam had lived in comfortable homes and had been surrounded by nice possessions their entire lives. Neither was ready to give that up, and they agreed that New Hampshire would be the best place to start as newlyweds.

What's more, Greg was ready to leave Florida for another reason. Pam and he had grown up in different kinds of families. The Wojas children were brought up with an independence from their parents that made it only seem natural if Beth or Pam or Jay went to school out of state and wound up living in some other part of the country. Bill and Judy Smart's children, though, never ventured too far from home after they grew up. Their strength came from the family, and they clung to it for as long as they could.

Greg also wanted to get back to the Northeast. Unlike Pam, he was happiest in the cold and the snow, skiing or cruising along in a snowmobile. He had had his adventure in Florida and now it was time to go home.

Pam's life was now in a swirl of change. School was ending. She would be getting married. And after chasing a dream of being a television reporter, Pam suddenly had to face the fact that she would probably have to put her ambitions on hold.

Once, Pam had spent hours in front of the mirror, simulating speaking into the camera. She told everyone how much she admired Barbara Walters and that she hoped to be the second coming of the ABC newswoman.

Now, Pam had to realize that she could not chase jobs all over the country, as most ambitious young television journalists must be willing to do. Pam was going back to New Hampshire, where only one station, WMUR in Manchester, was of any significance; and that station would ultimately reject her.

"It was really hard for her," recollected Sonia Simon, who would later be her maid of honor. "I remember her saying, 'Am I making a mistake? Should I be going and following my dream?' This is like everything she ever wanted to be and all of a sudden she was faced with choosing

Greg and New Hampshire or being an actual reporter.''

She chose Greg. Pam finished school that summer and
returned to her parents' home in Windham. "I was surprised
that she did it," said Terri Schnell, "because all she ever
talked about was the media and going on TV. Her ambitions
were huge."

Pam, who scarcely had the word "surrender" in her
vocabulary, was setting aside what she had set out to accomplish, all that she had worked for, because of Greg.

As it turned out, it was not all bad. She worked for a
temporary agency for a while, then that summer she was
hired by School Administrative Unit 21 in Hampton to be
the new media center director. The school board was looking
for someone to perform the usual duties, taking care of
equipment purchases, for example, and overseeing dis-
bursement of it to the schools.

But SAU 21 officials also wanted a person who could
bring a new dimension to the job. They thought it was time
to start generating more positive publicity about the school
board. And Pam looked like the person who could do it all.

She seemed to be an ideal hire. She was young, but she
brought with her obvious intelligence, energy, and a will-
ingness to learn. She was friendly, too, and around the SAU
21 building the staff felt protective toward her. She was,
after all, the baby of the office.

For Pam, the job was a good alternative to being a reporter. She was right out of college, and already she had
her own secretary, a state benefits package that her father
praised as better than his at Delta, and a $22,500 annual
salary. She basically was her own boss, worked at her own
pace, and had not strayed too far from journalism. She spent
a lot of time using the video equipment at the various
schools. And she was writing press releases, which was
almost the same as putting together actual stories.

Greg, meanwhile, started work that fall for Metropolitan
Life in Nashua, in his father's office. Greg had a way with
people, perhaps a trait he inherited being the son of a salesman. He had a self-assuredness that some saw as cocky,
but a smile that made customers feel at ease. He was also
a quick learner. That and the guidance of his dad made Greg
one of the young stars in his office.

Pam and Greg were both living with their parents, which
helped them save for their upcoming life together. "Of

course my parents charged me rent," recalled Pam. "They were still teaching me that lesson." Greg's parents let him stay for free.

The months passed. Greg's parents had gotten a smaller place, a condominium, in Derry, and in January 1989, Pam and Greg moved in together to their rented condo on Misty Morning Drive, a five-minute walk from the Smarts' home. It was also just down the road from Pinkerton Academy, Pam's high school.

In the meantime, the couple went through the counseling sessions required to marry in the Catholic Church, which Pam as a nonpracticing Catholic desired.

Before they knew it, the day of their marriage was almost upon them. But by this point the concept of being married was not completely foreign to either of them. Talk of tying the knot was cropping up all over among their friends: Sonia was married to Chris Simon. Tom Parilla was getting married that spring. Several other friends were engaged. It was almost as if getting married was now the thing to do.

Parilla and Greg had agreed that they would be one another's best man at Greg's wedding on May 7 and Tom's a week later. Rather than throw separate bachelor parties, the two grooms to be decided instead upon a joint farewell to the single life along with their fiancées. So the couples, their families, and friends got together at the Hanover House, a nightclub they frequented in Manchester.

It was a joyful evening, with lots of laughs and good fellowship. Tom's fiancée and Pam presented their men with a number of gag gifts, *de rigueur* at any such occasion. One was a specially baked cake in the shape of a woman's bosom. They each also received a G-string to model later.

And that night both Greg and Tom went home with special T-shirts from their future wives, which had drawn guffaws from their buddies: "Man is not complete until he's married," the message on the shirts read. "Then he's finished."

After a year and a half of preparations, Pam's and Greg's wedding took place on May 7, 1989, at Sacred Heart Church in Lowell, Massachusetts, where her parents had exchanged vows thirty years earlier.

Arriving at the church and waiting for the bride and groom to take their places, some of Greg's friends were mystified. Smart, they had always figured, was the freest of spirits and would certainly be the last of them to ever settle down. Instead, he would now be among the first. "Greg just wanted to have fun," said Terri Schnell. "Life was a party to him. That's all it was. I have no idea why he got married so soon."

It was a large wedding, with nearly two hundred and twenty-five guests and few expenses spared. The ostentatious exclamation point on the whole affair was the couple's limousine, called *The Starship*. It was so vast that it sat nearly a dozen people and even had a bar.

The driver picked up Greg and Parilla and the Smarts to take them to the church. On the way, the best man requested a stop so he could buy champagne—seven bottles. And all the way to Lowell and the church, the bubbly flowed . . . and flowed.

By the time they got there, a half-hour trip, Greg and his best man were feeling no pain. Greg's nose took on a rosy color, as it often did when he drank. They posed for some pictures, made a trip to the men's room, and waited, Parilla kidding the groom about how nervous he must be. Then they started to embark on a second trip to relieve themselves.

"All of a sudden, the priest goes, 'You're on,' " remembered Parilla. "And Greg and me, we're both like, 'Oh, man!' We're standing up at the altar and we had to go to the bathroom so bad. Plus, we were cocked. We were standing there going, 'Oh, jeez,' just trying to stay still."

All the same, the ceremony went off without any major problems and was a beautiful affair. Pam, as nervous as any bride, had been slightly perturbed because one bridesmaid's bouquet of flowers had not been delivered and had to be picked up. Also, her limousine had been late. Still, she and Greg made a handsome couple as they exchanged vows, Pam wearing a gorgeous pearl-covered gown and Greg in a gray tuxedo.

Later, at the reception at the Pelham Inn in Pelham, New Hampshire, Greg's buddies—many of them with hairstyles like heavy metal rockers, a stark contrast to the older people also in attendance—took full advantage of the open bar and ran up a tremendous tab for Pam's father. One of Greg's friends, in fact, had everyone's attention as he carried tray after tray back to his table, storing up for when the time limit on the free drinks was up. Parilla, meanwhile, offered up a mangled, inebriated toast to the newlyweds.

Pam and her father and Greg and his mother danced as the band played "Wind Beneath My Wings." Their wedding song, played on the stereo system, would be by the Christian heavy metal band Stryper. Its title: "Honestly."

Two weeks later, not long after their honeymoon in Bermuda, Judy Smart was over at their condo for a visit and Pam said she had something she wanted to show her mother-in-law. Pam went to a closet and came out with a pile of wedding cards. On them were notations of each person's gift or how much money they gave.

"First she went through her whole family's cards," Judy said. "This uncle so and so gave me three hundred dollars, aunt so and so gave me one hundred dollars and this friend from Florida gave me five hundred dollars.

"Now I'm getting madder and madder and I'm saying to myself that I'm not going to say anything because of Greg. I didn't want to get into a big argument with her.

"So, she got done with her side and she says, 'Now I want to show you this.' She says this person, and she's naming my husband's sisters and brothers and aunts and uncles, only gave fifty dollars. This person only gave thirty dollars. Do you know that thirty dollars doesn't even pay for the price of the meal?

"It got to the point where Greg said, 'That's enough, Pam,' and she still wouldn't stop.

"Finally I just got out of there. Never in my life have I seen anyone do such an awful thing."

Like a lot of new marriages, the union of Pam and Greg raised doubts among their friends and relations. Besides the husband's history with women, the couple simply did not seem to easily mesh, and a number of people wondered how long the marriage would last.

Before the wedding, Bill and Judy Smart said, Pam's parents called them, concerned that their son would not be able to give their daughter the things in life that she deserved. Greg, after all, had no college education and did not seem the type to set the world on fire. Greg's parents tried to allay their fears. Greg will make a good provider, they said. Everything will be fine. "We had to sell Greg to the Wojases, like he was a piece of merchandise," Judy Smart later said.

The differences between the two went deeper than

whether or not Greg could keep Pam in the life-style to which she had grown accustomed.

Both of the newlyweds liked to be noticed. Before they had even met, in fact, both had altered the spellings of their nicknames—she was "Pame" and he was "Gregg"—so as to set themselves apart from the crowd. Some people wondered how long there could be twin centers of attention.

The couple also seemed to have differing drives in life. Greg had always wanted to enjoy himself, to party or hang out with his friends. He took what came when it came. Pam, on the other hand, was organized. She was ambitious. She set goals.

"She's someone who had to be in control," said Brian Washburn. "The way she dealt with things was to organize things. The reason that they got along is that he didn't care, so if she planned something out and wanted to do something, he'd just do it. He didn't give a shit. With Greg it was always, 'Let's go, no problem, whatever.'"

Greg liked outdoor activities—riding his four-wheeler, snowmobiling, skiing. Pam preferred lying on the beach or waterskiing. Greg, like his father, found joy in trips to Atlantic City, where he would sit in the baccarat pits at the Trump Plaza, drinking draft beers and gambling contentedly for hours. Pam was less enthusiastic about gambling.

Each, however, was willing to try. Particularly early in the relationship, Pam agreed to go on skiing trips. And when they went to Atlantic City, Pam and her friends would shop or otherwise amuse themselves while the men gambled, and then they would get together for dinner and a show.

Early on, in fact, Pam came to depend on Greg for the bulk of her social life. Outside of Sonia, virtually all of her friendships were with Greg's buddies or their girlfriends and wives. "I don't even know who she hung around with before she met Greg," said Brian Washburn. "I don't have a clue."

As she'd been in high school, Pam was possessive of her man. She had few close male friends. As a result, Terri Schnell remained the couple's friend, but her closeness to Greg was limited. Indeed, the very thought of Terri making Greg breakfast like in the old days was unspokenly forbidden. "When they got married, Greg pretty much wasn't supposed to hang out with me," Terri said. "For a few months we lost touch because it just wasn't allowed. Pam did have a problem with that.''

Pam, however, felt threatened by a number of people. As with everything in his life, Greg took his friends as they came. But Pam could not get along with strong-minded individuals, such as Greg's friend Tom Parilla, for example. Pam's closest friends were often younger than she, less educated, and tended to admire Pam and her forceful personality. ''She liked to be the one who everyone would turn to, the dominating one, the leader,'' said one old friend.

Despite the differences, the marriage did seem to have some strengths. Mr. and Mrs. Gregory Smart were starting life together with few material needs. The gifts from the bridal shower and wedding had been overwhelming. Their seven hundred and fifty dollar a month condo in Derry was decorated as attractively as those of many couples who have been saving for years. Pam had her 1987 Honda CRX and Greg a 1989 Toyota pickup.

Pam, who signed the checks for most of the couple's bills, would eventually earn as much as $24,300 with the school board. Greg had a phenomenal year selling insurance for such a young man. He earned almost $42,000 his first year, eventually sharing MetLife's regional rookie-of-the-year awards with a friend from the Nashua office.

They were not wealthy, but they lived a life of privilege and middle-class respectability that they had known since childhood. Together they had at least $6,000 in the bank. They started looking for a house. The future seemed nothing but bright. ''They were typical yuppies,'' said John Wojas, ''up-and-coming people that were doing good.''

At the same time, both Pam and Greg had begun to gradually grow on their respective in-laws. Greg scored points one time by showing up at the Wojas house with individual roses for Pam, her mother, and sister, Beth. At other times he would help John Wojas work around the yard. Pam's father planned to take Greg to a boxing match in Las Vegas. And at Easter, Linda Wojas even made Greg his own candy bunny.

Living so close, the Smarts tended to see the couple more often, so much, in fact, that Linda Wojas felt a tug of jealousy. Early in their marriage Pam and Greg often had dinner with his parents. On summer weekends, Bill Smart would take them and their friends out on his yacht, the *Bill Me Later*, on Lake Winnipesaukee.

And Judy Smart agreed to take an aerobics class with her daughter-in-law. "It took me a while to warm up to her," Judy Smart later said, "but she would stop and visit and I grew very attached to her."

Both Greg and Pam were sticklers for cleanliness. Pam, according to Greg's pal Yvon Pellerin, used to fold her dirty clothes before she put them in the laundry hamper.

Greg, meanwhile, found pleasure in keeping the condo tidy. He took it as his duty, for example, to wash and brush the dog. He also used to tell his mother that he liked the neat lines the vacuum cleaner made on the carpet, so he would vacuum often. And friends would visit and inevitably smell one of Greg's beloved potpourri air fresheners. "What is this?" they asked. "A passion pit?"

The newlyweds had dinner out once or twice a week, occasionally having a limousine ferry them to some costly restaurant in Boston. Now and then Pam would join Greg on a trip to Atlantic City, taking in the casinos and nightlife.

At other times, they would hit the clubs, places like the Hanover House or T.R.'s Tavern, with their friends, usually other couples, like Brian Washburn and Tracy Collins or the Parillas. Less often, they would get together with Terri Schnell and her boyfriend.

Life was good. They seemed to be an idyllic couple. Pam had always been a person who liked to touch, often greeting her friends with hugs, and so she was with Greg, holding his hand and cuddling in public.

"I used to look at them and say, Wow, they've got two cars, two jobs, a nice little condo all neatly furnished," Pam's sister, Beth, told the *Boston Globe*. "And I thought, I hope that happens to me someday. I mean, the worst thing I can remember between them was him yelling once because there was macaroni on the floor."

Yet no couple is that blissful. Truth be told, Greg continued his distasteful practice of spitting beer in his wife's face on into the marriage. "I've seen that a few times," said Yvon Pellerin, one of Greg's longtime friends. "He'd have a can in his hand, spit a little beer in her face, and she'd go upstairs all pissed off. That was it, she'd leave us alone for the rest of the night. He could see it coming, that she was getting ready to bitch, and he wasn't in the mood to hear it.''

Pellerin, uncomfortable by what he would see, would sometimes try to talk to Greg about it. "He'd look at me and go, 'Ahh, forget about it,' put the TV back on, throw me a beer, and he'd forget about it. He'd make believe it didn't happen. I think he wanted to show her that he was the man, he was the boss, and you're not gonna tell me what to do or who I can have at my place.''

One night Greg and his pals Brian Washburn and Dave Bosse drove to Boston to see Ted Chappell's heavy metal band perform at one of the clubs. It was a joyful night for Greg, made even better by a credit card mixup in which he and his friends got all of their drinks for free.

When it was time to leave, Greg and Bosse, in their cups, could not find Washburn, so they left him behind. They pulled in around two in the morning to find Pam livid because Greg was so late and so drunk.

"He went straight up to bed," Bosse recalled. "He wanted to crash. They had an argument then and there. The next day she left him. I was hung over on the couch when he called me. She wrote him a note: *You can't find me. I'm not at my mother's. I'll be somewhere else. Don't even try to find me.*''

That dispute passed quickly. The couple, in fact, rarely had long-winded, public disputes.

Pam, however, did have to agree that sometimes her husband could be an irritant. The summer after Pam and Greg got married, Terri Schnell said she remembers complaining to Pam about her boyfriend. Some problem or other had come up, and Terri was angry and frustrated. Pam told her she empathized. Greg, too, had his moments.

"Why can't they just die and make our life easier?" Pam said. "No divorce. No nothing. Just disappear.''

Terri Schnell laughed. After all, sometimes she wondered the same thing.

Chapter 3

Like everyone in the detective bureau, twenty-eight-year-old Dan Pelletier had pushed aside almost everything he was working on and was putting in heavy overtime on the Smart homicide. Unlike the others, though, when Pelletier came on the job in the morning he kept finding police reports about the killing, written by his colleagues, piling up on his desk.

All of the detectives shared the same large office, and space was at a premium, so no one ever got too touchy about their "personal space." Pelletier was one of the more methodical of the investigators, though, and simply followed his nature: He started organizing the paperwork.

Then one day Jackson came by. "So what's going on with your case?" he said. "How's it going?"

"My case?" Pelletier said. "*What* case?"

"You know, the Smart murder."

Typical Jackson, Pelletier thought. Most of the detectives liked the captain because of his easygoing nature and disdain for supervisory formality. Still, Pelletier wondered if maybe Jackson could have let him in on the fact that he had been named lead investigator for Derry's lone killing of 1990.

Still, it was a good surprise. Pelletier—Danny to his fellow detectives—had been with the force for six years but only two as a detective. What's more, he had only been involved in three other murder cases, none as a major player. Yet everyone else—all three other general investigators, their sergeant, and Jackson—simply had other assignments that they were locked into.

Someone had to be cut free to handle all the paperwork the Smart case seemed certain to generate and to become intricately aware of all the nuances and players. Danny just happened to be in the right place at the right time.

Like any Derry detective and like any detective on any

small police department, Pelletier had worked all kinds of crimes—fraud, drugs, bad checks, rape, anything and everything.

He had also carved out a niche on sexual assault cases, in particular child abuse. Patience was one thing Pelletier had in abundance. And he could effortlessly downshift into layback mode. Called to a school, he would get down on the floor with some kid he just met and talk about puppies or Teenage Mutant Ninja Turtles, as if time was no consideration at all, winning trust and eventually progressing to the true reason he was there.

Not that it was all that hard to guess that Pelletier was a policeman. His boss, Jackson, could pass for a bartender at some local pub, but things would not be much different in life for Pelletier if he had his occupation stamped across his forehead. Every hair on his blown-back pelt was in place. Moustache trimmed. Posture straight. If there was a manufacturing plant somewhere that turned out frames of young cops, Pelletier would have came from one of the standard molds.

That was not a very far cry, in fact, from how Pelletier got into police work. When he was a high school student in Methuen, Massachusetts, near the New Hampshire state line, he had joined the Explorers Club and had spent a lot of time around the local police department. He liked the people. The work looked interesting.

So after high school, he drove a newspaper delivery truck, enrolled in the criminal justice program at a community college, took all the exams, and one day a job became available for a patrolman just up the interstate, in Derry.

It was 1984 when Pelletier joined the force and like any patrolman took to cruising the streets, a job that mostly entailed chasing noisy kids from one hangout to another, calming down the combatants of domestic wars, and handing out traffic tickets.

Things, however, were a little different these days. Now he was a detective. He worked nine to five. He and his wife, Robyn, had a six-month-old daughter.

And Dan Pelletier had a new assignment: He would spearhead the search for Gregory Smart's killer.

As it turned out, Pelletier's taking the ball had some advantages. For one thing, he was one of the better organized detectives around, and when the case file started becoming hundreds of pages long Pelletier could always pluck out any statement or report in an instant.

He had also established some rapport with the widow just hours after the killing. That was a plus, because as in any murder the odds were that Greg Smart knew his killer. That was where the investigation would have to start.

During the dinner break the night of the wake, Pelletier had met with Pam again, asking for a list of everyone who had been at the condo during the last month, so their fingerprints could be separated from any others that may have turned up. Pam was happy to oblige and gave him nine names—Tom and Heidi Parilla, Chris and Sonia Simon, Steve Payment, Yvon Pellerin, Rich LaFond, and Greg's parents. All, except of course her in-laws, were longtime friends of the couple.

On Saturday, the day after the funeral, Pelletier asked for more names, those of the people in Greg's and Pam's wedding a year ago and those of the pallbearers at his funeral. Again, Pam had no qualms about helping.

This time, in fact, she would offer more than just what Pelletier requested. She had been in the house that day preparing to move out, and came across some things she thought the police overlooked that might help their investigation.

She gave the detective a wobbly candlestick, apparently the one that had been under Greg's foot; she pointed out a crescent-shaped dent she said she discovered on one of the walls by the entrance; and she showed him some stains on the carpet that hadn't been there before.

Pam seemed anxious to be of assistance all right, but she was hurting the investigation more than helping. The problem was not her pointing out peculiarities at the crime scene, most of which the cops felt came *after* the state police processed the place anyway.

The real problem was that she seemed oblivious of what had become a litany by the cops: *Please* do not talk about the case to the media.

Jackson began a slow boil when Pam first went to Spencer. The captain then started bubbling over after the subsequent numerous newspaper articles. He had made it as clear as he could that releasing information about the crime could hinder the investigation. He even took Pam's father aside and pleaded with him to talk to his daughter.

Nothing seemed to register. Within a few days after the murder Pam had told reporters in exact detail about the crime scene, from the overturned drawers to the stereo speakers by the door, and that there were no witnesses. She also said that three hundred dollars worth of jewelry was stolen, and that it almost certainly was a botched burglary.

Enough was enough. The cops were fed up with hearing about how their investigation was going while they were publicly saying next to nothing. The week after Greg's death, Jackson ordered that Pam and her family be told no more about the progress of the investigation.

Most people figured it was Pam's way of handling her grief, but after a while it began to look as if she could not resist the attention, as if she enjoyed being in the spotlight. The local journalists picked up on it, too, and more and more reporters started leaving messages at the Wojas house in Windham. Virtually every request for an interview was granted.

Diane Rietman of the Nashua *Telegraph* was the first to talk with Pam at any length about herself and her life with Greg. Two days after the funeral, on Sunday, Pam gave Rietman a telephone interview.

The story came out the following day, May 7, the one-year wedding anniversary of the couple. "For Pamela Smart life must go on," read the headline over the page-one story.

The article and Rietman's notes reveal what seems to be a heroic young woman, who, strengthened by her dead husband's spirit, vows to gather the shattered pieces of her life and go on.

"We didn't have any problems," Pam said. "We were very happy. We just wanted to be together."

It was Greg she was hurrying to see the night of the murder to tell that her mass media course was approved. "I had talked to Greg that day, and he was really excited about whether or not I'd be able to do this," Pam said. "He knew how important this was to me. He wished me good luck at the meeting. While I was driving home, I was excited to get home and let him know it had been approved."

"I've had a lot of family and friends who have been around me, but most of my strength has come from inside. Just knowing that if Greg was here . . . if this was one of our friends he would be saying this was awful but that things would work out.

"He would always say that to me when I'd get upset about things: 'You don't need to worry about everything, it'll be OK, it'll work out,' and I know he'd be there trying to comfort me, remind me that life's not fair and you have to take what happens. You can't control everything.

"Knowing how short life can be—that's scary for me. I'll tell everybody until the day I die that from this tragedy I'll learn to live life to its fullest. If there ever comes a time I'm at a crossroads in my life and there's something in my heart that I want to do, I'm going to go ahead and do it. I'm not going to hesitate anymore. You never know when you won't have a life."

Over the next few days and on toward the summer, common strains ran through Pam's interviews. Most obvious was her explanation that Greg had unexpectedly walked in on a burglary. Pam never wavered about that and made sure every reporter knew it.

"Greg didn't have any enemies," she told the *Derry News*. "If he did, that person's name would be the first out of my mouth to the police."

She told the *Lawrence Eagle-Tribune*, "This was some jerk, some drug-addict person looking for a quick ten bucks."

She also put forth the image of the strong widow, who with Greg as her inspiration was going to forge onward.

That was the crux of her talk with Bill Spencer when he came out to the Wojas' house on Pam's wedding anniversary.

Spencer was a few years older, but the two seemed to get along well. One thing they had in common was their interest in television journalism. Right out of college, Pam had applied for a reporter opening at WMUR, but the more-traveled Spencer had gotten the job.

Chatting with the reporter on camera, Pam sat on the couch in a blue dress and silver hoop earrings and stroked the dog, Halen. Spencer himself remembered being on the verge of tears at the utter sadness of the story, but when he looked over at the widow he saw none of the same emotions.

" 'She's a public relations person, that's her job at the school,' " Spencer recalled thinking. "She studied media in college, and I thought, It's so bizarre but she's going to PR her husband's murder, she's going to manage the media on her husband's murder. I thought this was a way of her dealing with her incredible grief.''

Pam glanced over at Spencer, then down at her pet, the camera trained on her expressionless features. ''Well, today's a hard day because one year ago today we were married right about this, you know, at this time. And I remember on that day the feelings that I had and how different, in contrast, the feelings are that I have today.

''You know, I woke up with a bright outlook on the day a year ago, you know, facing one of the happiest days of my life. And the beginning of our future together. And today I have to wake up and realize that there is no future for us. There's a future for me, but not for us.

''Sometimes I ask myself, I can't figure out where the strength is coming from, but it seems like it's coming from inside maybe. Maybe it's a part of Greg or whatever that's helping me go on with everything, you know, and I feel like if this happened at any point in Greg's life it wouldn't be fair, and it wouldn't make sense then. It's just an awful tragedy and now, you know, there's no better time in his life for this to happen.

''And that's one of the things that I think is keeping me going, that if Greg was here right now he would be saying that things that, like, life's not always fair and you have to take what happens in stride and move on and move forward.''

It seemed to be the stereotypical grieving-widow story. The tragedy was evident. Her words sounded right. But did they?

There's no better time in his life for this to happen?

You have to take what happens in stride?

In stride?

Spencer paid no mind. After all, this was a victim and everyone knew it.

''You know, it's awful to just think about what happened in there,'' Pam said, talking about the murder. ''You know, the only comfort I have is that, you know, it just seems to have been a situation where Greg didn't know what was happening. And he just never knew, you know, and it was really quick.''

''Do you have any idea why somebody would pick your house of all houses?'' Spencer asked.

''No.''

"I'm sure you asked yourself that, and that probably didn't make sense either. . . ."

"The only thing I could think of is it's close to the field and it's an end unit and there was nobody home."

Pam begged off on any more questions about the police investigation. The cops were frustrated with her and she knew it. She also had other concerns. "I know the police are working their hardest on this case and everything, but right now I'm concentrating more on my loss than on the investigation, because if they caught the person tomorrow he'll never be back. Greg will never be here again."

Two other points came through in almost every interview. One was the Greg Smart Memorial Fund, which was in truth a fund-raiser for her own course. "Every kid who comes through this course will share a piece of Greg," she told the *Derry News*.

The other was her incredulity that her neighbors heard nothing that night. Surely someone knew more and was not talking, she said. "I know a gunshot isn't a common sound in Derry, New Hampshire," Pam complained, "but I'd at least look out the window."

"I'm hoping there's someone who is afraid to come in and I would hope that their conscience would get to them in the end."

Through it all, the young widow found a way to smile. "I kept the top layer of my wedding cake and put it in the freezer," she told Tami Plyler of the Manchester *Union Leader*. "Greg has complained about it since I put it there. Right before this happened, he said, 'I can't wait until our anniversary so we can get rid of this cake.'"

Pam conjured an image of a benevolent Greg watching her with approval from heaven now that she finally removed the year-old piece of cake.

"I can laugh," she said, "because I know Greg's looking down and saying, 'I'm glad you got that out of the freezer.'"

What few people knew at the time was what Pam did with that cake. Without much sentiment, she brought it over to Greg's parents and gave it to them, one of the numerous reminders and possessions of her dead husband, most of which had been placed in plastic garbage bags, that Pam would drop off.

"Here," she said, in a condescending tone that irked

Greg's father to no end. "You take this. I don't like cake anyway."

As she promised in her interviews, Pam was getting on with her life. As she told Spencer, Pam and Greg had no future but Pam had one.

First, however, the past had to be properly laid to rest.

Pam selected Greg's tombstone, a three-foot-high slab of New Hampshire granite. On one side it bore his name and the years of his birth and death. On the other was an engraved rose laid across a heart. Along the bottom it read: "A life that touches the hearts of others lives on forever." Pam had come up with the phrase after seeing a similar sentiment on a sympathy card she had received.

"I didn't want something like 'He lived, he loved, he died,'" Pam said. "I wanted something that made you, for a second, feel warm inside. It was for people to realize he's still alive in us."

Pam returned to the condo the day after the funeral. She was joined by her parents, the Smarts, and a claims adjuster from Metropolitan Life. Greg's father was using the pull of twenty-five years with the company to speed the processing of Pam's claim for property damage—some of the furniture had been ruined by fingerprint dust—and the missing jewelry.

Pam in the meantime did the laundry and made some calls to cancel services, time and again stepping carelessly on top of the towel that covered the bloodstain from Greg's head wound. Granted, it was impossible to get into the main living area without passing it, but the Smarts, who could hardly stand to look in the direction of the stain, simply could not understand Pam's lack of revulsion. "She flitted around there like a busy bee," Judy Smart would later recall.

Like the Smarts, Pam had much weighing on her mind. Her husband was dead, her life was in upheaval, and almost every day she was in contact with the police, coming to the station when beckoned and answering their many questions about herself and Greg and their friends. She also provided names, hair samples, and telephone bills.

She took some time off from work, and lived with her parents in Windham. Friends visited often, many times staying over and sleeping in Pam's bed with her so she would not have to be alone.

Pam's relationship with her mother and father, however, had long been tense, and even now the strain could be felt. Pam told friends that she felt smothered at home and decided early on that she would get back on her own as soon as she could.

Yet Pam's desire to get on with her life went beyond finding a new place. In the month after Greg's death, she would shop around at car dealerships, looking to trade in her practical Honda CRX and use some of the $140,000 in insurance money that was due her to buy a car with a little more muscle—an eight-cylinder Trans-Am, for example, or a Camaro.

She also hit a number of area night spots. All of the couple's friends were concerned about her, and they thought it was a positive step when less than three weeks after Greg's death Pam went with some of them to the Hanover House to have a drink or two and listen to the local top-forty band Joker.

Pam's high school boyfriend Paul Reis was lead singer. A construction worker by day, Reis tugged on the spandex at night and put on a fair imitation of the acrobatic David Lee Roth. Like Van Halen's former singer, Reis too liked to leap around in front of an audience, perform splits, and make his way into the crowd and sing right in the faces of all the pretty girls.

It was good for Pam to get out, but no one quite expected her to have such a good time. She happily showed off her photo with Eddie Van Halen to some of the band members. And then she got caught up in the music and the entreaties of Reis, stood up and started belting out several rock and roll tunes with her ex-boyfriend.

"It was weird," says Reis. "She was footloose and fancy-free."

Joseph O'Leary, the band's drummer, recalled Pam holding a bottle of Budweiser in one hand and the wireless microphone in the other as she joined Reis in singing the Van Halen standard "Dance the Night Away" and Motley Crue's "Wild Side," among others.

"The reason I remember it is because she couldn't sing for shit," said O'Leary.

Yet that night stuck in O'Leary's mind for another reason as well. He had heard that this woman's husband had been murdered less than a month ago and he did not know *what* to make of this behavior.

Maybe it was nothing, but O'Leary thought it might be a good idea to document the moment, just in case this widow ever became of interest to the police. The drummer called to a friend who had been taking pictures of the band and asked her to snap a few of the young woman with the singer, which she did.

The other members of the band finally convinced Reis to get back to singing by himself. "We were trying to tell Paul to knock it off," remembered O'Leary, "because she really didn't sound that good and new people were coming into the club. We didn't want them to think that she was the singer."

Before Pam left, she gave her former boyfriend her phone number and urged him to come out to Hampton and see her new condo. Reis told her he would, but said later he never followed up on it.

There were other nights out as well. Terri Schnell, who frequented the local clubs, remembered being at T.R.'s Tavern in Londonderry with Pam two weeks after Greg's murder. Schnell says that when Pam met people that night one of the first things out of her mouth was the matter-of-fact remark that her husband had recently been murdered.

Terri went clubbing with Pam several times after Greg's death. "She got pissed one time when a guy she was dancing with went and danced with someone else," Schnell remembered. "When she asked the guy why, the guy said it was because Pam had a fat ass. Then she started crying."

Around the middle of the month, a group of Pam's friends, her mother, and her sister, Beth—about a dozen people in all—joined her at the condo in Derry one Saturday to help her start moving. Pam was going to a similar sized condo in Hampton near work, and she wanted to get her lighter belongings out of the way before the movers took the heavy stuff.

The condo on Misty Morning Drive was a low-level disaster area. The couches were black with fingerprint dust. The couple's belongings were strewn around. And there at the edge of the dining area was the ever-present bloodstain from Greg's skull, covered by a towel but unsettling all the same.

Everyone went to work, boxing things and helping clean the place. Then, upstairs in the bedroom, Pam held court, handing out items she no longer wanted. To the Parillas she gave a humidifier. To the daughter of an old friend from junior high a cheerleading doll. But the main door prizes were her dead husband's belongings.

Some friends had wondered why they were invited in the first place. Nothing very heavy needed to be moved. They got the feeling that this everything-must-go giveaway was the real reason they were there. "She was just giving away everything that was his," remembered Ted Chappell, a friend of Greg's since boyhood.

Then, when it was time for lunch, a few people got some food and brought it back. They all sat around the dining room table, just feet from where Greg's blood still stained the carpet, talking, laughing, drinking sodas and beer, and eating chicken fingers, hot dogs, hamburgers, French fries, and onion rings.

"Pam wasn't upset," remembered Chappell. "She wasn't perfectly normal, but she was eating and laughing and joking. She was just having too good a time."

Chappell was not alone in these thoughts. Some of the neighbors noticed Pam running back and forth between the condo and the cars to take stuff away, and thought it odd how happy she seemed. "I guess I expected to see her come in slowly, a little bit wary, sad," said Mary Jane Woodside. "But she was bopping in and out of there, literally running up the front stairs into the house. I said to my husband, 'That's weird, that's really weird.' I said, 'If I had found you on the floor they would have to carry me kicking and screaming back into the house. There is no way I would go back in there.' "

One neighbor went over to wish her well. But Art Hughes, who had burst into the condo the night of Greg's murder without a thought for his own safety, was too irritated with the widow to do the same. He had read her complaints about the neighbors in the newspaper, statements that made it sound like no one cared, that people in the complex had information about the killing but were too afraid to come forward.

"I can understand her being mad at the world," Hughes told his wife. "But if she was going to say *anything* about the neighbors, she could at least acknowledge that a bunch of us came out to do whatever we could for her.''

With so little to go on, the cops were fanning out in every direction that seemed reasonable.

Street sources were questioned up and down about any scuttlebutt they were hearing regarding Smart's death.

Flyers with pictures of jewelry similar to that which was stolen, as Pam had described, were distributed to pawnshops and detectives all over. Earrings, bracelets, rings. One of the more identifiable pieces was a gold chain that Greg liked to wear on weekends. Attached to it was a little charm— the letter *P*—in honor of his wife.

And every new lead that dribbled in, as crazy as it might sound, stood a chance of breaking the case wide open.

Someone named Greg Smart called the cops claiming that he had recently been at odds with some very dangerous people. He was convinced that the killing in Derry was a mistake and that it was *he* who had been targeted to die.

One of the neighbors in the area, meanwhile, was discovered to have a criminal record for violent behavior and had to be checked out.

Then word came in that police in Fort Lee, New Jersey, had arrested a gang of blacks and Hispanics on weapons and drug charges. They were from Massachusetts and were suspects in a number of other crimes, among them a killing in Haverhill, Massachusetts. Included in the items confiscated at their arrest were hollow-point bullets, a car that had been purchased in Hudson, New Hampshire, and several handguns that could very well have been the type that killed Smart.

It was not so farfetched to think that these hoodlums could have broken into a condo and killed someone. Some of them had been in southern New Hampshire in recent months, trying to raise bail to free their leader who was in jail in Manchester. Apparently they had been posing as cops, storming the homes of drug dealers and ripping them off.

Next, in going through Greg's and Pam's telephone records, the detectives found Greg had made some calls to a business—as it turned out, a gambling junket service—that supposedly had ties to local organized crime.

Around the same time, word trickled in that not long before his death Greg had been at a huge party where drugs were being sold. Some people wondered if it had any connection to a recent assault on some residents at the same house.

The cops also looked into one of Greg's old girlfriends, whom a few years earlier he apparently had gotten pregnant but then refused to help pay for an abortion. Her father, enraged at Greg's behavior, spouted off that he had a good mind to go shoot the kid.

Painstakingly, one by one, each lead had to be weighed and checked out. And one by one, each was scratched off. Nothing was panning out.

On the night of May 14, with all the other leads still swirling around, a call came in at the Derry police department. When the dispatcher answered, a woman started telling how she had information into the recent murder. High-profile cases send all kinds of crazies to their telephones with "tips." When an investigation is going nowhere, though, even the most bizarre callers get heard.

The call was sent back to Dan Pelletier.

The woman, who at first refused to give her name, was nervous. She told Pelletier she did not want to get involved. But she had heard some things the police ought to know. Things were not as they may seem, she said, with the killing of the young man in the condo complex. And she had the name of someone who knew a lot more.

"His wife planned him to be killed," she said of Gregory Smart, "so she could collect the insurance money. And he was killed in home and she came home and she put on a wonderful performance. The person you can talk to about it is a minor."

Pelletier wanted to keep her talking, so he prodded her along with gentle affirmations. "Yeah," he said.

"She's fifteen years old."

"OK."

"But she knows the whole ordeal. The whole situation of what was going on."

"Is she a friend of this woman's?" Pelletier asked.

"Yeah. I—I'm sorry. I—I will not reveal my name or where I'm from, but I have heard this from hearsay, but I'm damned scared silly."

At first the caller said she thought the fifteen year old's name was Cecelia Perkins, but soon she corrected that. It was Cecelia Pierce.

Cecelia was a friend of the wife's, the caller said. The girl had even been at the funeral, she said. And she could be located out on the New Hampshire seacoast, in Seabrook.

Pelletier kept at her, probing for any information at all.

"I'm not positive, but from what I've heard the wife had planned it," the woman said. "She wanted the insurance money. From what I understand she's already gone out and bought a brand-new Trans-Am with the insurance money."

"OK," Pelletier said. "And do you know how long she was planning on doing this?"

"Not exactly. The last four or five weeks."

The detective was walking a tightrope. He wanted to cull as much as he could, yet not scare her off.

"I—I'm just trying to be helpful," the woman said. "I don't want to be involved."

"I understand, but I'm just . . . you got to understand, this is probably the last time I'll talk to you, so I've got to get as much information as I can right now."

"Yeah," she replied. "Well, if I hear other things I will get back in touch with you again."

"OK," Pelletier said. "Yeah, just for—"

"There's just been a gentleman killed," the caller interjected. "There's been a murder committed here and I don't like the idea of that."

A minute later she was gone. What she had left, however, was a tip that rang some bells.

Cecelia Pierce. The girl's name had come up before. In a routine interview just a few days after the murder, one of Pam's co-workers had mentioned that one of the students at Winnacunnet High School, Cecelia, had spent the week before Greg's murder at Pam's condo.

Pam, too, had brought up the girl's name. The widow had failed to mention Cecelia when Pelletier initially asked for names of anyone who had been in the condo the month before the murder. But she did pass the name along about a week later, when the detective had asked if Pam had any friends that were not Greg's as well.

Pam could think of just two, and though they were not related, both were named Pierce. Ann Pierce was Pam's college roommate. Cecelia Pierce was her student intern at work, a girl she had met through the drug- and alcohol-awareness program.

Now Pelletier figured that maybe investigators should get to know Cecelia Pierce a bit better.

Chapter 4

The late cartoonist Al Capp once said that Seabrook was where he "found the men to be the most ferocious and the women the most beautiful."

He also said, tongue in cheek, that Seabrook, where he and his wife often enjoyed the beach, was the model for Dogpatch, the comic-strip community of hillbillies where Capp's "Li'l Abner" took place.

A cartoonish figure in his own right, Capp was a raconteur who never let the truth ruin a good yarn, whether it involved his place of birth or the inspiration for his famous comic strip. "Li'l Abner" sprang from the cartoonist's travels through the South as a young man. His wife, daughter, lawyer, and a publisher of his cartoons in book form all insist that Capp was joshing about Seabrook.

Yet on the New Hampshire seacoast, the story persists as fact. For Al Capp was not the only one who scorned reality for the sake of an anecdote. In the minds of many, even some of its own residents, Seabrook has always been Dogpatch: a place that embodied a clannish, backwoods mentality and life-style, a chunk of Appalachia transplanted to New Hampshire, an hour from Boston.

It sits seven-thousand people strong, beside the ocean, the first New Hampshire town off Interstate 95 north. From the exit, it is just a short drive in one direction to Seabrook Greyhound Park, the dog track, and in the other, Seabrook Station, the infamous nuclear power plant.

The town's main drags—Route 1 and, by the Atlantic Ocean, Route 1A—are a seedy hodgepodge of tattoo parlors, fireworks stores, and fast-food joints. Big Al's Gun Shop here, Leather and Lace adult books and videos there.

First appearances notwithstanding, the town's coffers are far from bare. Tax dollars from the nuclear plant have brought healthy five- to six-million-dollar budgets and have allowed Seabrook to build facilities—a police station and a community center to name two—that are envied around the state.

North and south of Seabrook are popular recreational areas, Hampton Beach and Massachusetts' Salisbury Beach. "We're basically the town in between, the point in transit," said one citizen. From Memorial Day to Labor Day, as a result, the traffic in Seabrook can be ungodly and the visitors, often teenagers, hellish.

Summertime only adds to what is already a day-to-day struggle for a good number of Seabrook's residents, many of whom make their living from the sea on fishing boats, clamming, and catching lobsters. Others work at the nuclear plant or in factories in the surrounding communities. A handful hold professional positions. And many do not work at all. Seabrook's unemployment rate, and the number of its young people that fail to finish high school, is high.

The most impoverished, rough-and-tumble part of town is south Seabrook, a four-square-mile section that has long been a world unto itself. Hard by the Massachusetts border, south Seabrook is marked by blight, the front and backyards of many houses and mobile homes decorated with skeletons of old cars and parts. Barking dogs tethered by chains are ever present.

Outsiders regard this part of Seabrook as Dogpatch. This is where the natives proudly call themselves "Bubbas" or "Bubs." Outsiders derisively refer to them as "Seabrookers" or simply " 'Brookers." It is a neighborhood where even the local police tread carefully, never being quite sure when their cruisers might be stoned or egged.

Here, generations of the same families have lived. Unwed daughters raising their babies at home are not uncommon. And while the traditional family does not thrive, a wariness of strangers makes for a thick code of loyalty among family and neighbors alike.

That isolationism is exacerbated by a dialect seldom heard elsewhere in the vicinity.

When *New Hampshire Seacoast Sunday*, a weekly newspaper, published a critical article about the town, residents were outraged. One sent a lengthy letter to the editor and closed with a couple of paragraphs written in the native tongue.

Ike, even our "clipped dialect and homespun idioms" are a bone of contention with you. My answer is: I think it's bout time we start mouthing off in a mucker way, caus for ye-ars the carpetbaggers and cliff dwellers have tried to throw us out cross; it can't be done, boy. Berta, people like you try to stave us up with your written word, but it ain't gona work.

We ain't gonna be no bodies' larky. I can face a looking glass any day and be proud of my heritage. Berch, as far as our dialect and homespun idioms go we should never lose it, or try to disguise it. We should talk it to our children and grandchildren, caus it ott be taught um.

Sneers one newcomer: "If you can understand what they're saying, you've been here too long."

South Seabrook fought change when the rush was on from Massachusetts to southern New Hampshire. Often literally. The Seabrook cops spent many a night pulling apart upwardly mobile transplants and the Bubs when turf battles erupted in places like the pool hall.

To this day, many of the residents resist impingement by the outside. At the same time, the outside has not always been kind to those from Seabrook.

Nowhere has it been more evident over the years than at regional Winnacunnet High School in Hampton, where nine hundred kids, both working-class and wealthy, from five towns are poured together for grades nine through twelve.

The dyed-in-the-wool Seabrook kids have always stood apart, particularly from their classmates raised in affluent communities like North Hampton and Hampton Falls. A standing joke is that there are no minorities at Winnacunnet High School, except, of course, the 'Brookers.

The differences are as subtle as the Seabrook kids tending to keep their coats on all day in the winter instead of putting them in their lockers. They tend to wear a lot of leather. T-shirts. Blue jeans. The dialect and lack of concern about education in many Seabrook families only draws the line more sharply.

Whether the kids are ostracized or whether they shut themselves off is open to debate. But if a child is from Seabrook, no matter whether he is a native or not, he stands a good chance of being regarded as a 'Brooker. And while some of the kids find friendship in the larger community of the high school, many others remain strangers in a strange land, left to seek security with the kids from their own community.

As such, class differences play out even where the students have lunch. For years, the Seabrook kids have tended to eat in the lower part of Winnacunnet's two-level cafeteria, a section known as "the pit." The kids from the other communities sit above.

A number of the teachers and school officials, though, have a warm spot for the kids from Seabrook. Unlike many of their classmates, they lack certain pretensions. A lot of the students from Seabrook tend to show real appreciation when someone takes the extra time to care about them.

And even the troublemakers among them often have an ethical code unlike the rest of the students. "As a disciplinarian I never had much trouble with the Seabrook kids," recalled one former Winnacunnet official. "Usually when I called them in they'd say, 'Yeah, I did it.' It was the Hampton kids who gave me some phony story or tried to talk me out of punishing them."

Still, not many Seabrook kids have grand dreams for when they leave Winnacunnet High School, which is often long before graduation day.

"I hated to think what their future would hold for them," said the former school administrator.

The hangout was Vance and Diane Lattime's house on Upper Collins Street in the heart of south Seabrook. Their mobile home sits down a dirt driveway, off the road, with woods out back, an ideal place for the Lattime's seventeen-year-old son JR and his buddies. It was not expansive, but there was property enough for a few junk cars that the kids worked on and space to roughhouse or blast fireworks without driving too many neighbors crazy.

What made it perfect, though, was that Vance and Diane liked having the kids around. If their son was home, the parents figured, he wasn't off someplace else getting into trouble.

And, anyway, with the Lattimes it was always the more the merrier. Their place was never empty: Diane's mother was over regularly. Their daughter, who was not married, had a baby and they were planning to adopt him. And they had taken in one of JR's friends, Ralph Welch, who lived in the neighborhood and whose parents' place was in need of repair and overcrowded.

The elder Lattime was a laborer at the nuclear plant, and his wife was a warranty administrator for a car dealership. They had moved from Salisbury to escape the Massachusetts tax bite ten years earlier, and picked Seabrook because Diane's mother lived there. The couple, in fact, had planned to move the family to wooded northern New Hampshire in the summer of 1989.

But JR, who would enter his sophomore year at Winnacunnet that fall, convinced them to stay until he graduated. He didn't want to leave his friends.

Indeed, he and his pals had forged strong bonds over the years. Ever since they were little, JR, Ralph Welch, and Patrick Randall might as well have been brothers. Randall's family had moved to Connecticut for a while, but for the most part, they grew up together in Seabrook—brawny, tough talking, street smart.

They were joined by Billy Flynn, who had come to town three years earlier and who lived with his mother and two younger brothers near Seabrook Beach, a few miles away. Billy was from southern California. His parents were splitting up, and his mom had packed up the kids and headed east, settling in New Hampshire, not far from the little Massachusetts town where she grew up. It was not long after that, however, that Billy's father died out in California.

In less than a year, Billy Flynn's world had been turned inside out, and the boy, who had already been quiet, turned deep within himself. It was JR and Pat who helped pull him out, taking him into their circle of friends.

"For the lack of a better word," says JR's mother, Diane, "they decided to make Bill their project."

Other kids, of course, were always drifting in and out of the group, not to mention Vance Lattime's house. But as the summer of 1989 edged toward fall, the nucleus was Ralph, JR, Pat, and Bill.

They were 'Brookers. Together they were full of teenage bravado, smirk, and swagger. And what tied them together perhaps more than anything were the strains—always loud—of their favorite music, heavy metal rock and roll. The numbing guitars and defiant lyrics of bands like Van Halen, Guns 'n' Roses, Poison, and best of all, Motley Crue, were the background music to their daily lives.

They found comfort in the group, but it was their individuality that truly made the camaraderie click. They complemented each other.

Ralph, sinewy and with a broken face, was a little older and was always considered the strongest and best fighter. He was slowly pulling away from the group because his girlfriend did not care for the others.

JR, who wore thick glasses ever since he was one year old, was more thoughtful, a kid who devoured books, laying out his own cash for an anthology of Edgar Allan Poe, and who was eternally happy under the hood of a car or taking apart something to figure how it worked.

Pat was probably the most innately intelligent. He had a passion for reading, wrote well, and liked math. Yet he seemed bored at Winnacunnet, had to repeat his freshman year, and ended up in an alternative program designed to retain kids who looked as if they would drop out. His given name was Patrick Alan Randall, but he got a nickname when he was just a baby. His father, a fisherman, looked down at the kid one day and said matter-of-factly, "Looks like a Pete to me." And so Pete he became. Randall was a diehard, loyal friend. He was a handsome, clean-cut kid, too. But beneath it there seemed to be a seething anger and the promise of violence if pushed too far. Some people worried that Pete one day could end up behind bars.

Billy, meanwhile, was more of a dreamer. He liked to doodle cartoons, taught himself to play his electric guitar, and seemed more gentle, friendlier somehow, than the others. Beneath his dark eyebrows, his brown eyes were melancholy and his features soft. And sometimes when he was speaking, Billy's voice would drift off to such a quietness that you would think he was talking to himself. He also had a tendency to exaggerate about himself. Now and then, Billy would brag about his late father having been a biker, which was true only in that his dad owned and liked motorcycles. Flynn also told his friends that he had a quarter of a million dollars in trust waiting for him on his eighteenth birthday, the proceeds from his father's life insurance. His mother said it is closer to $24,000.

At JR's they would spend their spare time, digging into car engines or relaxing and letting heavy metal wash over them.

Now and then they would grab Mrs. Lattime's video

camera and record themselves in full-blown teenage silliness, albeit a roughneck kind of foolishness. Some footage shows them one by one riding bikes up a homemade ramp, flying into the air, and landing in some brush. Another scene shows them in a circle trying to catch an arrow they were tossing at each other.

But some segments seem worthy of those television shows in which people send in their home videos. Billy Flynn, for example, once did a mock commercial for the Ralph Welch School of Guerrilla Tactics. "This is the deadly foot," his voice intoned, as the kid's sneaker filled up the screen. "This is the deadly hand," and a hand came into view. "And most of all, the deadly toes!" And there was a set of toes wiggling away.

The Lattimes enjoyed the kids, trusted them, and in a pinch had no qualms about leaving Ryan, their daughter's baby, in their care. One time, Diane Lattime stepped out for a minute, giving JR and his friends command of the baby. When she came back, the walls were shaking to the roar of Motley Crue. In the kitchen were the boys, including the one year old, all of them pumping their fists in the air and shouting, "Crue! Crue! Crue!"

The kids adored the baby and never missed a chance to play with him. Ryan could even get away with calling Pete a name few kids at school would ever dare to pin on him: Pee-pee.

Yet angelic they were not, and in some people's eyes they were punks first and last. The kids had developed a nasty reputation as small-time thieves, stealing motorcycles or breaking into cars and taking radios. And if a stranger left his keys in his car, one of them might very well climb in, go for a ride, and leave the vehicle around the block, chuckling at the image of some guy wandering around looking for it.

None of them was overly excited about school, and their grades were for the most part middle-of-the-road. With the exception of Billy, they were physical kids, but none of them intended to go out for school sports. The idea of joining a club or running for class officer was a laugh.

As such, it was probably not 100 percent altruism that fall when Billy and JR, now sophomores, agreed to help out with Project Self-Esteem, Winnacunnet's drug- and alcohol-awareness program for freshmen.

It was, more likely than not, just something to do. And if nothing else, it wasn't a bad place to meet girls.

The first time Pamela Smart blipped across Billy Flynn's radar screen was at Winnacunnet High School during a meeting for Project Self-Esteem discussion leaders. One of the guidance counselors introduced the petite SAU 21 media center director to the group and the fifteen year old's hormones kicked into gear. He turned to Lattime and said softly, "I'm in love."

Billy's was not the only adolescent head to have been turned by Pam. At periodic meetings of the discussion leaders, which led up to the three-day program with the ninth graders later in the school year, lots of the boys would flutter around her flirtatiously.

Flynn made sure he got into Pam's group when the facilitators broke into units of four or five. At that point they would work on discussion exercises in which everyone told about themselves. It was then that Billy learned of Pam's mania for Van Halen and her experience as the Maiden of Metal.

Billy would talk about himself, too, saying that he also was a metalhead and that his favorite group was Motley Crue. He also talked some about losing his father. It had obviously caused him some pain.

Still, Flynn did not appear to take Project Self-Esteem very seriously. He joked around with Lattime a good part of the time, and out of school along with his buddies was drinking and snorting cocaine.

What he was interested in was Pam. "She's hot," he told his friends, then went off in typical teenage fashion about his utter desire for her. As time went on, Billy would skip lunch or study hall and with another friend from Project Self-Esteem, Tommy Sells, wander across the parking lot to the school board building to visit her.

Another student, meanwhile, had also developed an instant attraction to Pam. Cecelia Louise Pierce approached the media center director that first day and introduced herself. Cecelia, whom her mother had called "Critter" or "Crit" since she was a baby, was an affable, talkative kid. She was embarrassed by a problem with her weight, though, and her antennae were always up for slights, both real and imagined, about being from Seabrook.

From the very beginning it was obvious that Pam was unlike anyone in Cecelia's world. The girl had lived in Seabrook all of her fifteen years, and although she never was close to them she had known JR and Pete since she was little. Her parents had been divorced when she was a baby. Her mother, a woman of some heft who was also named Cecelia, remarried Allen Eaton (one of the more common surnames in Seabrook) who himself came from a family of sixteen kids.

Cecelia's mother and stepfather were working people, not particularly handsome, with educations that stopped at high school. There was nothing glamorous about them nor their day-in and day-out efforts to stay on top of the bills, keep food on the table for Cecelia and her younger sister, and now and then scrape enough together for a vacation or maybe a school ring for Crit.

But Pam was something else altogether. She was attractive, full of energy, and when Cecelia talked to her it was as if she listened, as if she cared.

Like Billy, Cecelia basked in Pam's glow. As they came to regularly work together in the meetings for facilitators, Pam and Cecelia became friends. And when the girl mentioned that she thought she might someday go into journalism and that Pam's job looked interesting, Pam threw out the idea of her working over at SAU 21 as her intern.

To Cecelia it sounded like a good idea. She could come over to Pam's basement office two periods a day and get credit for helping typeset the school board newsletter, edit, and whatever else needed to be done. What's more, she could be around her new friend.

More and more, as she started her internship that November, Cecelia came to cherish Pam's friendship. Since she was little, Cecelia had a best friend, Karen Crowley, but now room was being carved out for Pam, who was becoming almost like a big sister. She was Cecelia's confidante and role model, someone who knew what was out there beyond Seabrook.

At the same time, Pam could relate on Cecelia's level. For Christmas, for example, she gave her intern a Bon Jovi tape, *New Jersey*, a perfectly appropriate gift considering the nature of their relationship. But more than that, it was a present the kid actually liked.

What Cecelia took to more than anything, though, was

that Pam treated her with a basic kindness that she felt was lacking in her life. Pam would often hug Cecelia, which in itself went a long way to building trust and affection. And Smart was not above saying she was sorry.

"When we get in a fight, my best friend never apologizes to me," Cecelia would later say. "I always have to say, 'I'm sorry, please don't be mad.' And with Pam, we only really got in one fight and it wasn't even really a fight and she was like, 'Please, don't be mad at me, I'm sorry.' And all I was thinking was, 'Here's this girl, she's twenty-two, she's my friend, and she's actually apologizing to *me*.' "

For five years, the Florida Department of Citrus had been sponsoring a high school video competition. The idea was for kids around the country to compete for various prizes, including a trip to Disney World, by making a commercial touting the nutritional value of orange juice.

The competition had never gone over particularly well at Winnacunnet High School. But one day in December, Cecelia noticed a flyer for it on Pam's desk. They got to talking and decided it might be a fun project.

Pam got the school's permission, then she and Cecelia started recruiting kids. Cecelia got her friend Karen interested. Billy, who at first thought it a lame idea, was attracted enough to Pam to get a couple of school friends and take part.

By January, when the project got underway in earnest, only three high schoolers—Billy, Cecelia, and Karen—were involved. Flynn's pals had pulled out. One had moved and the other was involved in after-school sports. So Pam recruited Tracy Collins, the girlfriend of Greg's buddy Brian Washburn. Tracy was just out of high school herself.

The concept for their video was simple, and appropriately enough, sophomoric. The group had gotten together and tossed around ideas, settling on rap lyrics and acted-out scenes depicting orange juice's role in the life of modern and primitive man.

Throughout the winter, on Saturdays and after school, the group would meet several times a week for a few hours. As in most everything she took on, Pam was the driving force behind the video. She rounded up the kids, cajoled them when they weren't interested, and pushed it through to completion.

For the most part, Billy was the cameraman. It was a job he liked better than performing. Even when horsing around with his friends in the Lattimes' backyard, Billy was more comfortable behind the camera than in front of it. Playing the part of a caveman, say, was something that just was not in Billy's makeup. It was not cool. Running the equipment, he figured, at least had some dignity.

Without much enthusiasm, Billy did appear on the video at one point, shooting baskets for a scene apparently showing the youth of modern times hard at play.

He had a speaking part, too, though one less comedic than his promotion for the Ralph Welch School of Guerrilla Tactics: "Although times have changed, man still longs for the taste of refreshing Florida orange juice. Today, thanks to modern technology, the process of making freshly squeezed orange juice has become much simpler. Even though time has progressed, orange juice has maintained its nutritional value."

For taping, Pam drove the school board van, mostly around Seabrook—to the beach, Cecelia's grandmother's house, behind the recreation center, and to Billy's mother's apartment.

Billy's mother, Elaine Flynn, remembered one time that the kids came over to tape a scene, which was when she met Pam for the first time. "I thought, Ah-hah! *Now* I know why he's involved with this commercial, even on his weekends."

Everyone appeared in one scene or another. Pam, in particular, was an active participant. Once, while taping out behind Cecelia's grandmother's house, the media center director took the old woman aback when, in the dead of the New Hampshire winter, she stepped out of the bathroom and went outside in a skimpy leopard-skin patterned outfit, apparently to play the part of a cavewoman. In the commercial, Pam, who could almost pass for a teenager herself, can be seen gathering wood and wringing out her clothes by a stream, propelled no doubt by vitamin C.

Together they wrote the lyrics, which Pam fine-tuned: "We start each day with work to do/ We get our energy from orange juice/ We all need nutrition and there's no excuse/ Cause you can get plenty from orange juice. . . ." On and on it went.

Billy, who was taking a music class, helped pave the

way for Pam and the kids to use the electronic music lab to mix the thumping rap music and the vocals.

When it was completed, the video lasted a little more than two and a half minutes. Pam wrote a story for the SAU 21 spring newsletter, *On the Move*, about it and included a picture, taken in the music lab, of Billy and Cecelia. She told an assistant that the story was important and asked that it not be left out of the issue.

All the same, the video would win nothing in the competition. Even for a teenage production it seemed to lack punch.

What did happen in the three months that the video was produced, however, is that Pam developed a loyal little following. What seems to have started with good intent on Pam's part, a desire to work with kids, was gradually changing.

The kids never got much closer to one another as a result of the project, but everyone looked up to Pam. Unlike most adults, she never appeared to be patronizing them. She spoke their language and enjoyed the same music they did. Rather than lecture them or run on about her glory days at Pinkerton, Pam instead spoke of meeting Eddie Van Halen and of getting backstage passes for heavy metal concerts.

Then, when the work on the video was done for the day, she would take them out to eat at Wendy's or to hang around Salisbury Beach and talk. As time went on, she would even go with the kids to places like Sneakers, a teenage, non-alcoholic dance club in Salisbury.

Before long, Pam's role as an authority figure was all but nonexistent. In many ways, it was as if she were one of the kids herself. An older one to be sure, but popular, the one all the younger kids wanted as *their* friend.

All of Pam's charges showed signs of it, but by far the most vitriolic was Cecelia Pierce. The girl was proud of her relationship with the pretty media center director. She grew possessive, going out of her way to sit next to Pam in the van, for example, and became upset if anyone got there before her.

She even let her affection for Pam come between her longtime friendship with Karen, growing angry when her onetime best friend mentioned possibly becoming Pam's intern the following year and worrying aloud that she was trying to steal Pam from her.

Cecelia had never had a friend like Pam, someone who was pretty and intelligent and self-assured. She made Cecelia feel important just being with her. Pam paid for everything when they went out, be it lunch or whatever incidentals came up. And when Cecelia began to learn to drive, Pam would always let the teenager take the wheel of her Honda CRX.

It got to the point that the friendship soon came to affect the girl's home life. Cecelia saw her mother as overstrict. Pam, however, was fun. More and more, Pam's desires would come up against what Cecelia's mother wanted. For example, if the family was about to go shopping at the mall and Pam called, saying that it was time to work on the video, off Crit would go.

"As this relationship went on and on," said her mother, Cecelia Eaton, "I liked it less and less. I was actually getting angry. I even said to Crit: 'You'd think Pam was your mother. Well, I'm your mother, not Pam.' "

Cecelia's grades also began to dip, and Mrs. Eaton even went to talk to school officials about how much time her daughter was spending with the school board's media center director. "I noticed it, too," an assistant principal told her. Apparently it went little further.

Billy Flynn had also adjusted his life to spend more time around Pam, working on the video and obviously flirting when he would make his way down to her office for his daily visits.

He wore a black-leather jacket and an earring and he ran with a tough crowd in Pete, JR, and Ralph, but almost everyone who knew Billy thought that by himself he was as threatening as a golden retriever.

Carrying only one hundred and fifty pounds on his lanky five-foot eleven-inch frame—and most of that from a heavy diet of junk food—Billy was quick to help Pam carry equipment or boxes if he saw her struggling across the parking lot. If Pam or the girls were having a hard time crossing a patch of ice during the making of the video, he would come to their aid. Or if someone was cold, he would offer his coat.

Billy was hardly a problem in school. He had complained to some staffers at Winnacunnet about excruciating headaches, the result of a skateboarding accident. Fooling around with his buddies, Billy was on the board, being pulled by a truck, when the skateboard struck something in the road. Billy was sent crashing down on the back of his head. He was briefly unconscious and lost his memory for about a day.

Besides that, he seldom called attention to himself. If anything, his problem was being too quiet. A number of adults at the school, in fact, would wonder now and then if something was bothering him, perhaps something that could be traced back to home.

Indeed, by his sophomore year, Billy's home life was less than ideal. He was living with his mother, Elaine, and two younger brothers, Jimmy and Larry, in the basement apartment of a house near Seabrook Beach. For the most part, though, he was going his own way.

He was at a difficult age, fifteen, and did not talk much with his mother. After a while, she tended to look the other way. When Billy was around, he usually kept to himself. What he did show at home, which he did not reveal elsewhere, was his rage.

Elaine Flynn is a soft-spoken woman of around forty. At one time she might well have been one of the young women who take assignments from the modeling agency where Elaine does office work to supplement her income cleaning homes. She had once planned, in fact, to be a model.

It was not that Billy was violent, she said. In fact, she believed he had a lot of self-restraint. The problem, though, was that he could become incensed over the smallest difficulty, making him hard to communicate with, much less understand. "Outside of the family, people saw a kid that was polite and charming," she said. "That was one side of Billy that he projected to people that he wanted to impress. He wanted to be liked. Inside the family is where he took out his anger. At home he could be whatever he was feeling like and most of the time he was feeling like a prick."

Elaine laughed at her choice of words.

"He has an attitude when something's bothering him. He vibes out. You can just tell that he's angry. It's like a volcano waiting to erupt."

Elaine, a widow, would ask for advice from relatives and friends about how to handle Billy's moods, particularly when he would cause problems for her other sons. "Everybody's solution was, 'Beat the shit out of him,'" she said.

"And I could never go for that. So most of the time I would just try to create peace, whatever it took."

Billy Flynn's parents had come of age in northeast Massachusetts during the turmoil of the late 1960s. Elaine graduated from high school in 1969, worked in New York for the better part of a year, and came home to save some money before trying to make it in the city as a professional model. That changed in the summer of 1970 when some friends introduced her to James William Flynn, whom everyone called Bill.

Flynn was intelligent—an intellectual, said his wife—but in keeping with the times, he was scraggly haired and heavily into recreational drugs and riding his motorcycle. He had graduated from high school a few years earlier, served some time in the army, and was planning to start college that autumn.

Then he met Elaine. When she said she was going to southern California to visit her sister, Bill said he would come along. They drove across the country in an old Dodge, found a place together, and ended up staying.

They got married a couple years later and over time would live in a variety of places around the San Gabriel Valley before moving to canyon country and the desert.

Flynn was an intense individual, with dark eyebrows that only added to his serious-minded persona. He broke away from his hippie image, donned a coat and tie, and like his father held positions as a car salesman—of Cadillacs at first and then Chevys. Eventually he would end up running a construction company with his brother-in-law.

The couple was only married about a year when Elaine, working as a nurse's aide in a convalescent home, underwent a powerful Christian conversion. Overnight, she took on a whole new view of life and abandoned marijuana and swearing, two of her more enjoyable pastimes.

The change did not bode well with her husband, who always liked to drink and dabbled in pot and coke. Before long, Elaine's newfound religion became a constant source of discord. Major arguments ensued, and one day with Elaine six months pregnant with their first child, he ordered her to leave.

Elaine moved in with her sister, never telling her husband where she went. The night before she gave birth, the telephone rang. Bill had found her. He said he was furious that she had hidden from him. Growing more and more belligerent, he said that he was on his way over to blow her away.

He hurried to the sister's place, stormed in wild-eyed, and upon confronting his wife, reached into his pocket as if going for a gun. Elaine let loose a scream that she expected to be her final sound in this life. But when she looked Bill Flynn had taken his empty hand out of his empty pocket. He pointed his finger at her as if it were a pistol and smiled.

Their son, William Patrick Flynn, was born the next day, March 12, 1974. William was a popular name in the Flynn family, so that part of the process was easy. The nurse at the hospital, though, refused to allow the couple to depart until they decided on a middle name. It was near St. Patrick's Day, so Patrick it was.

The marriage would continue to be tumultuous. Usually, Billy would be at the center of the storm, with the arguments raging over what his mother saw as overbearing treatment by the father. Perhaps because of his own strict upbringing, Bill Flynn demanded perfection from his son, something the child was unable to give.

"Bill never treated him on his level," said Elaine. For example, she recalled, when Billy was about three, her husband had been washing his van and gave Billy the job of cleaning the back window. It should have been fun, but it ended in torment. The boy washed the window as one might expect, like a child, with the paper towel crumpled and rubbing it in little circles that streaked the glass. "Bill would not accept that," remembered Elaine. "So he just kept Billy there doing it over and over until it looked acceptable."

Billy attended parochial school in the first grade and one day he came home with a note saying the boy should work harder on his penmanship. So his father sat him down and made the six-year-old write the alphabet and the numbers one through ten. Every time he finished, however, his father said it was not good enough and commanded that he do it again. And again. And again. Nine times. Ten times. Eleven times. The lesson finally ended with the boy, and his mother, in tears.

A couple of days later, Elaine picked up Billy after school and the boy started weeping. As best as she could piece it together, Elaine says, a priest had spoken to Billy's class that day and talked about how God, like their earthly fathers, loved them so much that He would never give them more burdens than they could bear. "But Billy interpreted that to mean, 'My earthly dad doesn't love me because he always gives me more than I can bear,'" she said.

It was not a lack of love for Billy, but a demanding disposition that caused his father to push Billy so hard. "If things were going my husband's way, he was a great guy to be around," said Elaine Flynn. "But as soon as he had to deal with any inconvenience, forget it. We used to go down into the canyons on dirt bikes and spend the day. There's always problems with them. Well, once Billy had a problem with his bike. It was something as trivial as a spark plug. His dad told him how to fix it and it didn't go. It was blowup time. His father would start yelling, 'You couldn't have done what I said!'"

Billy grew up in the desert, far from the California coast, riding his dirt bike through washes and playing with the springer spaniel puppies his parents sometimes bred. He was shy even then and never had a lot of friends.

The Flynns would have two other boys, whom Elaine says the father never pushed as hard as the eldest son.

Still, the marriage was wracked with problems and finally it fell apart. Elaine says she learned that her husband had been cheating on her for years. In 1986, she decided to leave him.

Her husband agreed to send her a thousand dollars each month, and in September of that year Elaine prepared to start her life anew. She sent Jimmy, her middle son, east to her parents on a plane. Then, driving a souped-up Dodge with mag wheels, which her husband raced now and then at one of the local tracks, she took Billy and Larry on a cross-country drive to their new home.

Billy, who was twelve at the time, never wanted to leave California. "He was just going into junior high and he didn't want to move," recalled Elaine. "He was an angry little guy coming back with me."

Elaine would eventually find a place in New Hampshire, and Billy would enroll in seventh grade at Seabrook Elementary School. Unlike Pamela Wojas, who moved to Windham from Florida at around the same age, Billy never took his classmates by storm. He never possessed the outgoing personality to win over friends with his jokes or other attention-getting devices. If anything, he preferred to be in the background.

That Christmas, Billy's father came to visit and attempted to reconcile with Elaine and his family. Something had changed since they last saw him. Now Bill Flynn was more at peace somehow, more patient and understanding.

"I don't know what my husband went through during those months," Elaine said, "but for those ten days, he was Mr. Perfect Dad. I don't think he ever yelled at anyone once. I heard him tell Billy he loved him and I saw him with his arms around him. I think it was the first time that Billy ever felt, wow, maybe my dad does care about me."

Except for the formality of a divorce, the marriage was over. But by the time her husband headed back to California, Elaine and he had talked out many of their differences. They even discussed sending the boys west to stay with him for the summer.

That was never to be.

It was just after one in the morning on Wednesday, January 21, 1987. Bill Flynn had been out drinking all night. When it was time to go home, he refused all offers from his brother-in-law to stay at his house and drove off into the dark in his '85 Mercury Cougar.

Not much later, Flynn was pushing eighty miles per hour on the Antelope Valley Freeway, one exit from home, when a car pulled in front of his. He veered to avoid a collision and smashed into the back of a gasoline tanker carrying nearly nine thousand gallons of fuel.

At that instant the night seemed to become day. The rear tanker and Flynn's car roared into flames.

A couple passersby and two sheriff's deputies tried to save Flynn as the fire ripped through his car. To no avail. When it was over, only Bill Flynn's teeth would reveal his identity.

"The hardest thing I ever had to do was to tell those three boys that their dad was dead," said Elaine Flynn. "I shut the TV off and I told them. I remember that Billy was standing up and started to cry. Then he broke away from me and shut his door and wouldn't let me in."

For a long time, Billy Flynn let no one in. He and his mother went to California to retrieve his father's remains for burial in northern Massachusetts. When he returned to New Hampshire, Billy stayed by himself, scribbling in his room and fiddling with his Sears computer. He just wanted to be alone.

Chapter 5

It had long been coming. Like the nearly imperceptible chill in the summer twilight that speaks of autumn, something in the very air of Gregory and Pamela Smart's marriage was changing.

Greg and Pam were the same. It was true that they had full-time jobs now, careers. They wore their hair differently than they once did. They spoke of buying a house. They had, as people like to say, started to mature. As individuals, though, they were no different than they had been. Their personalities and attitudes and values had undergone no major overhauls.

Yet theirs was a relationship held by the most fragile of ties. Having so little in common, outside of similar social-class upbringings and their regard for heavy metal, Pam and Greg slowly began to pull away from one another.

Their jobs did not help. Every morning, Pam headed east toward the seacoast. Greg worked in the other direction, in Nashua. Most of his appointments were at night, so often Greg was not home before nine o'clock. And Pam, never one to like being by herself, was bothered by it. So much so that Greg complained to a friend, Yvon Pellerin, that Pam wanted him to quit the insurance business. Smart was happy in his job and was earning a good wage, though, and he refused.

Their free time, meanwhile, was seldom spent together by themselves. Greg could often be found with friends, playing cards or golfing or roaring his four-wheeler, an off-road recreational vehicle, down the trails by the power lines in Londonderry or along the old railroad bed in Windham.

Pam was never taken by such outdoor activities and leaned instead toward dance lessons or classes, such as in public relations, to further her career. She also liked to follow the news closely, reading five or six newspapers a day.

The common ground they did have was eroding. Dinners with Greg's parents were fewer. Greg would go to parties without his wife. They would even take separate vacations, with Greg and some friends going skiing in Canada and Pam taking a cruise to Mexico with her parents.

If other couples came to visit, often the women would do one activity and the men something else. Some of Greg's friends who needed a break from their girlfriends or spouses especially liked going to see the Smarts. But for the ones who hoped to get together as couples it became maddening.

"It ended up that they were never together," said Heidi Parilla.

Other changes were more damaging. Pam told people that Greg used to tease her about having an affair and, in a nonjoking way, he once told his friend Dave Bosse that if either of them was likely to cheat on the other it would be Pam.

But a week or so before Christmas 1989, Pam would later testify, Greg failed to come home one night. When he showed up a little after six the next morning, he told her he had been drinking and stayed at a male friend's place.

Pam went to work that day angry and certain that he was lying. At home that afternoon she demanded the truth. "You wouldn't like the truth," Greg replied. She continued to press, until, finally, Greg admitted that he had spent the evening with another woman. He had been drinking and one thing led to another. He hardly even remembered the whole matter, he said.

Pam was, as she would later tell a jury, devastated. When Greg tried to discuss it with her, she refused to listen. For a day she would not even talk to him.

The marriage was on shaky grounds, yet few, if anyone, outside of the couple seemed to have noticed. No one moved out. There were no massive public disagreements. Life went on for Greg and Pam, though the issue of husband's infidelity was no doubt always simmering near the surface.

A few days before Christmas, they even accompanied his parents to a holiday party at a relative's home in Nashua. Greg had been drinking heavily at the gathering and was acting silly on the ride home with his parents. Pam, who these days drank only in moderation if at all, was irritated by Greg's behavior at the party and afterward.

A bit later that night, Pam showed up at the Smarts'

condo obviously upset, having trekked over in the snow, wearing only her nightclothes and slippers.

Pam, according to Bill and Judy Smart, blurted out that Greg had slapped her in the face, had her bent over a railing upstairs, and tried to strangle her.

After several attempts, Bill Smart finally got into Greg's condo and confronted his son. "He had come out of the bathroom," the father remembered. "And I said, 'Did you hit Pam? What the hell are you doing?' You know, like a father would. He said, 'I haven't even touched her. She's a pain in the ass. I just told her to get the hell out of here.' So I said, 'OK, go to bed.' He jumped into bed, I turned the light off, and proceeded out the door. The next day I went up and down on him for three hours, telling him, 'You cannot drink hard liquor if indeed you did that last night and you don't even remember it.' I said, 'You've got a problem, so on and so on.'"

Pam would later say that Greg had accidentally slapped her, that he would never intentionally hit her.

Whatever happened that night, however, it was not enough to cause an immediate breakup. Pam said they had smoothed over their differences, though Greg would later complain that his wife never let him forget his breach of their eight-month-old marriage vows. And if Greg in fact did intentionally strike her, that too was not something Pam would easily set aside.

All the same, they stayed together, and virtually none of their closest friends thought the couple had any serious problems. Then again, few ever learned of the affair or Greg's having hit Pam until many months later.

Out on the seacoast, Pam had another life. She and her teenage friends eased into an existence that no doubt pleased Pam. Unlike home, this was her unchallenged domain.

In less than six months, Smart had become a central figure in the lives of Cecelia and Billy, two very different teens, each of whom was missing a piece or two in their emotional makeup and desperately longed for positive attention.

By February, the unfinished orange juice commercial was a constant presence, a project that continually drew them together. Now Pam's student aide Cecelia was at the media center for two periods each day. And Billy, never short of reasons to visit Pam, was also there daily, usually by himself but now and then with JR Lattime in tow.

Pam, in fact, encouraged Billy. She issued him passes to get out of his free-study periods. When Billy dropped by they would talk or he would help put labels on mailings or they would go to lunch.

One day, Pam brought in some film and gave it to Billy. The teenager had told her that Kenny and Karen Knight, his mother's landlords and upstairs neighbors, owned a one-hour photo shop in Seabrook. Billy said he could get Pam a discount and would see that the Knights got the film.

Pam and Billy drove over to the store on Route 1 to pick up the finished prints. In the CRX, Pam opened the package and laughed. Inside were photos of her and Tracy Collins posing in two-piece bathing suits on a bed. (Pam, heavily made up, wore a black and white bikini.) The two women had taken pictures of each other—for a modeling portfolio, Pam would later say—in a variety of poses, mimicking the kind found in men's magazines.

She brought the pictures to work the next day, telling Billy that neither she nor Tracy thought they were very good and if the fifteen-year-old wanted some of the pictures he could have them. Otherwise Pam would just throw them out.

Billy said why not. He took about fifteen.

He also took some heat from his mother after Karen Knight showed her a sampling of the kinds of pictures her oldest son had brought in to be developed. Indignant, Billy responded that the pictures were Pam's and that he was only doing her a favor in getting them developed. He assured her that he was not the cameraman in this particular venture.

It was not long after that when Pam called Cecelia to the room next to the media center office. By now, Pam and her intern were close and it was not unusual for either to come in with some tidbit about their personal lives for the other.

"Cecelia, sit down," Pam said. "I have to tell you something."

The teenager did as she was told and waited.

"I think I'm in love with Bill," Pam said.

A smile stretched across the teenager's oval face. She laughed at the notion. She was never part of Billy's crowd, but Cecelia had always liked him and she regarded Pam as her best friend. The idea of the two together, however, was ridiculous. Pam, after all, was an adult. Billy was fifteen years old.

"Cecelia, I'm serious. I think I'm in love with Bill."

"Get out of here."

"I'm *serious*."

As it would turn out, Cecelia was to tell Bill to come by the media center so that Pam could tell him herself of her newfound passion. When Billy came over after school to see what she wanted, Pam fluttered around the subject, never quite getting to what she wanted to say. Bewildered, Billy hurried out to catch the school bus home to Seabrook.

The next day, February 5, Billy skipped a study period and went to visit Pam again. Once more, she was evasive and seemed too nervous and embarrassed to talk about what was on her mind. She put her head down. She avoided eye contact. But Billy pressed the matter and Pam finally came out with it.

"Do you ever think about me when I'm not around?" she asked.

"Sure."

"Well, I think about you all the time."

Billy Flynn could not quite believe what he was hearing. Two minutes earlier, life was normal. He was putting in his time in high school, goofing around with his roughneck friends, and mooning over the pretty media center director. Now his fantasy was coming to life. Here was a woman—a *woman*—whom he had been attracted to from the moment he first saw her, whom he had been flirting with but with no real hope of getting anywhere, revealing how attracted she was to him. Pam said she did not know what to do about her feelings because she was married, but that Billy was constantly on her mind.

The boy was quiet. He was happy, but stunned. He walked back across the parking lot to class, giddy but not quite believing what had just occurred.

That was nothing, however, to the whirl of change his relationship with Pam would undergo in the next several weeks. At first, there was an awkwardness between the two, a period of readjustment between them. That would soon dissipate.

Pam, meanwhile, was openly discussing her unhappiness in her marriage. She spoke of verbal and physical abuse, about the night she had gone over to the Smarts' condo in the snow, saying that Greg had thrown her down and kicked her out in the cold in nothing but a long T-shirt and panties,

Billy would testify. She told him that they got married in the first place because so many in their circle of friends were doing it.

In time, as Billy Flynn learned more about the Smarts' marriage—whether it was truth or fiction that Pam was telling him—and as he came to love Pam, the boy admittedly developed a hatred toward her husband. For not only had Greg become Billy's rival, but Pam made it clear that he was a bastard as well.

Then one day, shortly after telling of her feelings for him, Pam reminded Billy of a conversation they had while working on the orange juice video. They had been driving in the van, Billy would later say, and Pam had asked if anyone knew where she could hire someone to kill her secretary. She wanted her eighteen-year-old friend Tracy to have the job.

Unknown to Flynn, that had been a trial balloon, the test for a reaction that carried no risk. Billy remembered the question as a joke, an obvious one, the kind people make everyday. Still, he commented that there was a guy in Seabrook, a serious badass, who would probably do something like that.

Now, however, Pam was behaving as if her earlier remarks had never been in jest. It was not her secretary she was looking to have killed, she told the boy.

It was Greg.

Although convinced of Pam's hostility toward her husband, Billy doubted that she wanted to go as far as to hire a hit man. It was like someone saying they were looking for a rocket launcher to eliminate their neighbor with the loud stereo. Angry yes, serious no.

Pam pressed on. She was in a quandary, she said. She wanted to be with Billy rather than her husband, and divorce seemed not to be a choice at all. Greg, she told Billy, would never easily give her up. Her husband would hound her, preventing her from establishing another relationship.

What's more, Greg would get everything they owned, from the cars and furniture on down to the dog, and she would be left with practically nothing. Besides that, her salary was scarcely enough to get a decent apartment. She would have to go home to her parents—a situation Pam no doubt wanted to avoid at all costs—and wouldn't be able to move to the seacoast to be near him.

Billy regarded Pam as a decent person. And he himself was just a fifteen-year-old kid. It was like an equation where none of the figures added up. Billy said he knew of no one who would kill for money. He figured Pam would soon let it go.

In the meantime, his relationship with Pam intensified.

One day, they would find themselves at Billy's place together, supposedly to work on the video. Pam and Elaine Flynn had met. The group had been to his mother's apartment on the beach a few times before, to tape a scene or two. Billy would put some music on and they would sit around his room talking about the orange juice project.

On this day, Billy would say, his mother and brothers were home when he locked his bedroom door behind him and Pam. Soon, they found themselves next to each other, stretched out on Billy's waterbed, while Motley Crue's "Starry Eyes" played on the compact disk player. The equipment, though, was malfunctioning and kept repeating the song.

They lay across the bed, picking up the conversation that started back in her office.

"Well, are you going to kiss me?" Pam finally asked.

"Yeah, I will," said Billy.

"Well? When? Do I have to come over there and rape you?"

"Yeah," he joked.

Then they kissed. "Starry Eyes" was finishing once again. Only now the CD went on to the next song.

Billy Flynn's life was changing. He seemed happier around school these days. His buddies at first refused to believe him when Billy said he was involved with Pam. Until they saw her dropping him off at the top of JR's driveway and kissing him good-bye. Then, they decided, she was probably using him. She couldn't be serious.

In Billy's eyes, however, his relationship with Pam was getting better every day.

Among other things, he and Pam started making plans to spend a night together. At one point she talked about the movie 9 1/2 Weeks, which Billy, who usually liked his films with a little more action, had not seen. There is a scene, she said, in which actress Kim Basinger seductively dances for Mickey Rourke. She longed to do that for someone, Pam said, but until now she had no one she cared for enough.

She planned to buy some sexy lingerie just for the occasion. "She told me she was gonna dance for me like that," Billy later recounted.

It wasn't long after, when they were together with Cecelia and Tracy Collins at a clothing store, that Pam took Billy aside.

"Do you see that?" she said, referring to what Billy would later describe as "a lingerie-lace-type thing" on a wall in the store.

"Yeah."

"Do you like it?"

"Yeah."

"Well, that's pretty much what I bought for us, only mine's turquoise and white."

Billy would remember it as a weekend in the middle of February, around Valentine's Day, when Pam invited him to spend the night at her condo. He testified that he believed Greg was skiing with his friends at the time. (Greg, in fact, had been on a ski trip in mid February.)

Cecelia was to come along as well. She was unaware, but the girl mainly was there to make it seem less suspicious that Pam was having a teenage boy sleep over at her place.

Like Billy, Crit had heard Pam complain bitterly about Greg. In fact, when Pam told Cecelia that she had finally made her feelings known to Billy, she added that she now had a choice: divorce Greg or kill him. The teenager said that divorce was probably a better idea. But Pam said she wasn't so sure. As she did with Billy, Pam told Cecelia that her husband would come away with everything in a divorce—even the dog, Halen.

That night, Billy called his mother from JR's and said he was spending the night at his friend's. Billy had done it so often that his mother did not give it a second thought. Then Pam and Cecelia picked up Billy and they headed to Derry, where they rented some videos, including *9 1/2 Weeks*, and went to 4E, Misty Morning Drive.

Pam and Billy sat on one couch watching the steamy film on the VCR. Cecelia was on the other. And when it was over, Pam and the boy went upstairs to her room. They brought the stereo from the guest bedroom into the master bedroom, so they could have some music. The fifteen-year-old lay on the bed naked while Pam went into the bathroom and slipped into the turquoise and white negligee.

After Billy's assurances that he wouldn't think she was overweight, Pam stepped out and danced to the Van Halen song "Black & Blue." Then she and the boy had sex. Billy had told Pam that he was experienced, but in reality he was a virgin.

That night, they had sex on the bed, then on the floor. At one point, Billy padded downstairs to get a glass of ice so he could rub it along Pam's body à la Mickey Rourke and Kim Basinger in the movie.

Pam took Billy and Cecelia home to Seabrook the next day. She dropped off the girl and then headed east, toward Seabrook Beach and Billy's home.

It is peaceful down near the sea in the winter. Traffic is mild. The crowds are gone. The year-round residents who live off the beach, most of whom are not natives of Seabrook, can tramp on the sand with their spouses, kids, or dogs in quiet solitude, with only the background sound of the waves rolling onto the shore.

Pam drove along. She told the boy sadly that this was probably the final time that they could be together. She wanted to be with Billy, but Greg did not go away all that often. The opportunities were too few. She said she just didn't know the answer.

Pam pulled in past Billy's house, down near one of the sandy entranceways that connect the beach with the road. By this time, both of them were sobbing. The teenager told her that he felt as she did. He wanted their relationship to continue. He wanted to be with her.

Then there was no choice, Pam said. The only way they could be together was if Billy killed Greg.

The boy figured that it was Pam's anger at her husband that was speaking, that she wasn't truly planning to carry out a murder plot.

After all, it had been an emotional discussion. All that had seemed so wonderful between them seemed on the verge of crumbling into the sea. Billy was in no mood to start debating moral or legal issues.

"Well, I agreed," the boy would later testify. "I wasn't about to start disagreeing with her."

As winter edged toward spring, Billy Flynn's world had a new order. He had had a girlfriend or two in the past, but they were always around his age and matters never became very serious. Now, he was chest deep in the throes of an *affair*, with a woman who worked for the school board no less.

There was, of course, the sex. Over the ensuing weeks, Billy and Pam would have encounters in a variety of places—his bedroom, a Seabrook ballpark, in the back of her Honda hatchback out behind a factory, and at Salisbury Beach.

Cecelia says Pam once told her about an instance in which she and Billy were making love on the ground near a secluded parking lot at Salisbury Beach when a car unexpectedly pulled in. Both of them supposedly scurried around naked, Cecelia says, and in the process Pam cut open her knee.

And Billy would tell friends about the time he was having sex with Pam in the back of her car and a guy who was mowing a nearby field caught them in the act and began yelling at them.

It had all the markings of a teenage romance, which made sense as far as Billy went, given his age. Pam, however, displayed a rampant immaturity—though some say it was an act—that belied her organized, achievement-oriented persona.

Besides the sex in out-of-the-way places, they took to trading love notes, a number of them sexually explicit. And at one point, amid the video games and other amusements down at the Salisbury Beach arcades, the two punched out cheap medallions for one another: "Pame and Bill Forever," read hers. "Bill and Pame Forever," read her teenage lover's.

The mystique was heightened by the secrecy that any extramarital affair involved. Added to the mix was the certainty that Pam would lose her job if the relationship ever came to the school board's attention.

Cecelia, of course, knew. But Pam's friends, such as Tracy Collins, who regularly took part in the orange juice commercial, remained unaware that anything was going on between the two. Pam had given the boy explicit orders not to let on in front of Collins or any of her friends. After all, most of them were Greg's friends as well. Even more than that, most of Pam's friends had been derived from her marriage to Greg.

No teenager, though, could be expected to say nothing

about such an incredible turn of events. It was inevitable that Billy would tell JR and Pete. Ever since eighth grade, when they started pestering him to stop moping around the house, Billy kept very little from them.

Pete Randall had only met Pam a few times and even then they had hardly talked. Unlike Billy, he saw nothing particularly fascinating in her. Something about Pam just irked him. In time, Pete and JR would come to consider Billy's affair as something of a joke. They would even come to rename the Van Halen song "Hot for Teacher" in honor of the lovers; they called it "Humping the Teacher."

Flynn, in fact, was far from secretive about the relationship. In the locker room one day he talked to Ralph Welch, who by now was seeing less of his old friends because he was spending more time with his girlfriend, about having had sex with Pam and their plans for more. He also kept Sal Parks, a friend from school, informed on occurrences.

Billy even mentioned it to JR's uncle once when the boy was over at the Lattimes' place. "He was wearing the biggest smile you ever saw," Donald Soule recalled for the *Boston Herald*. "He said he was smiling 'because I'm dating an older woman.' I said how old? And he answered, twenty-two. I said that's not old Billy. And he said: 'It's old to me—old when you're fifteen.'"

Often, the boy would carry Pam's letters with him. He allowed friends like JR and Jenny Charles, who befriended Billy back in seventh grade, to read them. Jenny had borrowed Billy's denim jacket one day and found a note from Pam to Billy. Pam had written about her jealousy of a high school girl that the boy apparently kissed while returning from a Motley Crue concert. A bit later, Billy showed Jenny a couple of other letters from Pam, these quite risqué. Finally, Jenny asked Billy if he was in love with the media center director. "He said that he didn't know," the girl would testify, "but the sex was great."

Pam tried to be careful as well. For Billy's sixteenth birthday on March 12, for example, she told him that she had considered buying him a gold-nugget bracelet. Because she was afraid that Greg would wonder where the five hundred dollars or so went, she decided instead on a more practical, more humble, gift—a subscription to *Guitar* magazine. Even then she paid for the subscription indirectly, giving Cecelia the money and having the girl pay for the subscription with her own check.

Five days later, on Salisbury Beach, Pam, Billy, Cecelia, and Tracy Collins were in Pam's car when another driver backed into her left front fender and sped away. While filling out the accident report, Pam omitted Billy's name when asked to list the occupants of her car at the time of the accident. Neither Greg nor the police, should they ever take an interest, would ever learn about his presence.

Despite such attempts at keeping the affair under wraps, Pam was often foolishly incautious out on the seacoast. Billy came over to the office every day. She left his letters in her desk. They went out to lunch together. When she dropped off Billy at JR's after school, a common occurrence, she would openly kiss him good-bye.

And one time, outside of a Seabrook convenience store, she let Billy, who was drunk, hang on her and nibble on her neck while she chatted with his friends. Pam had bought the boy a bottle of Southern Comfort that night, while she and Cecelia had wine coolers.

That same evening, Pam, Billy, and Cecelia had what was the affair's equivalent of a near miss. They passed Billy's mother on the road, but Elaine Flynn, heading the opposite direction, was preoccupied at that instant, yelling at one of Billy's little brothers. Everybody in the CRX breathed a little easier. Their "secret" was safe.

Organization had always been Pamela Smart's strong suit. Indeed, that was the key to her ability to balance four years of college packed into three, an internship and jobs, a steady boyfriend, and still come away with near-perfect grades.

It was also the first thing she tried to teach her young charges when they started to make the orange juice video. She sat them down and made them brainstorm, bouncing around concepts, and whittling away until they had a unified, workable vision.

It was no different when Pam began directing Billy Flynn to murder her husband. After the boy assented, Pam took the idea and began to ride it. As with the orange juice video, she became the propelling force. But also like the OJ commercial, there was an intangible that she was unable to reign in: She was counting on a confused teenager, not a hardened killer, to bring her plans to fruition.

Every day the plot would come up. Billy would drop by the media center and sooner or later Pam would start in about doing away with Greg.

In many ways, it was like an abstract game, the plotting of the perfect murder, and Billy chimed right in.

The possibilities were endless, but Pam liked the idea of making it appear as if Greg had interrupted a burglary. It was not the most creative concept. It was more like a variation on a theme. Plenty of crimes have been blamed on mysterious strangers, with none more prominent in recent months than the Boston slaying of Carol Stuart.

Pam talked about how the boy could dress in dark clothes, park a car up by Hood Commons, and sneak back toward the condominiums. Once inside, he could lie in wait for Greg.

"Well, it's gonna look pretty suspicious if a kid in dark clothes gets out of a car and goes behind the plaza," said Billy.

"OK," answered Pam. "Put the dark clothes in a bag and change behind the plaza. Then go down to the condo."

Each time they talked about it, the plot became more clear. Pam told the boy to tie his long dark hair back in a ponytail, so as to make later identification difficult. He should wear gloves, of course, to avoid leaving fingerprints. She would leave the cellar and rear doors open. Inside, the boy could tear the place end to end, take anything he wanted, and when Greg got there, kill him, preferably with a gun.

Pam's alibi would be beyond dispute: She would be surrounded by people at a school board meeting in Hampton.

At first, Cecelia usually was not around when Billy and Pam began laying the groundwork for the killing. She had classes when Billy dropped by, and he had classes during the periods she reported in for her internship. Still, Pam kept the girl up to date on the plan as well as on her faltering marriage.

From the winter on into the spring it continued. It happened now and then that one of their classes would be canceled and both Billy and Cecelia would be at the media center with Pam. Time and again, Pam would go over the plan and new ideas with Billy as Cecelia listened in.

Crit would come to know most of it, from the parking of the car behind the plaza to Billy tying his hair back.

As could be expected from Pam, not much would be left

to chance. She even took it upon herself to see that Billy took care of her beloved Shih-Tzu, Halen, who Pam sometimes called Haley. In one conversation, Cecelia heard Pam telling Billy that the dog might later react strangely to him if it actually saw the boy slay Greg. With that in mind as well as the possibility that the dog would bark, Pam ordered the boy to put the dog in the basement as soon as he got into the condo.

Cecelia would later say that she never expected the murder to actually be carried out. The reason was Billy himself. He simply was not a violent kid. It was ludicrous. "Why do you even bother?" she would say to Pam. "Billy's never gonna do it."

Still, the plotting went on. Perhaps it had become something of a perverse game that had nothing to do with reality for Billy and Cecelia. Maybe it was the thrill of flirting with danger, a dance along the edge of a precipice. Or maybe it was simply the lack of a sound-minded adult that the kids felt comfortable with, someone who could point out just how crazy it had all become.

Whatever the case, being around Pam, even with all the strange talk of murdering her husband, offered a form of sustenance. Pam provided it in different ways for the boy and the girl, but when it came right down to it, their needs were the same. Both Cecelia and Billy deeply wanted to feel that they were good and loved and special.

Pam gave them that. With Billy it was through sex. With Cecelia it was letting her be an intimate friend and part of Pam's little circle.

It was madness, but without abhorrence the kids continually accepted the small steps that in the end pointed to a death.

When the subject of a gun came up, for example, the teenagers named everyone they could think of who might have one. Cecelia said her father, whom she had not seen in a few years, had a shotgun. Then there was JR's dad. And supposedly Sal Parks' mother. And Billy's landlord. Cecelia mentioned a friend at Papa Gino's, a local pizza joint where Crit worked as a waitress, who was said to keep a handgun in the glove compartment of her car.

Of those, the best bet seemed to be Cecelia's co-worker. It got to the point that Billy went to Papa Gino's and rummaged through the woman's car, hoping to steal the gun.

He never found it. Not in the parking lot at Papa Gino's, nor later when he went through the vehicle again at her home.

Pam, Billy, and Cecelia had a secret. But as one might expect with teenagers, it did not last long. Cecelia for the most part said little to anyone about Pam's marital problems or what was starting to sound like an obsession with having Greg killed. But one night in the early spring, while Cecelia was on dinner break at Papa Gino's, something in the conversation with a co-worker made her think of the discussions about killing Greg.

Crit told Cindy Butt, who delivered pizzas, that she had a friend named Pam who had an unhappy marriage and was looking for someone to kill her husband. Butt, who was twenty years old, listened for a bit and considering everything from the fifteen-year-old source to the likelihood of the tale, decided not to take it too seriously. It was just too ridiculous.

Billy could not keep the plot under his hat either. So he, of course, let his buddies in on it. One day in March, Pete and JR were lounging around at the Lattimes' house, the stereo playing, when Bill told them that he wanted to kill Greg Smart.

The boys had known of the affair, and Billy had talked about some of Pam's marital problems. Now Billy was going on about how Greg abused Pam and how a divorce was out of the question because Pam would be left with nothing and how killing the husband was the only way to resolve it.

Knowing Billy as they did, the boys thought little of his talk about murder. He was not exactly the most fearsome kid they knew, though he was as likely as anyone to talk big.

Pete Randall figured he was just angry at Greg. "You're nuts," he told Billy. He figured that about summed it up.

Around this same time, Billy Flynn was plotting even more murders. At least hypothetically. That winter through the end of the school year, both he and JR were enrolled in Crime and Punishment, one of the most popular classes at Winnacunnet.

Taught by social studies teacher Leonard Barron, the class was an overall view of the American legal system, covering everything from criminal law to how the penal system works. The part of the class that most kids liked best involved mock crimes and trials. Everyone was assigned a role, be it as the criminal, the police, prosecuting attorney, and so on. Sometimes parents and others from outside of Winnacunnet took part, being called in, for instance, to testify.

Those who volunteered to be criminals also had to suggest a crime. If approved by Barron, the lesson would then be set into motion, from acting out the offense through the trial. With due warning, certain people around the school were told to brace themselves. It was "Crime and Punishment Crime Time."

Billy and JR Lattime took well to the course. They had B averages through most of it. Would-be bad guys, they proposed that the two of them go on a killing spree around the school. Barron rejected their idea, but not wanting them to lose their obvious enthusiasm, he assigned them key roles in the playing out of another pair of students' idea.

The mock crime was simple enough. A group of animal rights activists were upset about Winnacunnet's science department's using fetal pigs for laboratory work. First, they sent letters expressing this concern and threatened that if the practice continued, repercussions would follow.

Billy and JR were assigned to be hit men. Their mission was to "kill" one science teacher a day, which in reality involved little more than informing the person that he was dead and putting down a paper cutout outline of a body, until use of fetal pigs stopped. Three or four corpses had turned up before Billy and JR were arrested and put on trial. The verdict came back guilty.

Perhaps it is true everywhere, but along the New Hampshire coastline in particular the arrival of spring is always much welcomed. The Atlantic takes on a marvelous deep blue, drawing more and more loners and couples and children to gaze out and wonder. A few miles away, the athletic fields behind Winnacunnet High School—"Home of the Warriors"—recover quickly from the ice and the snow, revealing a vast expanse of green dotted with daffodils. It does not take long for two or three kids to make their way out there with gloves and a baseball. Or for the teenagers and adults inside the school to discover new energy as they head down the homestretch of the school year.

Such was the backdrop when Pamela Smart decided that

the time for her husband's demise had come.

Pam and Billy, of course, had talked at length about the plan. Unexpectedly one day—toward the end of March, says Flynn—she told him it should be carried out that very night.

To Pam, all seemed to be ready. She herself had a meeting. Greg would be getting home around nine o'clock. And she had left the bulkhead and rear doors open. After the deed was done, Pam told Billy, he should call her at the media center.

Fine, said Billy. The only problem was on his end. He was missing everything he needed to commit the crime, namely a gun and a car—ignoring that he was too young to have a driver's license—to get to Derry.

"Well, hurry up and get them by tonight," Pam said.

"I'll try."

But the boy did not try. He simply let it slide, like a skipped homework assignment. Pam had talked a lot about wanting Greg dead, but she gave no indications that it was this-minute urgent. "It's not something I wanted to do, for one thing," Billy would later say. "And I didn't think she'd be mad or anything if I didn't."

After school that day the boy followed his usual routine: He went over to JR's to hang out. When he finally went home, he waited for his mother to go to sleep, around ten o'clock, before he called Pam at the media center.

"Look, I'm sorry, but I didn't do it," Billy told her. "I couldn't get a gun and I couldn't get a car."

"You don't love me!" Pam exploded, giving a bizarre twist to an ageless complaint. "If you did, you would do this for me. It's the only way we can be together and if you loved me you'd want us to be together."

Until this point, Billy had only seen Pam's sweetness and her tears. That was all that had been needed. Now he met her fury.

Crying, he assured her that he cared about her and that he would kill Greg.

"I know you're never going to do this!" she said. "You don't have any intention of doing this. And I can't go on seeing you like this when I know we're never going to be able to really be together. So, that's it! It's over between us!" Then she hung up.

It was insanity. They were talking about snuffing out a human life, but Pam made it sound as if every woman should expect as much from a lover. What could be more simple? Love me, kill my husband.

Billy went to bed that night, wounded and bewildered. The next day at school he kept his distance from the media center. He was certain it was over with Pam.

Then Cecelia took him aside and said Smart wanted to talk to him.

Billy went over. Pam apologized for getting so angry. What's more, she told him not to worry. She had another meeting scheduled within the next month. Billy could kill Greg then.

"That's when I started getting serious about it," Billy would say in court, "because I thought that if I do something like not go up or anything again, she's gonna leave me and that's gonna be it. So this is the time that I really started talking to JR and Pete about it."

Pete Randall and JR Lattime were not going to win any most-likely-to-succeed awards at Winnacunnet High School. At the rate Pete was going, skipping school altogether on many days, he would be lucky to graduate. Randall had a sensitive side, but he also had a disrespect for authority that some people felt started with his being allowed to do whatever he wanted at home.

"He just gave out an air of constant arrogance," said one official who knew him. "He's a kid you'd look at just by his facial appearance and say punk." A number of people believed it was only going to get worse.

As for JR, he would probably have gotten through all right. Maybe his future held a job somewhere as a mechanic or even managing a garage.

Both of them talked about going into the armed services. JR was interested in getting a look at the mechanical guts of some of the military's tanks and other heavy artillery, maybe in the marines. Pete was intrigued by the army's elite Airborne Rangers. He wondered aloud to his friends sometimes what it would be like to kill somebody.

When April came to south Seabrook, though, what happened to them after high school was far away. For now they were content to be teenagers, hanging out with their girlfriends and the guys, listening to the screaming guitars of their favorite heavy metal bands, ripping off a car stereo when the mood struck, drinking, and scoring an occasional hit of cocaine.

Life had changed slightly. Ralph Welch, who had been like a brother to them, particularly to JR, was still staying at the Lattimes' house, but he usually was out with his girlfriend. And Billy, meanwhile, was often off somewhere with Pam. Still, JR's house remained the gathering place for them and their friends.

It was early in the month when Billy Flynn began to ask JR and Pete if they would help him kill Greg Smart. There was much to be gained if they did, he said. They could keep anything they could take from the condo, Flynn said, because insurance would cover it.

What's more, Pam would move to Hampton after Greg was dead. They could have another place to hang out and Pam would let them use the Trans-Am she was planning to buy as well as Greg's pickup truck, the Honda CRX, and Greg's four-wheeler.

Billy even told JR at one point that he could have anything he himself owned. The boys told him no.

Yet one day, Ralph Welch's cousin, Raymond Fowler, was over when Billy was making his pitch. Fowler, a high-school dropout, was the stereotypical Seabrooker. He was a tough kid, inarticulate, considered less than brilliant by most people who knew him. "He's slow," said one individual who had dealt with him. "Very slow."

Flynn had asked him about finding a gun. Ramey, as the kids called Fowler, replied that he thought there was one somewhere around his house. His late father had been a Seabrook cop and had owned a .357 Magnum handgun.

Although he was from the neighborhood, eighteen-year-old Ramey did not usually hang out with Billy, Pete, and JR. He had just gotten out of the Rockingham County Jail in January after doing four months on charges of receiving stolen property and conspiracy to receive stolen property. Besides that, he had a long laundry list of minor run-ins with the law, mostly motor vehicle offenses.

Fowler, Billy would later testify, took an interest in the proposition. It would be an easy break-in since Pam was in on it, and Ramey could take anything he wanted—the stereo system, television, video-cassette recorder, jewelry—anything at all. It was also understood that Pam would pay him a thousand dollars, Fowler later told a friend, according to court records.

Fowler was in, but he said he wanted to take care of the actual burglary and the murder by himself. Since Billy was romantically involved with Pam, he would be the first person the cops looked into. All he wanted Flynn to do, Ramey said, was lead him to the condo in Derry and be a lookout.

Given Fowler's criminal history of theft and other small-time capers, with virtually no propensity for violence, it is probable that Ramey was more interested in the burglary than the murder. (One court affidavit says that Fowler told Lattime at one point that "he would not kill Smart, but he did not care if Flynn did it, he just wanted the stereo.") Although it is impossible to be certain, Fowler might well have been thinking only of rounding up the goods and ignoring the matter of Greg altogether.

Still, he and Flynn began searching for a weapon, digging around in the Fowler attic and cellar for the old man's Ruger pistol. Nothing. As it turned out, the gun was in safekeeping with an uncle.

With no firearm, they would eventually go to Plan B. Fowler's brother had a knife collection. Ramey would bring one of them, Billy testified, and when the time came planned to simply slit Greg's throat.

One of the last items on their checklist was a car to make the cross-county haul to Derry. They asked around, but finally Billy told Pam that he and Ramey would accept her offer to use her Honda CRX. For obvious reasons, it had not been their top choice.

Pam said she would leave it behind the SAU 21 building, the keys in the ignition, and they could take it while she was in her meeting.

On the day Gregory Smart was marked to die, most likely around the middle of April, one of JR's friends from school, Johnny Mylo, was driving to the Newington Mall to get tickets for a Motley Crue concert that was coming up in Rhode Island. Billy, Ramey, Pete, JR, and Fowler's cousin, Danny Blake, all piled into Mylo's car. It was a madcap trip, with the lot of them packed together, cracking jokes, and laughing when Pete took someone up on their dare and dropped his pants, mooning a woman in another car.

The sky was just darkening when they got back. Ramey told Mylo to drop him and Billy off at SAU 21. Pete and

JR knew better, but for Mylo's and Blake's benefit, Fowler said that he and Flynn were helping Pam with a school project.

When Flynn and Fowler got out of the car behind the building, Billy could hear voices from upstairs. It sounded as if Pam's meeting was underway.

The two got in the unlocked silver CRX, with Billy on the driver's side. Mylo drove off.

As Pam had promised, the key was in the ignition. He turned it to start the car. Suddenly, Van Halen's "Black & Blue"—the tune Pam had played the first night they had sex—poured forth from the stereo. It was a special tape Billy had made for her. Now Pam had put it in the stereo to automatically play when the car started.

Billy pulled out of the lot and drove to his house where they picked up a red and black duffel bag loaded with dark clothing—sweat clothes mostly—and the knife. Fowler had also provided some old sneakers, to be disposed of later, just in case the police could establish shoe prints.

Fowler took over behind the wheel, Flynn testified. They stopped at a pharmacy, Freedom Drug, in Seabrook to get some gloves so as not to leave fingerprints. Billy asked the price of the latex surgical gloves. They were ten cents a pair, so Billy said he would take six. He told the guy it was for a magic trick.

Now nothing was left to do but go to 4E, Misty Morning Drive.

They got on Route 101 toward Derry. Billy generally knew the way. He had been to the condo with Pam and what's more, she had put the directions down on paper and told him to commit them to memory.

But now, as every mile passed beneath the wheels, Billy started to realize it was happening. Raymond seemed serious as hell. He might very well carry this thing out.

They were almost to Derry, straight ahead, when something in Billy's brain cried Abort. He told Ramey to hang a right.

Fowler turned. They drove . . . and drove.

"I don't see any signs that say Derry," Fowler said after a while.

"Yeah, I don't recognize anything," said Billy. "I guess we're lost."

"All right. Let's ask at this gas station."

Ramey got directions. This was not the way, all right. They were in the town of Raymond. Fowler turned the car around and got back on track.

It was edging toward ten o'clock when they finally got to their destination. The plan called for them to park back at the plaza, but Billy suggested they drive through the condo complex first—in Pam's car no less—to make sure all was clear. It was not. The silver Toyota pickup was there.

"Greg's home," said Billy, breathing easier. "We're gonna have to leave. We can't make it look like a burglary if the guy's here."

"Let's make sure," Fowler said.

They parked behind some trees in a lot across from the condo complex. They crossed the street and walked through the parking lot to Pam's building. In the darkness, they stepped on the lawn and went around back.

Upstairs the bedroom light was on. Their target was definitely home.

So they drove over to Hood Commons, where Billy got some change and from a pay phone called Pam's office in Hampton.

"We got here and we couldn't do it," Billy told her. "He was home."

The school board meeting had long since been over. Not wanting anyone to know she had given Billy and Raymond her car, Pam had gone into her office and was sitting in the dark, waiting for them to get back. She had heard someone starting to come in, she said, so she had to lie on the floor behind a bookshelf. Whoever it was, they had opened her desk. She told Billy that she wondered if anyone had come across his love letters.

"Hurry up and get back here," she finally said.

They did. Raymond wheeled into the Winnacunnet High School parking lot and Pam got in, sitting back toward the rear of the hatchback two-seater. She was curious about what had happened.

"You got lost?" she said to Billy. "You've been there before. You know the way."

"I don't know," answered Billy. "We just got lost."

They drove for a bit.

"Let me see the gun," said Pam. Billy had told her that

they were searching for the firearm that had belonged to Ramey's dad.

"Well, we couldn't find one," said Billy.

"Then how were you going to do it?"

Fowler displayed the sharp blade.

"You were going to use a *knife*?" she said incredulously. "Do you know how much of a mess that would make?"

"It would be quieter," said Raymond.

"I just can't believe it," said Pam.

Raymond was dropped off. Pam took the wheel and headed toward Billy's house. Billy had been relieved. She did not seem too upset that the plot had failed.

When they were alone, however, she started in on him.

"You knew the way!" she said. "You got lost on purpose. If you loved me, you would do this because you would want to be with me."

"Pam, I do love you." The last thing Billy wanted was to see her angry again. He was afraid that this time the romance would be over for good.

"If you're never going to do this, I want to know right now," she said. "That way we can end this right now because I don't want to go on like this."

"No, I'll do it."

"Well, there's another meeting on May first. You can do it then. But you have to do it then. It's the last meeting of the year. If you don't do it then, that's it."

Pam pulled down along the ocean onto the street that leads to Billy's house and stopped. She did not want Billy's mother seeing them together so late at night. Billy would have to walk the rest of the way.

In Pam's office the next morning, Smart was angry as she talked with Cecelia, recounting the events of the night before. Cecelia had known that Billy and Fowler had planned to use the CRX, but now Pam was telling her about the knife and how Greg had gotten home before they even arrived.

Smart said she could hardly believe the boys' stupidity.

By spring, Gregory and Pamela Smart's marriage was in trouble and they both knew it.

On the surface it generally appeared to be fine. Greg and Pam spoke by phone in the early afternoon almost every day. They occasionally had dinner with friends. In May they were planning to go to Florida for a vacation-conference that Greg had earned for being one of Metropolitan Life's top salesmen in the region. And Greg had even told a friend or two that he was planning a one-year anniversary party.

Increasingly, though, Greg was making comments to friends and even to some people to whom he was not very close that he and Pam were having problems. Toward the end of March, during a MetLife office party, Greg had been drinking and told some of the women staffers that the marriage had not been living up to expectations.

On an impromptu trip to Atlantic City in February, he told Yvon Pellerin, whom Greg had known since they worked together as boys at an area supermarket, that he wanted to buy a house and start having children, but that Pam was not interested. Greg mentioned to his old friend that it was possible that the marriage was falling apart, but that he might still buy a house. He wondered if Pellerin would consider moving in with him.

Pellerin worked second shift for a company that built computer circuit boards. He and Greg both had midday free and that spring would meet for long lunches two or three times a week at the 99 restaurant in Manchester. They also usually got together at least once on the weekends.

Greg told Pellerin that the marriage was taking a nosedive. Pam seemed more distant, Greg said. When he called Pam at work, she often was not around. He spoke of Pam coming home late with no real explanation.

One time that March, Pam had left a message on the answering machine that she had to work late. Pellerin got off work early that day and had dropped by hoping to go out drinking with Greg.

Instead, Pellerin says, they drove to SAU 21 in Hampton. Greg wanted to see what exactly his wife was doing. Plus, he had a few things he wanted to say about her behavior. Lately Pam had failed on several occasions to be where she said she would be. She was coming home late. Sometimes she wouldn't even return his messages.

When they pulled in the parking lot, however, Pam's car was not around. They waited about twenty minutes before she showed up, by herself.

"Where the hell have you been?" said Greg. "I came over to see you and you weren't here. I wanted to tell you what was going on for tonight and you're not even here. This is real nice.''

"What are you even doing here?" Pam fired back. "Checking up on me? You don't have to know what I do. You do what *you* want to do."

Pellerin says Pam launched an offensive immediately, deflating Greg before he could say all he had planned. "She turned everything around on him," says Yvon.

By April, Greg found himself coming home to an empty house and eating dinner alone more often. And one night, possibly around the time of Fowler's and Flynn's attempt on his life, Pellerin says Greg told him he had felt a god-awful chill of danger as he walked into the empty condo-minium. Something unexplainable was just wrong. He turned around and left. He went to his parents' place instead.

Out on the seacoast, meanwhile, complete strangers to the young man were observing his marriage's demise. Cecelia Pierce one day came into the media center while Pam's secretary was on break. Crit walked into the office to find Pam on the telephone arguing with someone.

"I said, 'Greg?' and she shook her head yes," Cecelia would later testify. "She was saying something about get-ting a divorce and then they started fighting over who was gonna take the dog and the furniture and everything. And then she said, 'Fine, take the dog' and hung up."

Cecelia saw this as a good sign. After all, talk of divorce sounded better than talk of murder. But moments later, Pam called Greg back to apologize. She told Cecelia that in her mind divorce still had its problems. She didn't want Greg telling his parents that the marriage was in trouble.

Billy Flynn obviously knew a lot about the marriage's problems as well. Pam, he claims, showed him a bruise she said Greg inflicted.

He too remembers hearing Pam and Greg arguing on the telephone one time. This conversation, he says, was also overheard by JR Lattime and Cecelia. (Pierce has no mem-ory of it.) They were at the media center when Greg called and Pam put him on the speaker phone.

Greg started right in, Billy would say, demanding to know where Pam had been when he called fifteen minutes earlier. "What do you care?" Pam replied.

"They just got into a big argument, yelling at each other back and forth," Billy testified. "And he said something like, 'Well, what do you want? A divorce?' And she said, 'Maybe I do,' or something like that and hung up.

"But then he called back I believe and she didn't put it on intercom this time. And, I don't know, I think they worked things out."

After Pam hung up, however, she looked up at the kids and said, "Now you see why I've got to have this done."

There was no mistaking what "this" meant.

Still, neither Greg's parents nor many of his closest friends believed the marriage was falling apart, sometimes even when Greg said as much.

In mid April, on Easter weekend, a group of Greg's family and friends took in the Trump Plaza in Atlantic City. Greg always loved the excitement of the casino, particularly playing baccarat, which seemed always to attract the highest rollers. He liked to watch the big shots lose tens of thousands of dollars in a single game, then plunk down tens of thousands more. Even when he was losing, Greg enjoyed himself.

But as he and Brian Washburn, a pudgy twenty-one year old with shoulder-length hair and a gentle, puppy-dog disposition, sat in the pits one morning, drinking icy beers, and playing baccarat, Washburn thought his friend was lacking his usual energy.

"What's wrong with you, man?" Washburn finally asked.

"Nothing," said Greg.

They sipped their beers, and played a little more.

"Oh, I don't know," Greg mumbled.

"Come on. What's going on? What's wrong?" asked Washburn.

"Everything's all screwed up."

"What are you talking about?"

"Between me and Pam. I wasn't gonna tell you this because I didn't want anybody to know, but I screwed this other chick."

"What? When?"

"It was a while ago, but all me and Pam do is fight about it. Everytime we fucking argue that's all she brings up."

"You fucking *told* her? What are you? An idiot? What do you think she's gonna bring up when you guys argue? If she had told you about something like that, you would bring it up, wouldn't you?"

"Well, I don't know."

"Bullshit. I'd bring it up in a heartbeat."

"Well, I don't have to worry about it much longer, I don't think, because she has, too."

Washburn understood that to mean that Pam also had an affair. He says he did not press his friend about it. They knew many of each other's secrets. He figured Greg would say more if and when he was ready.

A few minutes later, though, Pam and Tracy Collins came down, happy and laughing. They announced that they were off to go shopping. Washburn watched Pam and Greg interact and figured the affair was just a bad bump in their marriage. It sure didn't seem to be tearing them apart.

Indeed, Greg was not shouting it to the skies, but few people who are confronting the failure of their marriage do. Instead, Smart was turning back to his old friends for support, a number of whom he had largely separated from because of Pam.

One person he sought to renew ties with was Giraffe, his friend Terri Schnell, who had introduced him to his wife. By April, he was calling her more often and dropping by to visit. "Hey," Terri blurted out at one point, realizing that it was like old times. "You're Greggles again."

One Wednesday night, to Terri's surprise, Greg and Steve Payment even showed up at Decadance, a Manchester nightclub, to have a drink or two and dance with Terri and a girlfriend.

"Everything sucks," he said at one point, an unmistakable reference to his marriage. "I'll be divorced by the summer."

Terri said she took it as a joke and told him to cut it out. Greg had made similar remarks previously and Terri figured it was just Greg's way of complaining. "I think he was uncomfortable talking about it," said Schnell. "He would mention it and then we would get on to another, totally different, topic."

Before that Wednesday night was out Greg would say that after he got divorced, he and Terri would go out on a date some time, a remark he had also made before.

"I love you, you know that?" he told her.

"I love you, too," Schnell said, a bit miffed by the sudden sentimentality from a guy who usually was not sentimental.

The last week in April, Greg Smart went out of town to Warwick, Rhode Island, for a work-related training program, the Metropolitan Career Success School. He returned on Friday. That night he attended a party with about fifteen other people at Terri Schnell's, where he played quarters, a drinking game, and smoked some pot with a group of other people. Pam did not attend.

The next day, Greg and a friend went to Schnell's again to shoot some baskets and chat with her.

Then on Sunday morning, he called Giraffe once more. He wanted to have breakfast at her house, something they both used to enjoy immensely but which Greg had stopped once he got married. Schnell, though, was on her way out and said it would have to be another time.

They talked a little and then said good-bye. It was the last time Terri ever spoke to her friend.

No one, not even the participants themselves, may ever know for certain why JR Lattime and Pete Randall decided to assist Pamela Smart and Billy Flynn in the killing of Greg Smart. From the first the boys heard of it, all indications are that they thought the whole idea was idiotic, that Billy was being manipulated, and they wanted no part of it.

Shortly after Fowler and Flynn failed, though, the boys agreed to help. Randall would say that he got involved because he was worried that his friend Flynn was going to get caught by the police if someone did not help him. In defiance of all logic, Randall says he then decided that he himself would take part, presumably, to make sure that Greg got murdered the right way.

More likely, it was a number of factors that converged. Indeed, Pete and JR had a loyalty to Billy Flynn; he was their friend, no small word among this group of boys. After all, they had few other people whom they trusted and who were always there for them. In addition, JR and Pete could not have known the high level of pressure and manipulation Pam was employing on Billy.

Equally important, Raymond Fowler's involvement may well have legitimized the entire matter, making it now seem like not such a bad idea after all.

What's more, maybe Pete Randall, as he had said, truly was intrigued by what it would be like to kill someone.

And, if not, who is to say that a few rough-edged teenage

boys would not find some titillation in playing out the stages of a murder plot—even if their heart of hearts, as JR would say, they never actually expected someone to die.

Even Billy did not understand why his friends agreed, but Pete and JR finally told him, "All right." They would help, but they wanted to be paid. That could be arranged, Billy said, and assured them that Pam would give them one thousand dollars each. Pam had talked about there being at least one insurance policy on her husband's life, through Greg's job, so the boy knew that Pam was about to come into some big money. (In the weeks that followed it would be learned that Greg had carried $140,000 in coverage.)

Now, Billy went to Pam and said his buddies would help. "But my friends aren't just gonna do this for something to do on a Tuesday night," said Billy.

"I told you they could have everything in the house," said Pam.

"Well, they're probably gonna want some money."

"How much?"

"A thousand each."

Pam balked. All she needed was for the police to start scouring her banking records after the murder and to see an unexplained withdrawal of a couple grand. In what one newspaper reporter would later dub "murder on the installment plan," Pam said she would give them five hundred dollars each, in payments of fifty dollars a week, so that the cash flow from her bank account would not attract attention.

Business matters settled, their connection to Pam being all but completely through Billy, the boys would discuss the murder virtually every day.

JR's grandmother, Mary Chase, owned a camper that she kept adjacent to the Lattime's house, where the boys liked to kick back and talk. Inevitably, their conversations would drift onto how best to eliminate Pam's husband. Sometimes they talked about it at Raymond Fowler's house.

Some twenty discussions about the murder took place, mainly involving Billy, JR, and Pete. The boys spoke, for instance, about the most effective method. Someone mentioned having it look like a mugging gone wrong. Or they could make it a drive-by shooting; they could steal a car and gun down Greg outside of his office in Nashua.

In time, they would settle on Pam's basic plan, complete

with the wearing of dark clothes, the parking by the shopping plaza, and setting up the burglary.

Inherent in such a plot, however, were some problems: Pete and JR never completely accepted killing Greg with a gun and it caused some friction among the friends. Repeatedly, Flynn said that Pam wanted Greg shot, but Pam's desires carried less weight with the boys than they did with Billy. To them, it was as if Pam, who would be doing nothing but sitting in a meeting over in Hampton, wanted everything her way.

Like Fowler before him, Pete figured a knife would be quieter than a gun, no small matter since the murder was going to be in a high-density condo complex. A knife would also be more difficult for investigators to trace.

Where were they even going to get a gun? JR's father, of course, had a collection of firearms in his bedroom—among them more than a dozen rifles—shotguns to muzzle loaders—and two handguns, a .22-caliber Ruger and .38 Charter Arms.

Despite Billy's requests, JR told the boys to forget about using any of them. He knew full well that his father's guns were not to be touched without permission and the old man's word was law.

What's more, it was impractical to use one of those guns. Vance would know it was gone if they dumped it somewhere, which would bring a hell to pay all its own. And if they returned the weapon, ballistics tests might someday connect it to Greg's death.

So the boys asked around. Pete Randall would say in court that he knew a drug dealer in nearby Haverhill, Massachusetts, known as Zeppelin, who had plenty of street connections. Besides selling cocaine, Zeppelin also bought stolen goods and moved them into the black market. When Billy and Pete Randall inquired about a gun, Zeppelin said he might be able to help, but the price could be as steep as $300. Billy reported that to Pam, who said it was too expensive. She would not pay.

The boys also talked about transportation. Someone suggested Pete's mother's car, but that was soon rejected. Stealing one was also out, as the last thing they would need on the night of the murder was to be pulled over in a hot vehicle. Pam's CRX, easily identified with its vanity plate, was also inadequate.

Soon, however, the final plan began to materialize. JR had hesitated to commit himself, but by Monday, April 30, he said OK. He would later say that he thought his friends would never kill someone anyway, so he might as well come along.

Certainly, the murder seemed dubious. Among other things, simply too many people knew the crime was in the offing. There was, of course, the three boys and Pam. But Raymond Fowler was on the fringes as well. And Cecelia. And Billy's friend Sal Parks, to whom Flynn revealed much and at one point even tried to talk into driving. Raymond Fowler, court records show, had mentioned bits and pieces of the previous attempt to others as well.

Equally troublesome—or at least it should have been— was that at least a dozen other teenagers, probably more, had seen evidence or heard rumors of Billy's affair with Pam.

But events marched on, and Lattime, who figured his friends lacked the cold-bloodedness to kill someone, became the linchpin of the whole matter.

JR was the only one of the three boys with a driver's license, and he often borrowed his grandmother's 1978 Chevrolet Impala, a yellow four-door. Originally, toward the end of April, JR had planned to use Mary Chase's car to go job hunting, but now he agreed to drive it to Derry.

Lattime's grandmother owned a place in Seabrook, but she was staying in Bradford, Massachusetts, a little town just over the state line, near Haverhill, where she was caring for an elderly woman. Mary Chase had planned to bring the vehicle to JR's house on May 1, so the car would be there when the boys returned from school. JR, in turn, would take her back to Bradford.

As for the murder weapon, Randall had made up his mind that he would stab Greg, using whatever cutlery he could find around the condo. JR agreed that his father's .38-caliber Charter Arms revolver could serve as a backup.

Pamela, in the meantime, was also making sure that her end was hammered down.

Although Pam might well have felt something similar to affection for Cecelia Pierce and Billy Flynn, her first priority appeared to have been making sure that the kids, easily malleable thus far, stayed in her camp as her husband's final day edged closer.

While Greg was in Rhode Island, Pam allowed Cecelia

Pierce to stay with her in Derry the week of Monday, April 23. Cecelia got permission from her mother—Pam, after all, could drive her to and from school every day—and in so doing won at least four nights of freedom from her family, plenty of time to drive Pam's car to practice for her upcoming driver's test, and a chance, quite simply, to play at being a grown-up. That Monday night, Cecelia's friend Karen joined them at the condo, and they watched some videos and talked.

Tuesday night and part of Wednesday night, Billy also stayed, and had sex with Pam again. They also went out to see *Pretty Woman* and watched some videos.

At one point, Pam, Billy, and Cecelia took the CRX and cruised around Hood Commons. Pam pointed out where Flynn and the boys could park the car, the dumpsters behind which they could change their clothes, and the grassy hill that would lead them to the back of Summerhill Condominiums.

On Wednesday morning, Billy called his mother from school to explain why he failed to make it home the night before. He had been at a party, he said, and with everyone drunk, he thought it would be safer to stay put than to have someone drive him.

Pamela was busy providing explanations for her activities as well.

That spring, Winnacunnet High School and Pam's employer SAU 21 were moving toward honoring her request to teach a course, "Mass Media: An Introduction to TV Production," the following September. Pam lacked teaching credentials, but permission was likely to be granted based on her education in television work. Her wanting to get involved seemed to be positive. Most schools appreciate it when talented people can help out in select places.

At the same time, the SAU 21 building, where Pam worked, was to be renovated. The media center's space would be cut back so that the business staff could have more room. Her employers had discussed the matter with her at length and Pam agreed with the plans.

What was mildly unusual, though, was Pam's interest in following these matters through by attending a series of school board meetings, both at the high school and at SAU 21. For the most part, the meetings were administrative, sometimes for no other purpose than setting the agenda for other meetings.

She had gone to one interminable SAU 21 meeting on April 5, a struggle no doubt for even some of those who were supposed to be in attendance, and was planning to be at the continuation on April 12, possibly the day that Flynn and Fowler drove to Derry. Her boss, Norman Katner, then superintendent of SAU 21, vaguely recollects taking her aside. Pam had no reason to attend that evening's Administrative Operations Committee meeting, he said. Nonadministrators rarely came to such sessions.

It was true that several matters that involved Pam were scheduled for discussion—her new course, a pay raise, and the renovations. But the committee was only making recommendations and setting the agenda for the larger school board meeting on May 1.

Still, Pam attended. The session lasted three hours. The committee overwhelmingly agreed to recommend that she be allowed to teach the course and that she receive a pay raise to $26,000. As Katner had said, her attendance was not needed.

As for the upcoming May 1 meeting, Pam again did not have to be there. The recommending committee obviously supported both her course and her pay raise, relatively minor matters. They were all but shoo-ins for approval by the larger board.

The renovation questions, meanwhile, simply were out of Pam's bailiwick. She had given her opinion long before and now it was an administrative matter.

On Monday, April 30, though, Pam told Fred Engelbach, an assistant superintendent, that after all the planning she now had second thoughts. Out of the blue, almost at the last minute, she no longer was willing to surrender the office space for the business staff. She needed more storage space, a problem Engelbach saw as minuscule.

Yet to Pam it was a most important issue. "I do recall that she indicated a very, I would say, violent objection to the whole plan," Engelbach would later testify.

Disturbed, Katner called a meeting with Pam and the assistant superintendent for Tuesday. The matter had to be ironed out before that evening's session.

* * *

For many people, autumn is the loveliest season in New Hampshire. That is strange somehow because the fall signals that an ending is near. The October chill warns of winter and its hardships. The brilliant foliage in the end is simply leaves that are dying. All around, autumn is a reminder that nothing survives forever.

Less renowned is the New Hampshire spring, when life comes to those same leaves. Anyone who has seen the month of May arrive in the state knows well that green in all its shades can inspire as much wonder and awe as any offering of reds and yellows.

Spring in the Granite State is not about retreat or hibernation or dying. It is about living. It is about being young, laughing a silly laugh with your friends, and knowing even that if your life has become an embarrassing mess that you can always start anew.

Yet danger lurks in the New Hampshire spring. For sometimes, even on the most beautiful days, electrical storms kick up out of nowhere. With the mountains and trees covering the distant skyline, storms can creep in undetected, leaving boaters, for instance, who were tranquilly dropping lines out on a pristine lake one minute, madly paddling for shore the next.

And it is strange to think that on such a day, such a deadly force can be rolling ever closer without your even knowing it is coming.

On May 1, 1990, Gregory Smart was back in the routine of selling life insurance. Around nine, he left for work for his usual morning of phone calls, paperwork, and an appointment or two.

As was his custom, Smart took the afternoon off and planned to see some customers that night. He was driving home on Route 102 when he saw Tom Parilla, his best man at his wedding just a year earlier, heading the other way. Greg flicked his headlights on and off. "Hey!" Parilla yelled. The two friends waved as they passed each other.

The day, which had started out cloudy, had turned nicer by the time Greg dropped by to see his parents. He talked with Bill and Judy Smart for a bit, romped around the house with his younger brother's baby daughter, fixed a flat tire, then slapped the old man on the back and said he would see him later.

That night, Greg had scheduled two appointments, one

in Salem and another in Pelham. He pulled on a pair of gray slacks, gray sports coat, and a light green shirt and a green plaid tie. Around dinnertime, he got in his Toyota pickup and headed out.

His last sales call of the day was to customers he had never met, Charles and Nancy Sargent of Pelham. Smart was to review their existing policy and talk to them about supplementing it. Greg had arrived at 7:30, about a half hour early, and sat down with the Sargents at their kitchen table to make his pitch.

They talked business for a while and by the time Greg was through, the husband, who had turned sixty-five that day, was writing out a check for the new policy. Before Greg left, he chatted with the couple a bit about basketball— the Chicago Bulls were on television—and some aspect of the Sargents' television remote control that intrigued him.

Finally, he said good-bye and climbed into his truck for the half-hour drive home to Derry. It was 8:30.

On most mornings, Pam was the first one out the door at 4E, Misty Morning Drive. On May 1, though, she had the evening meeting and stayed around the condo until quarter to ten before leaving for Hampton.

Billy Flynn would later say that Pam dropped by his locker at the high school that day. She told the boy that she had left the bulkhead doors open at her place. Everything was set and ready to go.

At work that morning, Pam met with Katner and Engelbach to discuss her sudden change of mind about the renovation plans, but by the time the meeting was over neither of the men was exactly sure what her strenuous objections were all about. Still, she insisted that she would be at that evening's meeting in case any of the board members had questions for her.

Katner was agitated. "Pam, you do what you have to do tonight and I'll do what I have to do tomorrow," he said.

The superintendent was sending a message: If Pam dared to go over his head and voice her concerns directly to the board, there would be hell to pay in the morning. He was prepared to call her on the carpet and give her a lesson in protocol. The renovation question was an administrative matter and she was out of line, particularly since it seemed to be such a minor dispute.

Fine, Pam said, but she would be at the meeting all the same.

For the remainder of the workday, Pam did not accomplish much. At lunchtime, most of the SAU 21 staff, about fifteen people, got together at the Library Restaurant in nearby Portsmouth. The supervisors, including Pam, were taking their secretaries out for a long lunch. It was about 2:30 when Pam got back to work.

When she did, it was not very long before the telephone rang. It was Billy Flynn. A snag had come up.

Flynn, JR, and Pete had taken the school bus to Lattime's house that afternoon. When they arrived, though, Mary Chase's car was not there. JR's grandmother had forgotten to drive it over and when Lattime called she told him that if he wanted to borrow it he would have to find a ride to Bradford.

Billy asked Pam if she would give them a lift. She said OK. She would be over in a little while.

Vance and Diane Lattime were at work that afternoon when their seventeen-year-old son stepped into their bedroom, went to the dresser, and pulled open the top drawer. There before him was his father's underwear, a coin collection, some rolls of quarters, and, in the right-hand corner, on top of some personal papers, the gun, a Charter Arms .38-caliber snubnose revolver, in its holster.

The gun, dubbed Undercover by the manufacturer, was stainless steel with a brown grip, and had originally belonged to JR's great-grandparents, Naomi and Don Rogers.

Naomi had been sixty-five when she bought it at Big Al's Gun Shop in Seabrook in 1981. Her husband had been a hefty, active man until he became bedridden with cancer. Then one night someone broke into their home on rough-and-tumble Collins Street. When the old man managed to make his way into the hallway to see what was going on, the hoodlums easily knocked him down. Worried afterwards that he was unable to protect his wife, Don Rogers instructed her to buy the gun, just in case.

As far as the Lattimes know, neither of JR's great-grandparents ever fired the handgun.

Then in 1983 after Don Rogers died, Vance Lattime paid the widow about two hundred dollars for it. Lattime, who liked to hunt and target shoot, did not need the gun for protection. There were enough weapons around his house to stave off a small invasion force. Vance wanted the gun for sentimental reasons; he wanted something to remind him of Don, one of his favorite relatives.

JR most likely was the first person to fire the gun. It had stayed in its box for several years. Then Vance took to bringing it along when he and JR would go bow hunting in the backwoods of northern New Hampshire, an extra precaution should they ever stumble upon an angry bear or some such threat.

The son would regularly pester his father about letting him try out the .38. Finally, one day in 1988 at a gravel pit in Pittsburg, New Hampshire, near the Canadian border, Vance said OK. JR set up some doughnuts as targets and at a distance of about thirty yards fired off less than thirty rounds.

After that, the gun was left in the bedroom dresser and largely forgotten.

Now, however, JR took the weapon from its holster and closed the drawer. He strode out to the kitchen and set the gun, unloaded, on the table, so either Bill or Pete could pick it up when they came in.

Then JR went down the hall to Ralph Welch's bedroom to distract him. Welch, to whom they all had been so close, was now too far out of the circle—especially to be told about something like this.

Ralph had been in on his share of scams all right. But none of the boys thought he would be so crazy about this one.

JR Lattime loved cars. He loved to drive them, work on them, talk about them. It mattered little what kind of car you owned. JR wanted to know how you liked it, how fast it could go, and any specs you could remember.

So when Pam pulled up in her Honda CRX, JR saw a golden opportunity. He didn't care to scrunch up in the back with Billy. And he had his license, so what the heck. He asked Pam to let him drive to Bradford.

Pam agreed and stretched out in the back of the car with Flynn, their legs between the front seats and their heads toward the rear. Pete Randall got in the front passenger seat. And off JR drove.

Lattime had a notorious "need for speed." He already had a couple of speeding tickets on his driving record. But no matter. Merging into the Massachusetts-bound highway traffic, he wanted to get a feel for the CRX's power. He gave it some gas. Then some more. And more.

If the final result of that day was not so tragic it would be the stuff of comedy. For there was JR Lattime, Coke-bottle bespectacled, pushing eighty-five miles per hour—possibly even faster—as he drove along a busy highway to pick up a getaway car from his grandmother to be used in a murder that evening.

Pam saw no humor in it. She finally told Lattime to slow the hell down. That was all she needed—to have a state trooper pull him over in her car, with her in it, with an overload of passengers, one of them carrying a gun no less, on the same day that her husband was to be murdered.

Randall, in the meantime, was nervous about other matters. He had not talked with Pam about the plan, and he asked her to review it.

Everything was ready, Pam said. The rear doors and the bulkhead doors to the basement were unlocked. The only glitch might come if Greg, who would be home in the afternoon, locked them. If anything, he would probably only check the rear doors.

The bracelets, chains, rings, and earrings would be left in the jewelry box in the upstairs bathroom, she said. She had tossed a lot of stuff in the same box, even items that usually were kept elsewhere, so they would not have to search for very long. Her favorite pieces were safe—she was wearing rings that day on almost every finger—but they should find some items that would be worth some money.

Once they got inside the condo, the boys were to be certain to put the dog in the basement and keep the place dark. "Greg's a wimp," said Pam. "He won't go in the house if the light's on."

Pam asked to see the gun, and Billy reached into the left inside pocket of his jean jacket and showed her.

"Would you freak out if I used a knife?" Randall asked at one point, uncertain of how Pam would respond to the sight of blood.

"I don't want to know the details," Pam replied, her voice rising. "But why don't you just use the gun? If you stab him it's going to get blood all over the place. And whatever you do, don't get blood on the sofa."

"Don't worry," Billy said, trying to calm her down. "We'll use the gun. Everything's set."

Yet Pam herself had a mission that night and as JR Lattime would recall, she had not decided how to handle it.

"How should I react when I come home and find him?" she said. "I mean, should I scream or run to the other condos for help or just run in and call the police?"

"Just act natural," JR replied. "Let your reactions come as they normally would if you were to find someone dead."

They pulled onto Lovejoy Street in Bradford and the house where Mary Chase was staying. JR went inside and got the keys to the Impala and some gas money from his grandmother.

He and Pete climbed in the Chevy and pulled out, followed by Pam and Billy in the CRX. Both cars stopped for gas, then headed back to Seabrook, JR leaving Pam in the dust.

It was late afternoon when the boys regrouped and rounded up everything they needed so they could leave for Derry. First, they had to go to Billy's to pick up the duffel bag with the clothes and gloves that Pete and Billy would wear when they went into the condo.

Then, they had to get Raymond Fowler, who had not been in on most of the planning this time but whom JR wanted to have as company while he waited for Billy and Pete to take care of business. Fowler was on Collins Street, helping Ralph Welch's dad put a windshield in a pickup truck.

"Ramey!" Randall yelled. "We're going! Are you coming or not?"

Fowler said he was and got in the car.

Lattime stopped one more time, for gas, then pointed the Impala west for their rendezvous with Greg Smart.

The ride was uneventful. Billy and Pete talked about the condo's layout and again whether a knife or gun would be better. It was agreed that Pete would kill Greg with the knife and Billy would bring the gun just in case they needed it— to show, for example, if a neighbor or someone tried to apprehend them.

The highlight of the drive, though, was when JR missed his exit off of Route 101 and Billy and Ramey ended up arguing about the correct way to go.

Eventually the boys found their way—again Billy had been wrong with his directions—and pulled into Derry while it was still light.

JR drove into Hood Commons, then took a reconnaissance ride around back and down toward Summerhill Condominiums. On the way, they noticed a lot of cars over near Hood Memorial Junior High School, where a sporting event was underway.

Once they reached the complex, Billy pointed out the end unit on one of the buildings set back from the road. That was 4E, Misty Morning Drive.

They went back to the shopping plaza parking lot. One of the first orders of business was to buy some Scotch tape, which Randall had suggested he and Billy use to cover their fingertips before going into the condo.

Earlier, JR had reached into Billy's duffel bag and pulled out one of the thin latex gloves. He put his hand in one of them and pressed a finger against the car window, leaving a fingerprint.

JR and Fowler had gotten a kick out of that and started laughing and chiding Flynn. "I figured with all this planning he was supposedly doing for this murder that he wanted so bad that he'd have a better set of gloves than them," JR later said.

The boys hardly seemed like a gang of killers. They wandered around in Ames, a department store, laughing and cutting up, before they finally bought the tape.

Ramey was hungry, so he hit up Billy for some money and they all wandered into Papa Gino's, where Fowler ordered some pizza with extra cheese and everyone piled into the men's room.

Fowler sat in the restaurant, making small talk with a blonde waitress, while the others waited around for it to get dark.

JR, Flynn, and Randall went back to the car. More somber now and tense, Billy and Pete got in back, where they methodically taped each of their fingers and Flynn loaded the gun.

He had a handful of hollow-point bullets that the boys had talked a friend of JR's uncle into buying under the pretense that they wanted them for target practice. One by one, Flynn dropped the bullets into the five chambers and closed the cylinder. He slipped the revolver into the front waistband of his jeans and closed his jacket to cover it.

Darkness was beginning to fall. Billy grabbed the duffel bag. It was time.

*   *   *

No one is completely certain what happened in Pam and Greg Smart's condominium on the night of May 1, 1990. The crime scene itself would pose as many questions as it would provide answers. All anyone has to go on is the information later given by Billy Flynn and Pete Randall, accounts which have gone largely unchallenged, but which suffer from lapses—perhaps as a result of their panicked state that night, perhaps a matter of selective recollection.

After they left JR, Billy and Pete walked behind the plaza to a row of dumpsters. All was quiet. No people or cars were anywhere. They went behind the bins and slipped out of their street clothes and into the sweats Billy had brought. Randall wore the gray outfit and an old pair of sneakers. Billy tugged on black sweatpants, a T-shirt, a black winter coat, and the beatup footwear that Fowler had given him. The plan was to dispose of the old clothes later.

Flynn eased the gun into his left inside jacket pocket, then set the duffel bag, stuffed with their clothing, into a stairwell behind the plaza.

The boys began walking down Peabody Road Annex, behind the plaza and alongside the condominiums. Then they noticed two people coming toward them, so the boys started trotting to appear as if they were out for a run.

They jogged around the condos once and ended up on the side of Pam's unit. As daylight faded, the boys crouched in the shadow of a garage twenty feet from the Smart's bulkhead doors. They watched some people on a nearby driveway saying goodbye to friends. Flynn and Randall slipped on the latex gloves and waited.

When all was clear, they crept to the gray metal doors that led to the Smarts' basement. All Billy had to do was pull up the handle, but for some reason he could not figure how to open it.

Finally, it gave way. They padded down the concrete steps, closing the doors behind them, pushed open a second door, and stepped into the dark cellar.

Number one on their list was the dog. The boys went upstairs, but when Billy stooped to pick up Halen, the Shih-Tzu began to bark and growl and scampered away. Flynn chased the dog around the couch before he finally got his hands on it. The boys would later laugh that they threw the animal into the basement and heard the thump-thump-thump as it tumbled down the stairs.

Upstairs, they ripped apart the master bedroom. Then, they went into the bathroom, which was windowless, closed the door, and flicked on the light. Randall unloaded Pam's jewelry box into a blue, flower-patterned pillowcase he had removed from the bed. They grabbed a small portable television that was in the bathroom as well.

Next, they stepped into the guest bedroom, but let it be.

They started downstairs, the pillowcase holding the jewelry and a pair of sunglasses that had caught Pete's fancy.

In the living area, Billy opened one of the rear doors a crack in anticipation of a hurried departure. They looked around the kitchen cabinets for a flashlight, but could not find one.

Randall busied himself with the VCR, pulling it off its shelf on the entertainment center. He could not reach the outlet to unplug it, though, so he left it upside down on the floor. Easier to move were a small pair of stereo speakers, which Pete set by the doors. He planned to bring them with him when he left.

With a black-handled carving knife from the kitchen butcher block, Randall then sliced open a black pillow from the couch and emptied the stuffing on the floor. The flowered pillowcase was too conspicuous, so he unloaded the jewelry and sunglasses, as well as some compact disks, into the black pillowcase. He tossed the flowered one aside.

At the plaza, Lattime and Fowler were killing time. They window-shopped, then wandered down where some new stores were under construction and surveyed the workmanship. They went back to Ames, where JR got some motor oil and poured it into his grandmother's car. They checked out the cars in the parking lot to see if any had radios worth ripping off. They sat around listening to golden oldies on the Impala's AM radio, belting out their favorites as loud as they could. They talked about whether or not they should take the wheelchair that JR's grandmother kept in the trunk and push each other around the parking lot. They sliced up plastic bottles with a razor blade.

And at one point, they drove around the condo to see if Greg had returned. His truck wasn't there, so they went back to the plaza.

Around eight o'clock, meanwhile, Sergeant Vincent Byron of the Derry police department's detective bureau had been out with his wife and two kids and as he was driving home decided to take a brief detour.

After work some days, Byron, then thirty-seven, liked to take a golf club or two and go to the athletic field at Hood Junior High and smack balls. He saved the money that a driving range would charge and usually no one was around to bother him. Byron told his wife that he wanted to see if the field was available.

The sergeant, who is built like a linebacker, turned into the Hood Commons parking lot, quite possibly passing JR and Fowler, taking a shortcut to the junior high. Byron drove up to the school, which overlooks Summerhill Condominiums. Billy and Pete were just a couple hundred yards away, in the Smarts' condo. But all the sergeant saw was the field filled with baseball players, apparently a softball game in progress. "Not a good night for golf," he said, and headed home.

Less than an hour later, close to nine, Greg Smart's friend Dave Bosse, whom Smart had met back when he was working construction, was also at Hood Commons, picking up a baseball magazine at a bookstore. Since he was in the neighborhood, Bosse figured he might as well drop in to see Smart. He drove past the condo, but like JR and Fowler, didn't see Greg's pickup. Bosse decided to just go home.

Billy Flynn was also keeping an eye out for the Toyota pickup, sitting on the kitchen counter and peering out the blinds. Pete was in the living room, trying to figure out how he could remove the stereo system.

As the seconds ticked away, the boys talked, trying to decide how best to subdue Smart. Billy said maybe they should use Pam's plan of Flynn's hiding in the closet and then pouncing on Greg when he went to hang up his jacket.

At one point, Billy grabbed a towel from the upstairs bathroom. The plan was to cover Greg's head with it when they ambushed him at the door and then yank him in. But then for some reason they changed their mind and Flynn tossed the blue towel on the carpet.

Billy then took one of the heavy brass candlesticks from the dining room table and said maybe he should hit Greg over the head with it.

A second later, though, he had another idea. What if they unscrewed the lightbulb in the foyer, so Greg would be unable to turn it on? Billy set the candlestick on the floor and went over to the door to look. But that idea also went by the wayside. If they ever got caught, he said, it would look like a premeditated killing, not a burglary gone wrong. He never picked up the candlestick again, Billy said.

Finally, they agreed on a plan. Randall, who was burlier, would hide behind the entranceway door. Billy would stand at the base of the stairs that led to the second floor. When Greg came in, Pete would pounce on him and Billy would turn off the lights and shut the door.

They waited. Flynn continued looking out from the kitchen. Randall, nervous about fingerprints, had wrapped and then rewrapped the knife handle in paper towels from the kitchen, discarding the used ones on the carpet. He sat at the dining room table, anticipating cutting Greg's throat.

Suddenly, the Toyota pickup appeared outside. Greg pulled into his parking place.

"Jesus, Pete, he's here!" Billy said. "He's here!"

"Calm down," Randall said, standing. "Let's go."

In the excitement of the moment, they ended up in each other's place. Billy stood behind the door and Pete got on the landing by the stairs.

Billy could hear Greg's footsteps outside as he climbed the steps, then the jangle of his keys, and the metallic click of the door unlocking.

The door opened.

Greg took a step inside and flicked on the light.

"Haley!" Smart called, to the dog.

No response.

For seconds they all stood there—Greg, Billy, and Pete—suspended on the cusp of the most critical moment of each of their lives.

Then Flynn leaped out. He grabbed Smart by the shoulders of his coat. Stunned, Smart hollered and tried to retreat.

Randall bounded down and shoved Smart completely into the foyer, then turned to shut the door and extinguish the lights. The doormat, though, was caught in the door and he had to kick it free. When Pete looked again, Billy had Smart over by the stairwell wall, the boy flailing away while Greg tried to cover his face to block the blows.

Randall rushed over and in one violent motion seized

Greg by the hair and slammed the back of his head against the wall.

"Get down on your knees!" Randall said, lurching before him with the knife in his right hand and Greg's hair tangled in his left.

Smart dropped to his knees, his back toward the stairwell wall, his hands in his lap. Flynn stood to his left.

"Don't hurt me, dude," Smart said, almost in a whimper. "What do you want, dude?"

"Just shut up!" Randall said, waving the blade before his face. "Shut up!"

"Where's the dog? What did you do with my dog?"

"Your dog's OK," Randall fired back. "No one hurt your dog."

Randall guessed that Smart was wearing a chain around his neck. He demanded that Greg hand it over, but Smart denied he was wearing one.

Then Pete told him to remove the ring on his left hand. It turned out to be his wedding band.

"I can't give it to you," Smart said. "My wife would kill me."

Pete decided to let it go. The boys turned instead to his wallet. Greg took out the billfold, monogrammed G.W.S., and Billy rooted through it, removing his money, most likely only five dollars.

The moment had arrived to kill him, but as Randall would later say, Greg's remarks about his wedding band and his pleadings to spare his life were playing on Pete's mind. It was not as easy to stab someone face-to-face as it was to boast about it.

Randall could not slit Smart's throat. Pete looked over at Billy, who motioned with his right hand toward where the revolver sat in his inside jacket pocket. The movement was a question.

Pete, still grasping Greg by the hair, nodded yes.

Flynn removed the gun while Randall and Smart traded words, babble now to the boy who held the power of life and death in his hand.

Billy cocked the hammer of the dual-action pistol. Now the trigger was far less resistant to pull.

The boy stood there—"a hundred years, it seemed like," Flynn later said—the gun two or three inches from the top of Greg's skull.

"God, forgive me," Billy said.

He squeezed. There was a loud report and a flash.

At that instant, Randall let go of Smart's hair.

Mysteriously, Greg's head came to rest partly on the discarded blue towel. Perhaps it was a coincidence. Or, perhaps one of the boys, worried about Pam's admonishments about causing a mess, placed it there, consciously or unconsciously. Neither of the boys says he remembers.

Also strange, though more likely a coincidence, was that Greg's foot came to rest on the candlestick.

Greg's right ring finger would show an abrasion, as if his ring was pried off of him. And the ring from that hand would end up beneath his body, along with his keys and his wallet. Yet neither of the boys would recall seeing it, much less forcibly removing it.

And most baffling would be the forensic evidence. Bullet fragments under the scalp and a lack of gunpowder in and around the wound strongly suggest that Smart was indeed shot at close range, as Billy and Pete would say, but that an object was placed between the gun barrel and Greg's head.

Was something used to muffle the sound of the gun? Was Smart's head covered, perhaps with a towel, so that he didn't know what was coming? Was he somehow tortured? No physical signs of such an object remained at the scene. And the boys say that nothing, absolutely nothing, was in front of the gun.

What is generally agreed upon, though, is that when the shot was fired, it did not take long for the boys to bolt for the back door. Billy went first, with Randall grabbing the black pillowcase from the floor, and following at full tilt. They catapulted over the back porch railing and broke for the field and the shopping plaza.

Billy gripped the gun as he ran. Pete sprinted with the knife in one hand and the pillowcase in the other.

Suddenly, they saw headlights. The original plan was for Flynn and Randall to change back to their street clothes and then meet JR and Fowler in the front of the plaza. JR was then to drive back to wherever they had left the stolen stereo equipment to be picked up.

Now, however, there was JR and Fowler, cruising along behind the shopping center in the Impala, on a second trip to see if Greg had come home.

Fowler had, in fact, seen Smart's truck, and they were going back so he could point it out to JR when he saw the dark outlines of his friends in the field and told JR to stop.

Flynn and Randall sprinted through the grass toward the car. Then Billy went down. His legs had been churning too fast for the terrain. Pete passed him and as he ran he hurled the knife into the turf at the top of the hill. He just wanted to be rid of it. Seconds later, just before he reached the car, Randall also fell, face first.

Finally, they scampered into the backseat.

"Go! Go! Go!" Pete yelled.

Lattime and Fowler all but yawned. "Why?" said Lattime. "What are you talking about? Did you do it?"

"We did it!" said Pete. "We killed him!"

"Sure, sure," said JR, not moving the car an inch. He assumed it was all a big put-on.

"Go!" Billy screamed. Something unmistakably real and scared was in his voice. "We did it!"

JR realized it was true. He followed Pete's instructions and drove to the dumpsters. Randall got out and grabbed the duffel bag.

Then JR pulled out onto the street to head home and noticed that the Derry police station was right around the corner from the plaza.

Lattime could not believe it. "Why didn't you tell us the police station was right there?" he snapped at Billy.

They got on the backroads toward Seabrook, the car filled with excitement, fear, and paranoia.

A truck happened to be taking the same circuitous route as JR. When he turned, the headlights behind him followed along. They worried that someone was trailing them.

"I can't believe I killed a guy," said Flynn. "Feel the gun. It's still hot."

"You almost blew my hand off!" said Randall.

They changed clothes in the backseat, throwing some out as they went, and getting rid of the rest and the duffel bag in the woods when JR stopped to urinate. It was in the car on the way home that Flynn realized something was missing. He had lost one of the gloves.

They finally found their way back near the seacoast, on Death Highway, around where Route 51 and Route 101 come together. Pam would later tell Billy that she had seen their car on the road as she was going home from Hampton and had even flicked her lights in greeting.

Randall and Flynn, though, were too shaken up by the whole affair to even know where they were. The car was filled with tension. So Lattime and Fowler thought they would take the edge off. They started singing one of the old songs they had heard on the radio while they were sitting around the Hood Commons parking lot—"Shoofly Pie and Apple Pan Dowdy."

Billy Flynn could not help but smile at the song, which among other things credits "shoofly pie and apple pan dowdy" with making "your eyes light up, your stomach say 'Howdy.'"

Randall, however, was only irritated by the tune. He repeatedly told his friends to stop singing.

Months later, in court, much would be made of the boys' behavior in the hour or so after the killing; J.R. Lattime would say that, since he did not know Greg Smart, the murder wasn't particularly bothersome. As he drove home to Seabrook, his main concern was getting away. Pete Randall would recall how Billy spoke excitedly about "the power" he felt in committing the murder, almost as if he was in awe of his own destructive capabilities. Flynn, in the meantime, would say that he remembered little of the ride home, and insisted that it was dubious that he would be boasting or laughing about the crime.

"Shut up!"

The Impala rolled into Seabrook. JR parked in front of Fowler's house. The four youths went down to Fowler's room in the basement, emptied out the bag and poked around through what was mostly worthless costume jewelry, and listened as Pete and Billy recounted what happened inside. Fowler, JR would later say, was given the CDs.

They got back in the car. JR dropped off Pete, who had the bag, at his parents' place. When Pete walked in, his mother, Patricia Randall, asked what was with the bag. It was from a break-in, said the boy. When his mother started to get angry, Pete told her not to worry. It hadn't been his idea.

JR next went to Billy's, where Flynn emptied the gun, took the remaining bullets for disposal, and handed the weapon over to Lattime and Fowler.

JR drove Ramey home and asked if he could clean the

revolver tomorrow while the boys were at school. JR wanted to return it to his father's drawer in good shape. Then Lattime went home himself, left the murder weapon in the camper for Ramey, and went to bed.

The next morning, JR, Pete, and Billy went to school, thinking that it would seem less suspicious if their lives proceeded as normal. Randall had been up late after the killing because he and Fowler had gotten together after everyone was dropped off; they walked down to Hampton Beach to try to trade some of the stolen gold chains for cocaine. Pete's connection had not been around, though, and now the boys were planning to make an after-school trip to Haverhill to see what their contacts there would pay for the jewelry.

It was about quarter after seven that morning, at their lockers, that Billy and JR saw Sal Parks. Billy's friend lived in North Hampton. Parks' father, ironically, had been a Derry cop before he and Sal's mother divorced. For the last month, Flynn had been telling Parks about the plot, even going so far as to bring a bullet to school and tell Sal it was the kind that would end Greg's life. Moreover, Billy would sketch maps of the condo and its environs for Sal and JR in biology class.

The day of the murder, Bill had told Parks that Greg was going to die that night. As always, Sal had listened, but he also knew Billy. He doubted it would ever happen.

"Well, did you do it?" Sal asked Flynn the morning of May 2.

"Yeah, I did it," Billy said nervously, but he revealed little more.

Cecelia, in the meantime, was also aware that the murder was to have gone down. Pam, she would say, had told her the morning of May 1. Cecelia and a friend had also dropped by the media center and said hello to Pam just before Smart went into the evening meeting.

Yet as classes got underway at Winnacunnet that Wednesday, Pierce had no idea what had happened. During second period, however, guidance counselor Barbara Kinsman poked her head into Crit's class and asked to see Cecelia and Karen Crowley. It was an emergency.

Kinsman, fifty-four years old and a guidance counselor for nearly two decades, had been sent as a member of the school's crisis assistance committee to gather some of the

Police evidence photo of Greg Smart's body.

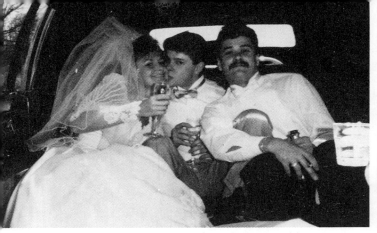

(Left to right) Pam Smart, Greg Smart, and best man
Tom Parilla on the way to the wedding reception.
(Tom Parilla)

Leaving the church after the funeral: (left to right)
John Wojas, Linda Wojas, Pam, and Beth Wojas.
(Don Hemsel/ *Nashua Telegraph*)

Derry Police stand guard outside 4E Misty Morning
Drive the morning after the murder.
(Don Hemsel/ *Nashua Telegraph*)

Billy Flynn and Cecelia
Pierce in a public
relations photo taken
by Pam for the orange
juice video competition.

JR Lattime examines his father's .38, the gun that Billy Flynn used to kill Greg Smart. (Mike Ross/ *Foster's Daily Democrat*)

Raymond Fowler leaves the Rockingham County Superior Court after an appearance. (Nick Thomas/ *The Hampton Union*)

Pete Randall eyes the black pillowcase stuffed with jewelry that he stole the night of the murder. (Mike Ross/ *Foster's Daily Democrat*)

Assistant Attorney General Paul Maggiotto at a post-verdict press conference.
(Mike Ross/*Foster's Daily Democrat*)

Assistant Attorney General Diane Nicolosi was involved with the case, often behind the scenes, from the night of the murder to the conviction.
(Mike Ross/
Foster's Daily Democrat)

Defense Attorney Paul Twomey. He described Pam as "a woman who had been emotionally drawn and quartered." (Brian K. Goyne, *The Daily News*)

Defense Attorney Mark Sisti referred to the state's case as "a toxic soup" based on the testimony of "young, thrill-killers." (Mike Ross/ *Foster's Daily Democrat*)

The Derry, New Hampshire, P.D. Detective Squad.
(Left to right) Mike Raymond, Sgt. Vincent Byron,
Capt. Loring Jackson, Michael Surette, Dan Pelletier,
Paul Lussier, Sgt. Barry Charewicz.
(Jim Paiva/ *The Derry News*)

One of the pictures that Pam gave to Billy Flynn.

students who had gotten close to Pam through Project Self-Esteem and the orange juice video project.

"What's going on?" Cecelia asked when they got in the hall. "What's happened?"

"Cecelia, I'll tell you in just a minute. We have to get Bill and Vance first."

Down the corridor they walked until they got to the biology classroom. Kinsman went in.

"Bill, Vance," she said quietly, "can I speak to you for a moment?"

Kinsman led the students to the group-counseling room in the guidance area.

"There's been an accident," Kinsman finally said. "Mrs. Smart's husband was killed last night."

"My god, no!" said Cecelia, only partly acting.

JR and Billy, in the meantime, were behaving so shocked that Cecelia thought they were giving themselves away.

"Do they have any clues?" Billy asked. "Do they know who did it?"

Kinsman did not know much, Cecelia remembered, just that Greg Smart apparently had been struck over the head.

They talked for a while about what they could do for Pam, such as get a sympathy card, and Kinsman told them that they could come to see her anytime if this tragedy was upsetting them.

That day at lunch, Billy Flynn bought Sal Parks a meal with the five dollars he said he took from Greg's wallet. Before the day was out, he would reveal to Sal almost everything that had happened in the condo. And Parks, stunned that it had happened at all, decided it was best to say nothing to anyone—for fear that he himself was in trouble as much as to protect Billy.

After school that day, JR went to the camper, where he found the revolver had been cleaned. He slipped it back into the holster in his dad's room.

Before heading to Haverhill to sell the stolen items, the boys decided to run two of the stolen chains and two bracelets through a mixture of bleach and water to test if they were truly gold. A black film rose to the surface. What had looked like the only pieces of jewelry of any value were in reality gold-plated. Junk.

Pete Randall tossed the chains and bracelets off a bridge and into Seabrook's Blackwater River, where the current most likely washed them away into Seabrook Harbor and perhaps even the sea. Oddly, however, he would keep the black pillowcase and its worthless, yet incriminating, collection of costume jewelry.

Cecelia, meanwhile, went through her day as she always did, but as the hours passed, she kept thinking about Billy and the boys and Pam's husband. She could not believe it. They had done it. They'd actually done it.

At Papa Gino's after school, Cecelia was finding it hard to keep her mind on waitressing. Cindy Butt came into the back room to see why she was so upset.

Her friend Pam's husband had been killed the night before during a break-in, Pierce said. It was just so sad.

Cindy suggested that Cecelia come with her on a pizza delivery when Crit had her break. They could talk more then. Cecelia agreed and later that night she got in Butt's car to join her.

"Didn't you tell me about a friend that was planning on having her husband killed?" Cindy asked, thinking back to their conversation during dinner a month or so earlier.

"Oh, shit!" said Cecelia. "I had forgotten that I told you that."

They talked about it for a while, and when they were through, Cindy Butt thought it was best to not get involved. If Cecelia was telling her, Cindy figured, she probably told other people as well and *they* would go to the police.

So Butt kept quiet. About two weeks later, though, she had a couple of friends from work, who also happened to live in the same Seabrook apartment complex, by her place for drinks. Cindy told her co-workers that Cecelia knew a woman from Derry who had had her husband killed for the insurance money.

Louise Coleman, thirty-one years old, pregnant and single, who worked as a waitress at Papa Gino's, was shocked by what she was hearing. Someone, she thought, had to tell the police.

"I left Cindy's apartment," Coleman remembered. "I walked across the yard, I went into my apartment, and I made the phone call."

Coleman did not get all the facts correct. She told the police that Cecelia attended Greg's funeral, when the girl in fact only attended the wake. She said Pam had purchased a new car, when the truth was that Pam was still looking for one.

But Coleman knew one thing damn straight: "Someone was killed and that bothered me," she said. "To hear what I had heard, I figured any little bit was gonna help 'em, because at that point the police didn't know much of anything.

"Like I told them, I says, it's hearsay; if it helps, it helps; if it don't, it don't. But I feel like I did my civic duty."

Chapter 6

For Dan Pelletier, there was no escaping the Gregory Smart homicide. The investigation was entering its third week, and the detective seemed unable to wrangle a full day off to spend with his wife and new baby daughter.

Pelletier might wake up believing that he need not go in, but inevitably the call would come, and it was back to the Derry police department. Robyn Pelletier would roll her eyes in disbelief.

Most of the time, the work was drudgery—leads that went nowhere, interviews that illuminated little, background checks of Pam and Greg that mostly painted a picture of a troublefree young couple.

Pelletier's only solace was that he had company. Every available investigator—five detectives and a patrolman who was on a training program in the bureau—was thrown on to the case. Only one, who at the time was working undercover drug cases with a regional task force, was kept off.

Generally, investigators seek to break a murder case in the first day and a half. After that, the odds that anyone will be apprehended begin to diminish. Killers can flee the state, even the country. Evidence can be destroyed. Witnesses move on, and the memories of those who remain begin to fade.

Time was marching on. What's more, all the detectives had other cases in limbo, which could not be left there forever. Pelletier himself had to carve out time to work a few rape cases that had been on his desk when Greg Smart was shot.

At the Summerhill Condominiums, meanwhile, residents began receiving sales calls from security-system installation companies. Some of the neighbors put new locks on their doors. Others placed Louisville Sluggers in strategic locations around their homes. And, a number called the Derry police with concerns about their safety and questions about what was being done to solve this crime.

The residents' fears were not allayed when Derry Police Chief Edward Garone and New Hampshire Attorney General John Arnold issued a press release that seemed to say that the investigation was at a standstill. The statement asked anyone with information to please come forward. And it refused to rule out the possibility that Smart had indeed interrupted a burglary.

Otherwise, neither the cops nor the AG's office was commenting to the press, a silence that was worrisome in itself.

In contrast, the widow continued to tell journalists, friends, and family that her husband had surely surprised robbers; she was certain of it.

With no surefire answers, the Derry detectives were all but forced to keep Pamela on their list of possible suspects.

Pam and her family had already been closed out from learning more about the case because Pam had revealed too much to the media. Linda Wojas would call the detectives on her daughter's behalf, asking for details on the investigation but would come away politely rebuffed.

Now, after the call from Louise Coleman, the Derry cops decided to look closer at Pam. Their first stop was Seabrook.

Talking to Cecelia Pierce became a priority. The phone call, of course, was one reason. But Cecelia had stayed with Pam the week before Greg's murder, which was interesting in itself. After all, how often do students get that close to teachers and other school officials?

On Monday, May 21, Detective Barry Charewicz, a lean man with closely cropped hair, sat down with the teenager at her parents' rented condo in Seabrook. He came to get fingerprints, which the police were collecting from everyone who was said to have been in the condo prior to Greg's murder. He also had a few questions.

Cecelia, three days shy of her sixteenth birthday, talked about her friendship with Pam and admitted that she had stayed at the Smarts' condo while Greg was out of town. She insisted, however, that she knew nothing about the murder, and anyone who said she did was a liar. Charewicz got Cecelia's prints and returned to Derry.

Before long, however, he was back at the seacoast. With Pelletier having finally taken a vacation, Charewicz picked up the slack, dropping in at Winnacunnet High School and the Seabrook police department, seeking anything he could learn about Cecelia Pierce.

Around the same time, Charewicz questioned Pam about Cecelia and her close friend Karen Crowley. Pam maintained that it was incomprehensible for the girls, who Pam regarded as good kids, to have somehow taken part in Greg's death. Anyway, she said, Cecelia still lacked a driver's license.

Captain Jackson, in the meantime, felt that he needed someone relatively close to Pam to read her moods and keep investigators informed about her activities. His best bet was Greg's father.

By now, Bill Smart was beginning to have a doubt or two about Pam having been his son's loving wife. Her behavior the day after the funeral, when she had casually strolled over the towel covering the bloodstain at 4E, Misty Morning Drive, had appalled Bill. He had also been disturbed when Pam brought over Greg's belongings in plastic garbage bags. Still, Smart and his wife talked to their daughter-in-law regularly.

One day, as it became obvious that Pam needed closer scrutiny, the captain contacted Smart and laid his cards on the table. "Look, I need your help," Jackson said. "I'm going to take a chance here. Are you willing to help me and keep your mouth shut about it? Even to your wife?"

Bill Smart agreed and Jackson broke the news to him that Pam was the main suspect. What the police needed, he told Greg's father, was someone to monitor Pam's behavior and moods, someone to report back what she was saying and asking family members. In short, Jackson wanted to know what Pam's concerns were about the investigation and when she would be most vulnerable.

"I more or less had to act like an agent of the state," says Bill Smart.

But it was now June and the investigation was at a crawl. Most of the leads had fizzled out. And now the strongest one—Pam's relationship with Cecelia—was murky at best.

Toward the end of the first full week of the month, Jackson met with Sergeant Byron to discuss the logistics of a round-the-clock, perhaps week-long, surveillance on Pam in the near future.

They were interested in her schedule, where she went,

with whom she spent time, even if it was just to eliminate her as a suspect, which by now seemed increasingly unlikely.

After the murder, it did not take Pamela Smart very long to reestablish her ties with Billy Flynn, her teenage coterie, and the seacoast.

Her initial contact with the kids was at the wake. Barbara Kinsman had suggested that Billy, JR, and Cecelia come with her to the funeral home to pay their respects. None of them thought it would look good to refuse.

Billy and JR had knelt beside Greg's coffin and later, according to Cecelia, both commented on what a good job the mortician had done on Greg. The dead man showed hardly a trace of having taken a bullet in the skull.

Pam was flabbergasted when the kids walked through the funeral home door, but she greeted them with great animation. Like any of the mourners, the teenagers told Pam how sorry they were and moved quietly away. "Then afterwards she came up to me and JR," Billy Flynn recalled, "and she said, 'I can't believe you guys came to the wake,' When we walked in the door, I think she said she was shitting bricks."

The kids stayed only ten or fifteen minutes. Pam took Cecelia aside and told her that while she was happy to see her, the situation was causing Pam great discomfort. "Tell Mrs. Kinsman that you're ready to leave," Pam said.

Kinsman drove the teenagers back to her own house in Hampton Falls. The guidance counselor was going to the theater in Boston that night and had told the kids that she would not have time to drive them home. But she gave them sodas and said they could stay at her place for a bit with her father, until JR's aunt and uncle picked them up.

The teens were in the backyard when JR stepped inside to get something in the kitchen.

"Billy, what happened?" Cecelia said, all but certain that the boys had killed Pam's husband, but needing to hear it firsthand.

"Ah, Greg was an asshole," Flynn replied. "He didn't even care about Pam. All he cared about was his dog. He was saying, 'Where's my dog, where's my dog. . . .' " Lattime started to come back out and Billy stopped. "I don't want to talk about it in front of JR," Flynn said.

About a week later, Pam was at the seacoast herself,

checking in at SAU 21 and dropping by the lockers at Winnacunnet High School to assure Billy and JR that all was going according to plan.

She told the boys, first of all, that the police were chasing leads far off track. The cops, she said, thought that Greg had either interrupted a burglary or that it had been a professional hit.

It was also likely that she would be living nearby soon, Pam said. Her friends were encouraging her to move out of the condo in Derry, and Pam was already telling everyone that it was important for her to carry on in the wake of the tragedy. Before the month was out, she found a place in the Seabury Condominiums in Hampton, just across the athletic fields from Winnacunnet High School.

Around the same time that the Derry police began looking in Seabrook, Pam returned to work full-time. She was soon back into her routine with Billy, seeing him daily and keeping him informed of anything she had learned about the investigation before the cops cut her off, such as the lead in New Jersey.

At one point, Pam happily told the boy that Greg had carried more insurance than she'd anticipated. In mid May, Pam received $90,000 from a group life insurance plan that Greg had at work. She was due to get another $50,000 from a personal policy her husband had purchased.

Billy never told Pam the details of the murder. She said she would rather not know, and Billy preferred not to tell her. Still, Pam did talk about how on the night of the killing, she simply could not bring herself to weep. Instead, she told Billy, all she could think was to repeatedly ask for her dog, Halen.

Pam also discussed what she knew of the murder with Cecelia: Smart described coming home and finding Greg. She spoke of the fingerprint dust ruining her furniture. And how she could not believe that Billy had so stupidly dropped a glove.

For Cecelia's birthday, not long after Charewicz's visit to her and his questions about the girl to Pamela, Smart took Cecelia to the Fox Run Mall in Newington for a bit of a shopping spree. What was important now for Pam was to keep the girl as an ally.

"Pam had everything," said Cecelia, "and now she wanted to buy me everything. That's what it seemed like."

Smart told Cecelia to pick anything she wanted and that Pam would get it for her. Underscoring their differences in upbringing and age, Pam suggested an eighty-dollar crystal item, but Cecelia preferred a pair of sneakers—her old ones had gotten ratty—and a Bart Simpson T-shirt that read "Where the hell's the party, man?"

A few days later, Pam had Cecelia stay with her at her parents' home in Windham and then spend a day at a nearby amusement park, Canobie Lake Park. And there, less than a month after Greg's death, Pam and Cecelia would have their picture taken, happily smiling into the camera.

Pam was making little secret of her friendships with the teenagers. Even old friends who knew Greg, like Terri Schnell, Sonia Simon, and Tracy Collins, were aware of Pam's spending time with the teens after Greg's death. To them, it seemed that Pam was simply trying to help kids who were less fortunate. None of them knew about her affair with Billy.

"I could see that they were close," remembered Sonia Simon, "but I thought it was because she was dealing with them with this awareness program. I thought that maybe she felt a need to be there for them, like they looked up to her."

On a number of occasions, in fact, these friends would even join Pam on outings with Billy and JR or Cecelia. Terri Schnell wondered at one point if the school didn't mind Smart spending so much time with the students, but then let it go.

Toward the end of May, Pam had made up her mind to rid herself of Greg's truck. She would simply let it be repossessed. But first she wanted the stereo removed. And to save money, she accepted Billy's offer to do it for free.

By now, Pam seemed less concerned about who saw her with the kids, almost in defiance of common sense. The degree to which she was socializing with high schoolers in itself was inappropriate, not to mention somewhat strange. But then there was the fact that she seemed to have shed her widow's weeds rather quickly, especially considering that no one seemed to know the reasons behind Greg's death.

At the end of May, Pam drove the pickup to JR's house, where amid a crowd of kids—Billy, JR, Pete, Ralph, and their girlfriends—JR removed the stereo system. He took an instant shine to Greg's dark gray Kenwood speakers and came out and asked Pam if he could have them.

She said no, but JR pressed on, saying he was willing to have two hundred and fifty dollars dropped from his expected five-hundred-dollar payoff for the killing. Still Pam refused, claiming that it would be too difficult to explain to her friends why she gave the expensive speakers to some kid she knew at Winnacunnet. Anyway, the speakers were going to go in the new car that she wanted to buy with her insurance windfall.

That day, Pam drove Billy, Pete, JR, and his girlfriend to Dreher-Holloway, the Exeter, New Hampshire, auto dealership where JR's mother worked, to look at cars, one of numerous trips that Pam would make to price Trans-Ams and Camaros.

They were waiting in the showroom for a salesman to help when Pam noticed a barrel of lollipops that the dealership keeps for customers. With Pete Randall standing nearby, she turned to Billy and ordered, "Go get me a lollipop."

Flynn was not sure whether Pam was putting on a bossy show in front of Randall or if she truly wanted the candy, but it still came down to the same thing—she was trying to embarrass him in front of Pete. So Billy ignored her.

"Fine, be that way," Pam said, not seeming too concerned.

When they were through looking at cars, Pam drove the kids back to Lattime's, then went with Billy to park down at a secluded spot at a nearby marsh. Before Billy knew it, Pam started in on him about his refusal to get her the lollipop.

"You don't love me," she said. "If you did, you would have gotten that for me."

"Well, to me it looked like you were just trying to be sarcastic," Billy answered.

They argued about it for a while, with Billy finally displaying a modicum of self-respect and not backing down. Pam, furious, drove him back to JR's. Billy started down the driveway when she beeped her car horn, signaling for him to return.

"So I went back up there," Flynn recalled, "and she said, 'I was this close to going, taking back my first and last month's rent at the condo and just not move down here anymore and that would be it between us,' like that. And she asked me if that's what I wanted. And I said no. And I apologized for not getting her a lollipop.''

Not long after that, in the beginning of June, Pam did settle into her rented Hampton condominium, beautifully adorned with furniture from her place in Derry. She also had new pieces to replace those damaged by fingerprint dust, which of course had been covered by Metropolitan Life. And true to her word, Pam would have Billy drop by to see her, as well as Pete and JR now and then, and many of her old friends like Terri Schnell and Tracy Collins.

JR, meanwhile, through Billy, kept up the pressure for Greg's speakers. Pam had yet to pay the boys for the murder and Lattime wanted the equipment more than the cash. Again, JR made the offer to have the payment for his part in the slaying lowered by half in exchange for the Kenwoods. He was hoping to get a job soon, he told Billy. All Pam had to tell her friends, he said, was that JR was buying them.

Pam's resistance began to waver. But before giving in, she made sure her tracks were covered. One day, Pam took Tracy Collins on a special trip to price similar speakers, thereby making it clear that the sale to JR was imminent.

Finally, Pam and Billy drove over to JR's house in the CRX and gave him the speakers. JR brought them into his room, where he had his own unique sound system—a car stereo hooked up to a car battery connected to a battery charger plugged into an electrical outlet. Now Lattime added the finishing touch: a dead man's truck speakers. Something in it seemed ideal for JR, the mechanically minded lover of Edgar Allan Poe.

With investigators saying next to nothing for the record, reporters were finding little to tell about the death of Greg Smart. On June 6, around midday, WMUR's Bill Spencer and a cameraman came to Hampton for a prearranged interview with Pam, their third meeting.

On the phone, Spencer had convinced her to grant the interview by saying that it was important to keep the murder in the news. It would maintain pressure on the police, he said, and might lead potential witnesses to come forward.

Upon entering the two-story condo, Spencer said, he was surprised to see no reminders of Pam's husband. ''I just found it funny that she had this gorgeous place and there's not one picture of Greg,'' said the newsman. ''Usually when you go into somebody's house who's just lost a loved one, they might even have a tribute up, like flowers or candles. Here, there was nothing.''

On the news that evening, WMUR's report began with Pam, dressed in a pink pullover and jeans, talking about the aftermath of her husband's killing.

''It's just frustrating because there's so many unanswered questions,'' she said, ''and there's so much speculation.''

Spencer then intoned, in voiceover: ''More than a month after her newlywed husband, Gregory, was gunned down just inside the front door of his Derry condominium, Pamela Smart is frustrated. Police have yet to make an arrest in connection with the killing.''

Pam continued: ''I've been told just that they are interviewing people and that it's a process of elimination. They do have to explore all kinds of different avenues. They have had some leads. A lot of them have turned up to be, turned out to be dead ends.''

Spencer then said: ''Along with the frustration, Pamela has also felt fear. After all, the killer is still out there. She worries it could happen to someone else.''

''Am I afraid that somebody else might go through something like this at the hands of the same person?'' said Pam. ''Yes. I do, I do think about that sometimes. I would never wish anything like this upon anyone.''

Spencer closed his report on an ominous note: ''And as far as the Derry police investigation goes, Pamela says the detectives in this department have made her husband's murder case their number-one priority.

''She says though they've been sensitive, they have not let anyone off the list of potential suspects. That includes friends of Greg Smart's, people he worked with, even Pamela herself.''

Diane and Vance Lattime had seen a spark of something in their son's friend Ralph Welch.

The boy had lived with his family in what was little more than a shack, a place with automobile parts strewn around out front, a house or two away from the Lattimes, on the opposite side of Upper Collins Street.

The Welch family was poor, with a gaggle of kids and even some of their children's children living under the roof of the same little dwelling. Ralph's father picked up what work was available, sometimes fishing, sometimes working in the junk business. His mother was a factory hand.

As he grew up, Ralph started to spend more and more time over at the Lattimes' house. There was, of course, his friend JR. Also, Vance and Diane had hot running water and Ralph liked to use their shower. He was also attracted to the sense of family that was evident at the Lattimes'.

Like most people who met Ralph, Diane and Vance saw a likable kid. Welch, rawboned, with a face that is best described as a mug—the kind that would fit in among the Bowery Boys—was rough around the edges, to be sure. At the same time, he could be friendly and respectful. Ralph had potential, perhaps not to set the world on fire, but certainly to go beyond the physical blight of his upbringing.

Before long, Welch was spending most of his time at the Lattime house, so Diane worked out a deal. She told Ralph he could live with them if he returned to high school, from which he had dropped out.

Ralph agreed and in the process found himself with a second family. Vance and Diane treated him like a son. He had a place at the dinner table. And for the first time in his life, Ralph enjoyed a traditional family Christmas, becoming an integral part of the Lattimes' annual hunt for what became known as the "elusive perfect Christmas tree."

For Ralph, it had not been a bad trade, considering that all that was expected of him was to go back to Winnacunnet, which he basically liked anyway.

Welch, of course, had his moments. In school one time he raised a few eyebrows when after an argument with his girlfriend he heaved a desk across the room. He had also come along on a number of car radio rip offs with Pete, JR, and Billy, and had, in fact, plotted a storage warehouse break-in that proved to be rather fruitful.

Ralph Welch was a realist. Maybe it was because he knew true poverty, but Welch tended to view the world in terms of the concrete. He wasn't a kid who complained about his lot in life. Nor was he a dreamer like Billy. Ralph, for example, thought that running a junkyard might not be a bad future.

Welch knew Billy was involved with Pam Smart. Flynn had told him as much, but Ralph had also seen the good-bye kisses at the top of JR's driveway. And once, a week or so before Greg Smart was killed, he had seen Billy coming out of the Lattimes' house joking around and saying, "We're gonna go do Greg." He even heard that Pam Smart's husband had been murdered, but dismissed any possibility that Billy or his friends were involved.

That is, Welch would later testify, until the afternoon of Saturday, June 9.

Ralph was working on his car in the Lattimes' driveway when Danny Blake, a cousin of both Raymond Fowler and Ralph, wheeled up on his bicycle. "Man, if I was Bill Flynn, I'd punch Raymond's face in," said Blake.

"How come?" asked Ralph.

"Raymond's been going around shooting his mouth off about killing that guy."

Danny Blake was a Seabrook hang around, a swarthy twenty-year-old high school dropout who ran with an older crowd but who spent a fair share of time in and out of the Lattimes' place, mainly to visit Ralph.

As far back as April, Blake had heard Raymond Fowler rambling on about this supposed murder for hire for Bill Flynn's girlfriend. About a week after the failed attempt, Blake said Ramey had said something about a plan to murder someone, but Danny had written it off to Raymond's tendency to try to make himself sound like a tough guy.

Then, in early May, Fowler had spoken to Blake about how Billy, Pete, JR, and he had driven to Derry and actually murdered Pam's husband. Blake said he again thought Raymond was lying.

"Raymond's the type who will tell you stories," said Blake. "He tells stories that aren't true. He'll tell you one thing and do the opposite. He exaggerates."

Again, Blake ignored him.

Yet toward the end of the month, Blake heard a news report that mentioned the murder of Greg Smart. Around Memorial Day, he asked Fowler about it again. Raymond repeated the story, saying that Billy and Pete had gone inside and killed Smart.

Blake, not wanting to get involved in a police investigation, said he elected to keep the information to himself.

By June, Fowler had left town, perhaps to put some distance between himself and the boys should the heat eventually come down, moving in with relatives just over the Maine border. In the meantime, though, he had already talked to a number of people about the murder. Word was leaking out.

Now, the story reached Ralph Welch. Somehow, Ralph thought, Blake's words had a ring of truth to them, but the only way to know for certain was to ask his buddies.

So that evening, after JR's parents and the baby, Ryan, had gone to sleep, Ralph came home to find JR and Pete in the bedroom. It was close to 11:30 and the two had just returned from being at the movies with Pam Smart and Billy.

Welch went in and asked the boys about what Blake had said. Was it true? Were they involved in this murder? Pete and JR were incredulous. They would never have something to do with anything like that, they said. No way.

Ralph said OK, that was all he wanted to hear, and stepped out, closing the door behind him. He walked away, then crept back and listened at the door.

"Billy is gonna be pissed!" he heard one hushed voice say.

"Yeah, you know who's gonna be next."

With that, Ralph burst into the room and jumped on top of Pete, mock wrestling and tickling his friend.

"I heard you!" Welch said. "I heard you! I can't believe you lied to me about this. Tell me now."

Welch climbed off Pete, who went over and shut the door. The three sat on the beds facing each other and Randall quietly recounted the night of the murder. JR chimed in periodically, to provide a detail or two, but mostly he remained silent.

Pete spoke of ransacking the condo to make it appear burglarized, putting the dog in the cellar, and Greg's futile attempt to escape and his pleas for mercy.

Then Randall described how Billy shot Smart. "Greg didn't even see it coming," he said.

Welch could not believe his ears. Why? What made them go so far?

Greg Smart was an asshole toward Pam, Randall replied. "Greg was worth more dead than alive," he said. Pam was paying them five hundred dollars each, out of her insurance payoff, for killing him.

"How do you think I got these?" said JR, holding up his hands to point out Greg Smart's Kenwood truck speakers between his windows.

The conversation soon moved outside to the driveway.

Ralph needed air and Pete thought it best to be away from anyone who might overhear.

That night Ralph learned that Randall had planned to slit Smart's throat with a knife from the guy's own kitchen, that one of JR's father's .38-caliber guns and a hollow-tip bullet did the job, and that on the ride home JR and Ramey had belted out "Shoofly Pie." They told him that Sal Parks knew everything as well.

"How could you do something like this?" Ralph said, growing more angry.

"That's what they do in the army," Pete replied. "People do it every day."

"That's *not* what they do in the army!" Welch fired back.

Ralph was bewildered that they had done it at all, but what struck him as even stranger was that they could discuss it in such normal, even tones, almost as if it was just another scam. At one point Pete said, "Me and Bill said our Hail Marys before we did it," as if killing someone was one big joke.

"Did it make you feel good to watch this guy's head come apart?" Ralph asked sarcastically.

"It didn't come apart," said Randall. "There was just lots of blood."

Ralph was responding worse than Pete and JR had expected. They'd thought he would protect them if he knew the full story. But now quite the opposite seemed likely.

"So, what are you gonna do?" asked JR.

"I don't know," said Ralph. "I gotta do something."

"You don't have to do anything," said JR. "Just forget you ever heard about it."

"I can't," said Ralph. "I can't keep something like this inside. What are *you* gonna do if I tell?"

"We'll be out of here like that," said JR.

They stood at the top of the driveway for nearly half an hour, talking back and forth, before Ralph Welch got in his car and left.

Ralph needed time to clear his head and, more important, to find Raymond Fowler and warn him that his life might be in danger. When he had heard one of the boys say, "You know who's gonna be next," he was certain that they were talking about killing Ramey.

Welch drove for a quarter mile, just down the road, and parked near Seabrook's former fire station. Then, trying to be inconspicuous, he walked back to his father's house. Ralph bummed five dollars from his dad and when he stepped out, Pete and JR were on a motorcycle, slowly cruising back and forth, almost as if they were sizing up what Welch was going to do.

Ralph went back to his car and set out to find Fowler. But first he stopped on South Main Street at a local hangout, to find Danny Blake and get directions to where Fowler was staying in Maine. Then Blake climbed in the car and said he would come along for the ride.

It was close to three in the morning when they got to Maine. Fowler's relatives woke him up and Welch spoke to Ramey. "Ralph went in and told Raymond that they were looking for him," recalled Blake. "Raymond said he didn't care."

Pete and JR, in the meantime, had driven the motorcycle to Pam's complex in Hampton. In the early hours of the morning, they knocked on her condo door, but no one answered. The boys wanted to warn Pam and Billy that the dam was about to burst. But all they could do was go home to bed and see what the morning brought.

As dawn approached, Ralph dropped off Blake and returned to the Lattimes' house, where he lay down for a bit and fell asleep, only to be awakened Sunday morning by JR. Welch's father was outside and wanted him for something.

When Ralph returned, he went into where Pete Randall was sleeping over and sat beside him.

"I don't want you and Bill around here anymore," said Welch. "I don't want you anywhere near Ryan."

"I'll come around here whenever I feel like it," Pete replied.

"Well, if you don't stay away, I'll make you stay away."

"I'll come around when I feel like it."

"Well, then we're gonna fight. Maybe we should go outside right now."

"I'll step outside with you," said Pete.

So they did. Randall and Welch started up the Lattimes' driveway, with JR trailing along, when all of a sudden, Ralph grabbed Randall's shirt and shoved him, as if he was pushing him off the Lattimes' property.

"You're not gonna come around here anymore!" said Ralph.

Randall snapped. When they were little, Ralph pushed Pete around and Randall used to run home crying. But now Pete was flailing away, driving his fists into Ralph's face. Then, grabbing Ralph from behind, Pete took to strangling him. In seconds, they both thunked to the ground, with Welch's skull smashing against a rock.

Ralph blacked out for a moment. When he opened his eyes, Pete was still choking him, but then let up and got off him.

Gazing up, Ralph saw JR standing nearby crying.

Battered, with a gash over his left eye and his clothes now filthy, Welch raised himself to his feet and staggered down the driveway toward the house. Pete and JR headed in the direction of Randall's place.

"I don't want either one of you coming back here!" Welch shouted, seeming to forget that it was JR's house.

Crying, Ralph stumbled inside. When Diane Lattime saw him, her first thought was that the boy had been working on his car and that it fell off the jack onto him.

"What's the matter?" she asked.

"They used Vance's gun to kill someone!" said Ralph, sobbing.

Diane, a slight, thoughtful woman of thirty-six, could make no sense of what Welch was saying. She called for her husband, who had been sitting in the living room with a friend.

In another setting, Vance, thirty-nine, would easily pass for a lumberjack. He was tall and husky, with a full head of beginning-to-gray hair, a moustache, and a slow baritone voice.

"What's wrong?" he said, stepping into the kitchen.

"They used your gun to kill someone!" blurted Ralph. Now he was nearly hysterical, blubbering and running on and on. Bill and Pete were robbing this guy, Ralph sobbed. JR wasn't there but he drove. Then the guy came in and they used Lattime's gun. It must be true because he himself had gone to Maine to check it out. But they said it was a joke.

All Vance understood was that the boys seemed to have shot someone with one of his weapons.

"Which gun did they use?" said Vance.

"I don't know," said Ralph. "A thirty-eight maybe. I'm not sure."

Lattime entered his bedroom to see if his .38 caliber rifle and pistol were still there. Ralph, who had been leaning against the kitchen wall, slid down to the floor in tears.

Vance did not know what to think. Ralph was talking crazy, but it sounded like the guy who was shot, if there was someone shot, might still be alive. He guessed that it was a gas-station holdup, maybe in Maine.

All Lattime knew for certain was that the kids never fought each other. If they had come to blows there had to be something to Ralph's story.

The guns were there. When Vance checked the .38 pistol, though, one thing struck him as odd. Lattime did not remember cleaning the weapon after JR had fired it that day up in northern New Hampshire. Now, not a trace of gunpowder was on it.

Vance called to his friend Dave in the living room. He needed help moving Ralph to the couch.

"What happened?" said his friend.

"You wouldn't want to know," replied Lattime.

When Vance finally got Ralph settled down, he turned around and Dave was gone. "If I don't want to know, then I'm *outta* here," Dave had told Diane before he hustled out the door.

After talking to Ralph further, Lattime grabbed the rifle and the handgun. *Something* had happened involving the boys. He did not want to believe that his son was tied up in a murder, but he did want to know the truth—good, bad, anything.

Lattime decided that there was only one way to unravel the matter: He was going to the police.

Ralph, in the meantime, said he was going to his girlfriend's house. The Lattimes said they would call him when it was time to go down himself.

It was around noon, a relatively sleepy Sunday for the Seabrook police, when Vance and Diane Lattime walked through the door, the husband clutching the handgun. He had left the rifle in his car.

Sergeant Carlene Thompson, who ran the department's detective bureau, had come in to put in three hours on paperwork. She was in her office when a dispatcher called on the intercom to say that Thompson should probably talk to the couple who had just come in. They had what they thought might be a murder weapon, she said.

Thompson came out and talked to the Lattimes. "A lot of things started falling together when she started talking," said Vance. "She said the Derry police thought there might be a Seabrook connection to a certain teacher they were looking into. And then she asked, 'Have you ever heard the name Smart?'

"That's when my wife said that she was the one who came with the boys a couple weeks back to look at a new car. Then that started the whole thing off."

To say the least.

What had happened was that Thompson remembered that Jackson's men had been in Seabrook following up on the tip from Louise Coleman. Thompson secured the gun and made a call to the Derry police.

Thompson's three hours of paperwork on a Sunday afternoon was about to become several sleepless days.

Pete and JR knew that everything was spinning out of control. After they left Ralph, the boys got back on the motorcycle, which they had stolen, and roared off again for Pam's condo.

Pam and Billy were awake, lounging in bed, when they heard the motorcycle outside and then the knocking. It was obviously Billy's friends.

At first, he thought to ignore them and maybe they would disappear, but they persisted. Finally, Billy angrily pulled on his sweatpants and went downstairs to see what they wanted. By their faces alone he could tell disaster had struck.

Their words affirmed it: Pete had told Ralph everything. Ralph had flipped out. He's probably going to go to the police.

Flynn stood frightened and angry and disbelieving. How could they be so stupid as to tell Ralph?

The boys were in the living room, trying to figure out what to do next, when Pam padded downstairs to the shocking news. While she had been spending the night with her teenage lover, hell had ripped loose on Upper Collins Street.

Panicked, they decided to take a stab at damage control, which by now was like applying the brakes as your truck careens off a bridge.

Billy managed to track down Welch by telephone at his girlfriend's house. "Ralph, what's going on?" he asked as

Pam, who was beside him, and everyone else in the room sat nervous and quiet.

"I know what you guys did," Welch said. "Pete told me everything."

"Who did you tell?" asked Billy. "What did you say?"

"The truth," said Ralph.

Billy Flynn, not the most practiced of liars, then began to unfurl a convoluted explanation:

A vicious rumor was going around that Billy and Pam were involved in Greg's death. Pete and JR—whom Billy said had dropped by but were now gone—only affirmed the rumor because they thought Ralph would want to protect Billy and therefore not repeat it. But it was just a rumor.

Pam—whom Billy said was with him but in the other room, out of hearing distance—meant everything to him. If she learned about the rumor, she would leave him. And if Pam dumped him, Billy said, he would kill himself.

"Ralph, you know I didn't do it," he said. "You know I wouldn't do anything like that."

"I know you *did* do it," said Ralph.

Welch might not have been class valedictorian, but he recognized a line of garbage when he heard it. Why would Pete and JR say they'd done something so awful unless they'd truly done it? What's more, he could hear whispering voices on Billy's end of the line. Ralph knew Flynn was not alone.

So when Billy, sounding scared and desperate, repeatedly insisted on meeting him somewhere, Welch refused. Finally, he hung up. He did not want to be the next corpse.

Figuring that Ralph was a lost cause, Pam and the boys decided they had to find Raymond Fowler, to fill him in on the turn of events and to come up with a mutually acceptable story for the police.

The plan was for Ramey to meet JR at Tuck's Field, not far from Winnacunnet High School, where graduation ceremonies were underway, and JR would bring him to Pam's condo. They called Maine several times and Fowler repeatedly said he was on his way. Forewarned of imminent danger by Welch, though, he never showed up.

At mid afternoon, JR called his parents to get a feel for the size of the avalanche that Ralph had begun. Diane Lattime told him to come home immediately. There was a family emergency, she said. JR said he was at Pam Smart's condo, but that he could not come home right now.

That afternoon, Pam drove the boys back to Seabrook. She dropped off JR at his house and drove over to a convenience store on nearby Route 286.

Lattime walked down his driveway and saw his uncle, whose house was in front of the Lattimes' place. When JR asked if his parents were around, his uncle said no. They had gone back to the police station.

JR hurried to the convenience store and found Billy and Pete playing video games in an arcade next door. Pam, they told him, said she saw Cecelia's parents at the laundry adjacent to the store and took off in her CRX. She would be back in a few minutes.

Pete Randall, in the meantime, called his mother, who was at work in another Seabrook convenience store. He and his friends were in a lot of trouble, he said, and he needed her to come right now. He would be watching for her on Route 286.

The boys walked to the road and hid in the bushes alongside a small bridge to wait.

Suddenly, Randall spotted his mother and waved her down. Pete had always been fiercely close to Patricia Randall. When he stopped, Patricia recalled, he told her of the murder and that he and his friends were planning to flee.

Mrs. Randall, a small, reserved woman, said she was nearly in shock. She didn't know what to think. But this was her only son. She gave him all the cash she had—one hundred dollars.

Pete then went back and waited with his friends until Pam returned. When she did, the foursome headed back toward her condo in Hampton, all of them nervous and trying to decide what to do.

Suddenly, at a traffic light near the condo complex, Pam ordered them all out of her car. With the police hot on their trail, she said, she wanted nothing to do with them. They should just stay away.

Pete and JR got the motorcycle out of Pam's garage. Billy, whose heart had dropped when Pam seemed to have abandoned them, went to say good-bye to her.

Billy told her that if he was arrested he would never tell on her. She, in turn, told him not to worry. The boys were juveniles, she said. Even if they were found to be involved in the murder they could only be held until they were eighteen.

Randall and JR took off toward Seabrook to get Patricia Randall's car. Their plan was to take the car, meet Billy, and leave the state.

When they got into town, they spotted Mrs. Randall's 1983 Sunbird on South Main Street. Both the boys and Pete's mother headed for Randall's house. In the meantime, though, a Seabrook cop driving in the other direction inexplicably turned around. He may have altered his course for any reason, but that didn't matter to them.

The boys panicked.

Adrenaline running amok, JR dropped off Pete at his house and told him to meet him on a dirt side street that they both knew. Then he roared away, with the cruiser zooming behind.

Randall went inside with his mother. She gave him the keys to the Sunbird, and Pete took off to find his friends. "He's my kid," said Mrs. Randall. "I would do anything that I could to help him."

Originally, the boys had planned to take both the motorcycle and the car, but by the time Pete hooked up with JR, who had lost the cop, they decided to abandon the bike. The police had already seen it.

Next, they headed to Winnacunnet High School, where they met Billy Flynn. Then they filled up the Sunbird with gas and headed south—not to South America, as one might guess, but to Connecticut.

Detective Barry Charewicz was considered by Captain Jackson to be the "last of the pure hearts." At thirty years old, Charewicz was the kind of cop who did everything by the letter. Even if his supervisor was not around, Charewicz refused to relax. Instead, he would diligently complete the tedious paperwork that most people would leave for tomorrow, working to the very end of his shift. And when he said he was going to be somewhere, invariably he would be there.

Growing up in Andover, Massachusetts, Charewicz had hoped to be a veterinarian, but because of the cost of vet school, he drifted toward criminal justice, which he found interesting as well. He had started as a patrolman in Derry eight years earlier and had been a detective since the end of 1987.

On Sunday, June 10, Charewicz was erecting a fence—to enclose his Rhodesian Ridgeback dog—in his Derry backyard. It was an interminable project that had become a target of gentle humor among his fellow detectives. Charewicz had decided that this was the weekend it would be finished. Providing, of course, that nothing came up. Barry was the detective on call.

It was early afternoon when the telephone rang. Someone had strolled into the Seabrook PD with a pistol that might have been used in the Smart homicide. Charewicz had to get out to the seacoast to see if the call had any merit before calling in the rest of the bureau. The fence would have to wait.

When Barry got to Seabrook, the parade began. First, Vance and Diane Lattime laid out their story.

Charewicz called Captain Jackson and said it looked serious.

Then, a battered Ralph Welch—driven to the police station with his father by JR's father—came in, and his statement was taken on videotape.

Welch was sobbing as he spoke to the detective. After all, he was breaking an unwritten code of loyalty, providing information that most likely would send his buddies, including the Lattimes' son, to prison.

By the time Charewicz was through, gently coaxing Welch along, gathering as many facts as he could and trying to make sense of it all, the detective knew the case was breaking wide open.

Everyone from the Derry detective bureau would drop what he was doing—Pelletier's beeper went off while he and his wife were helping out at a local Special Olympics—and head east.

The attorney general's office was contacted, too. Assistant Attorney General Diane Nicolosi as well as William Lyons, a senior assistant AG, came down from Concord.

Everyone was converging on the seacoast. A two-day offensive on the Seabrook, New Hampshire, beachhead had commenced.

Billy Flynn, Pete Randall, and JR Lattime were making their great escape to a little town south of Worcester, Massachusetts. North Grosvenordale, Connecticut, was where Pete and his parents had lived for a few years before coming back to Seabrook. And it was where the boy's grandparents and a couple of his aunts still called home.

The boys had no set plan other than that they were going to steal some motorcycles while they were in town and continue with their now several hours old life on the lam.

When they arrived in Connecticut, Randall spoke to one of his aunts, telling her that he and his friends were in a little trouble with the law over some stolen road bikes and hoped to stay until things cooled off in New Hampshire.

One of the first things the boys did was stop at some pay phones. Flynn chose not to call anyone, but Pete and JR telephoned their mothers, collect, and assured them that they were safe. JR refused to say where he was but told Diane Lattime that he and Pete had been only joking with Ralph. JR promised to contact her again soon.

The boys were grabbing a bite to eat at a pizzeria in the nearby town of Putnam when Randall's grandfather came in and took Pete aside. He had just spoken to Pete's father, the old man said, and his dad was not pleased.

So Pete called his father, who was livid. His wife had been too frightened to tell him, so Frank Randall was unaware of the murder. All he knew was that the car was gone and if it was not back by 9:30 that night, he would call the Connecticut state police, report the car stolen, and have his son arrested. Pete argued for a bit, but to no avail.

So, the three teenage boys—who would later be slammed as cold-blooded thrill killers—all piled back into the car and with JR at the wheel, went home to their parents.

With the walls tumbling around her, Pamela Smart, like the boys, was scared. But her character, whatever the odds, had always been to fight rather than flee, so she sat tight in her Hampton condominium and waited for her opening.

That night, at around nine o'clock—around the time that the boys were returning home—Cecelia Pierce and a friend, Robby Fields, dropped by Pam's place after a rock concert at one of the clubs on Hampton Beach. Pam ushered the girl upstairs to the guest bedroom, where they could speak in private.

Everything was going crazy, Pam said. Talking a mile a minute and quaking nervously, she told Cecelia about the events of the last twenty-four hours, from Ralph Welch having learned about the killing onward.

If the boys had a whit of sense, Pam said, they would try to pin the killing on Raymond Fowler and Welch. After all, if those two knew so much, maybe the police would buy that they'd done it.

It was around this time that Detectives Pelletier and Paul Lussier cruised by Pam's complex in an unmarked car, just to see what kind of activity might be going on. They jotted down Robby Fields' license plate number and looked up at Pam's window to see what seemed to be the silhouette of a female looking down, then moved on.

Not wanting to be alone, Pam asked Cecelia if she would stay the night. So Pierce got her pocketbook from Fields' car and she and Pam drove in the CRX to the girl's home in Seabrook to get a change of clothes.

Cecelia was driving back on Route 1A, in front of Hampton Beach, when suddenly an army of cops descended. Word had gone out to area police departments to be on the lookout for Pam's silver Honda in relation to a homicide. The Derry cops had guessed that the boys would be driving it.

Now, the Hampton police spotted the car, and practically every available cop was speeding to the scene. Several cruisers, motorcycles, mounted police, and a paddy wagon all surrounded the CRX, bathing it and its occupants in spotlights.

Cecelia wanted to know why she was being stopped. A cop barked that they would tell her in a minute, but in the meantime neither of them was to move.

Not thinking, Pam reached down to grab her dog, who had been growling. One of the officers screamed for her to put her hands up and not move again.

It was a tense scene, with the Hampton cops behaving as if they had captured a couple of the FBI's most wanted, only to find upon checking in over the radio that they stopped the car they wanted but with the wrong people in it.

A woman officer returned to Pam's car to say they could go. But before she could lower the volume on her walkie-talkie, a dispatcher's voice crackled with the information that the cops were seeking three male juveniles.

"Just tell her we pulled over the wrong car," came the message.

"We pulled over the wrong car," the officer said. "You can go."

The Derry cops offered Ralph Welch protective custody, drove him halfway across the state, and put him up for a couple days at a motel in Salem, New Hampshire, where he is said to have eaten heartily and run up a sizable phone bill with calls to his girlfriend.

In the meantime, investigators had talked to Danny Blake. And by eleven o'clock, Raymond Fowler and his mother were at the Seabrook police station. Detective Michael Surette, a baby-faced former MP, sat across from him, with the tape recorder running. Fowler said he did not need a lawyer; he was willing to talk.

And talk he did. He told Surette that he had been in the car with Billy, Pete, and JR the night of the murder; he revealed how he and JR had waited around the parking lot at Hood Commons and how he'd eaten pizza and hit on the cute waitress; and he told of picking the boys up after the killing and of the frantic ride home to Seabrook.

Raymond, in fact, told the cops just about everything.

Except of his own involvement. He said he was just going along for the ride—the forty-five-minute ride from Seabrook to Derry—and had no idea that a killing was to occur. He said he only learned about that when Pete and Billy jumped in the car and screamed that they did it.

Surette urged him to come clean, that this was his chance. But Fowler stuck to his story: He had no idea a killing was going down that night. No sir, no way.

JR Lattime was probably wishing he had stayed in Connecticut.

All day long, Vance Lattime had been trying to do the right thing, helping the police in any way he could to get to the bottom of this. He had brought in the pistol, driven Ralph Welch to be interviewed, and turned in some of his ammunition that he thought could have been used in the crime. It was eventually determined that this was not the ammunition used in the murder.

"My biggest thing was I wanted the facts and I wanted the truth," said the father.

But now, in his living room, he was fed up with the

whole situation. Vance was a working man, not Columbo, and he had had enough.

JR was sitting solemnly on the living room couch. The boy's mother was over near the corner, sobbing. And Vance was storming around the room, shouting at his son, hardly taking a second to grab a breath, and throwing in every few minutes, "Why won't you answer me?!"

The boy had tried to explain, saying, essentially, that Billy was having an affair with Pam Smart, but before he could say much more, his father burst in.

"Then it's a good thing she didn't gang bang all of you!" he yelled. "What would you have done then? Wiped out the town of Derry?"

When his father composed himself, JR did the best he could to explain, using aliases, obvious lies, and refusals to answer to help his dad understand what had happened without telling the whole story.

As far as Vance could make out, no one ever expected the killing to actually occur, if for no other reason than that the kid who wanted Greg Smart dead was Billy Flynn.

"Did he do it?" asked Vance.

"He said he did," said JR.

"Do you believe that he could do it?"

"Do *you* think he could do it?"

"I'd bet everything that I own," said Vance. "I'd bet one million bucks that he couldn't do it."

"Well, I know him better than you," said JR, "and I'd never believe he'd do it."

"But *did* he do it?"

"Yes," said JR. "He said he did."

That night, Vance Lattime returned to the Seabrook police department and told the detectives that it was apparent that the kids were involved in the murder.

Before he left for home, Lattime said he told the cops that his son was willing to talk, but only to a Mike Frost whom JR had mentioned.

JR's father was unfamiliar with him, but Frost was a Seabrook juvenile officer. He knew and had developed a rapport with all of the boys and with JR in particular.

His son never got to talk to Frost that night. Lattime said that the Derry cops rejected the offer. Some say the decision was a matter of territoriality, that with the case breaking, Derry wanted the glory to itself; others say the investigators did not want officers who were not up to speed with the case talking to key witnesses; and it did not help that Frost was out of town.

What is certain is that the connection was never made and an opportunity fell by the wayside. JR refused to come forward to any other law enforcement officials. The door would be slammed shut the next day when the Lattimes hired an attorney, who was aghast at the extent to which the family had already cooperated. And JR, at least for the time being, would be confessing to no one.

That Sunday night, Vance Lattime walked out of the Seabrook police department and drove home, thinking about the events of the day and what now seemed like the direction of the investigation.

Lattime remembered: "When I left that police station I didn't make it halfway down that road when I said to myself, 'What the hell have I done?' "

When the boys had returned from Connecticut, JR dropped off Billy outside his home. Elaine Flynn came out and met her son. As soon as the boy saw her it was obvious that she knew. Diane Lattime had called earlier in the day, in fact, and the parents of the three boys had met.

With a crisis at hand, Elaine Flynn asked her son if he needed a lawyer, then told him he should go upstairs to talk to their landlord and family friend, Kenny Knight. She and her son had been too far apart the past few years to expect anything to change now. Elaine figured Billy might explain to a man what had happened.

But first, fearing that the police might search her residence, Elaine told Billy to get rid of any and everything that "looked bad," or in other words, that tied the boy to Pam Smart.

Billy rummaged through his room with a brown paper bag and loaded it with Pam's love letters, the bikini photographs, the medallion that read "Bill and Pame Forever," and dozens of passes that Pam had issued him to get out of study hall. He gave it to his mother to throw away.

Then he went upstairs. That night, Kenny Knight contacted Boston lawyer James Merberg, who had represented Knight in some past misadventures. Merberg, who had once worked with F. Lee Bailey, had himself handled a variety of high-profile cases over the years, including a good number of homicides. Merberg, in fact, was once the lawyer for punk rocker Sid Vicious, who was accused of killing a girlfriend and who died of a drug overdose before going to trial.

Merberg's advice, according to Elaine Flynn's later court testimony, was that she "take Billy out of town somewhere until he saw what was going to happen."

That night, fearing that someone might follow her, Elaine drove Kenny Knight's car rather than her own and took Billy to her brother's place in Haverhill, where the boy stayed until Monday, when Elaine picked him up to return to Seabrook.

All the way home, the mother and son said nothing about the situation at hand.

"I didn't know how to deal with this," Elaine Flynn said later in court, "and I suppose I didn't want to deal with it at the time. I didn't want to know."

The investigators worked through the night. Pelletier, Surette, and Fowler drove along South Main Street in Seabrook, searching in vain for the duffel bag that Fowler said his friends had discarded on the night of the murder. Other witnesses were interviewed. When a lull came, some of the detectives stretched out for an hour or two on mats in the Seabrook PD's workout room.

Then, not long before sunrise, a harbinger of doom for Flynn, Randall, and JR arrived at the station in the unlikely form of a young woman named Ellen Carter. She was a clerk for the Derry police and she had come to type the warrants for arrest that the AG's people were beginning to draft.

On the morning of Monday, June 11, the Derry cops went to Winnacunnet High School and interviewed the girlfriends of Pete and JR. A little later, at the Seabrook police department, they met with Sal Parks.

Pete Randall was the only one of the three boys who'd gone to school that day. He stayed for a while, got into an argument with Ralph Welch's girlfriend over the events of the previous day, and then, when he saw the Derry cops were there, called his mother to have him dismissed.

Randall spent a few hours with his mom and JR, driving around in preparation for his driver's test. The boy would pass his exam and receive his driver's license that day.

Detective Paul Lussier, meanwhile, had delivered Vance Lattime's .38-caliber revolver to the New Hampshire state police forensic laboratory in Concord. Firearms examiner Roger Klose microscopically compared the bullet that had been removed from Greg Smart's skull to one that he test fired from Lattime's gun. They had a match.

By late afternoon, Captain Jackson had decided that it was time to try Cecelia Pierce again. Around four o'clock, the girl's mother received a telephone call from Dan Pelletier asking her to bring Cecelia to the Seabrook police department.

Mrs. Eaton, who was thirty-five, said she would bring her daughter over, but first she had to track her down. The last she had heard, Crit was with Pam. The teenager had a driver's education class that evening and had told her mother that it would be easier to go from Pam's place rather than have her mother drive over.

When Mrs. Eaton called Pam though, she said Cecelia had already left.

"Well," said Mrs. Eaton, "the detectives just called here and they want to ask her some questions."

"They did?" said Pam, obviously agitated. "What did they want?"

"I don't know. They just wanted to know if I could bring her over to the Seabrook police station."

"Look, why don't you just let me take her over there?" said Pam. "I can go and find her. I'll take her over."

"Pam, *I'll* find her and *I* can take her over," said Mrs. Eaton. "I want to know what's going on here."

Sure enough, the mother would locate her daughter at a friend's house just down the road. Before leaving to get Cecelia, though, Mrs. Eaton called Pam back.

"Pam, I found her and I'm going to bring her to the police station now," she said.

"Don't take her over until I get there!" said Pam, almost screaming now, her voice filled with panic. "Let me go with you so we can all go together."

"I'm a victim here! I have a right to know everything that the police know and they're not telling me anything! I'm getting tired of being treated this way and I want to know what's going on!"

By this time, Mrs. Eaton was holding the phone away

from her ear because of the volume of Pam's voice. Finally, she gave in.

"If you want to meet us there, fine," said Mrs. Eaton. "I'm driving over now."

Mrs. Eaton and her husband got in their car, picked up Cecelia, and drove in rush hour traffic about two miles to the Seabrook police station. Pam had three times as far to travel from her apartment in Hampton.

Yet when the Eatons' car pulled into the parking lot, Pam had already arrived. Immediately, she buttonholed Cecelia as they walked toward the door, the girl's mother lagging behind.

"I'm not sure why they're calling you in again," said Pam. "But don't panic. I'm sure it's nothing big. They do this with everybody."

They entered the building, and Cecelia's mother could hear Pam ranting about how the police were treating her so poorly. "I have a right to know what's going on!" said Smart. "I'm not being treated like the victim that I am. The police aren't telling me anything. Captain Jackson is nothing but an asshole."

A moment later, the door opened and Pelletier stepped out, a bit miffed to see who Cecelia had in tow. Pam demanded that the detective tell her what was going on, but Pelletier turned to Smart and snapped, "I can't talk to you now; I want to talk to *her*." Then, he ushered Cecelia and her mother inside.

It was around a quarter to five when Cecelia and her mom sat down with Pelletier and Charewicz at a conference table. Jackson sat back, out of the way, and let his men conduct the interview.

Both naturally amiable, the two detectives told Cecelia that it appeared that she had been less than honest when she had talked with Charewicz three weeks earlier. Now was the time to come clean.

Cecelia again said she knew nothing about the murder and denied any awareness of Pam having a relationship with Billy Flynn.

The only new bit of information she revealed was a fabricated story that Pam had told her to tell about how Cecelia and Billy had gone over to the Smarts' condo back in February. Cecelia told the police that as part of the orange juice video they had gone to tape Pam's husband on his four-wheeler, but that Greg had canceled because of an appointment. Pam had wanted this story out, and would repeat it herself as an explanation should Flynn's fingerprints be discovered at the crime scene.

Again and again, Pelletier and Charewicz urged Cecelia to say what she knew. It seemed clear that she was lying. Among other things, one of the veins in her neck was bulging out in response to the stress.

More obvious was her classically defiant body language. Arms and legs crossed, leaning back in her chair, Cecelia insisted that she knew nothing else.

Repeatedly, she glanced at her watch, concerned that she was going to be late for her driver's education class. Then, Cecelia looked around the room and up at the ceiling. "Like she had something better to do," Pelletier later said. (Her annoying pretension of disinterest, it would turn out, was Cecelia's way of coping with tense situations.)

Jackson had enough. He suddenly pushed himself out of his chair and came toward the girl, surprising everyone.

"I'm getting tired of listening to this shit!" he roared. "We don't need your smart-ass attitude."

"Do you think we're playing a game here? Don't you think this is serious?

"Let me tell you something, young lady. Do you realize that if you're lying to us, if you're jerking us around, that you can be in trouble yourself? Do you know that if you're lying we could charge you with hindering an investigation? And don't think we won't do it.

"You've got one opportunity and it's right now. This is your chance to come clean."

Cecelia's mother came to life. Like a mother bear protecting her cub, she too began to roar. "Now just wait a damn minute!"

She glared at Pelletier and Charewicz. "I don't mind you two asking her questions in a normal tone of voice. But I'm not gonna put up with *his* shit. I'll tell you people right now, just in case you forgot, this is a minor. She is sixteen years old. And I'm not going to sit here and listen to this *smart ass*.

"What's more, I don't think Cecelia's gonna answer any more questions for you. Maybe I'd be better off having a lawyer in here."

Jackson looked to Cecelia's mother, who seemed only to

be getting started, and nodded toward the door.

"Can I speak with you out in the hall for a minute?" he asked.

They stepped out of the room and Jackson's attitude changed, going from combative to conciliatory in one minute flat.

"Look," he said, "don't get upset about the way I was talking to her in there. It's a role. It's an act. From what information we have so far, we don't believe that Cecelia's done anything wrong. To me, she seems like a normal, typical teenage kid. But I also feel that there's something that she knows that she's not telling. And what I'm trying to do is to get her to pay attention and realize how serious this really is."

Jackson's anger had sounded authentic enough to Mrs. Eaton, but she said she understood. Calmer now, she said she would try to talk to her daughter at home.

The interview complete, the mother and daughter walked out only to be met by Pam again.

"Well, what's going on?" Smart asked Cecelia.

"Nothing," replied the girl. "They just asked me the same questions they asked me before."

That night, Pam called Captain Jackson at the Seabrook police department, demanding to know why her car had been stopped the night before and just what was going on with the investigation. Jackson replied that he could tell her nothing. And as for her car, well, they'd pulled over the wrong vehicle. "I'm not that stupid," Pam replied.

By 8 P.M., propelled mostly be adrenaline and caffeine, Jackson and his men had arrest and search warrants in their hands. They had the murder weapon. They had a handful of statements against the boys. All that was left was to bring them in.

The cops split up. Sergeant Byron, Surette, Lussier, and some Seabrook officers went to Pete Randall's home on South Main Street, looking for the black and red bag in which the boys had carried their clothes on the night of the murder. They came away with a knapsack, but it proved to be worthless. Patricia Randall told the cops she had recently bought it for her son.

For the most part, the search at the Randall's house went smoothly, until one of the detectives asked burly Frank Randall if he was hiding anything and suggested that he could be prosecuted if he was. "When they knocked on the door, this was the first my husband knew about anything," said Patricia Randall. "So when the cop said that to him, he freaked. He got really mad."

At the same time, Captain Jackson, Pelletier, Charewicz, and Seabrook Sergeant Thompson, along with some patrolmen, showed up at the Lattimes', searching for Greg's Kenwood truck speakers and the package of ammunition from which the killing bullet had been taken.

Of all Jackson's strengths, his people skills ranked highest. Blowing up, as he appeared to have done with Cecelia earlier, was out of form for the captain. He was more in character making small talk and showing an interest in folks. Jackson was the kind of guy who took the edge off any conversation by just being himself, telling an anecdote or politely chuckling at even the weakest attempts at humor.

So while his detectives ran their eyes and fingers through the Lattimes' personal possessions—a tense situation under any circumstances—Jackson stood off to the side, chatting with Vance, as if they were neighbors comparing notes on their rhododendrons.

"It was like he knew what I was going through," remembered Lattime. "It was like one father talking to another and one of them suddenly remembering he was a captain on the police force. He was looking for the truth, but he had to follow the guidelines."

Added Diane Lattime: "When they were getting ready to leave, Captain Jackson had tears in his eyes."

The Derry police departed that night with Greg's truck speakers, but they failed to find the bullets.

They also failed to find the boys. All afternoon, Billy, JR, and Pete had sat around the Lattimes' house, waiting endlessly for the rap at the door that meant they were under arrest.

All of the mothers had come by that day as well. "Diane called me up and said, 'No sense sitting home alone, why don't you come over?'" recalled Patricia Randall. "So I said OK. I went over and she said, 'Do you want to talk first or cry first?' I said, 'Cry' and that's what we did."

There had been discussions that day among the parents about sending the kids out of the country. Without passports, their choices were mainly Canada and Mexico. The idea was eventually voted down: The thought of the boys spending the rest of their days on the run was repellent. Plus, who could afford what it certainly would cost?

Instead, Billy, Pete, and JR settled on the movies. They asked their parents for permission to go to the cinema in Salisbury, if for no other reason than to break the tedium. First, the boys watched *Total Recall*. They came back out and bought tickets for *Another 48 Hours*.

With the cops holding arrest warrants, Patricia Randall and Diane Lattime agreed to get the boys and bring them to the station. Diane found the kids playing video games, killing time between movies, and told them that the police had arrest warrants. They had to go to the Seabrook PD.

The boys came along peacefully, except for Billy Flynn, who got into a brief argument with Diane.

He did not mind going down to be arrested for murder, but Flynn said if he could not see *Another 48 Hours*, he wanted his money back.

"I think Billy was focusing on staying normal," said Patricia Randall. "I think he was holding the murder apart. I think if he didn't, he'd crack up."

The two mothers and the boys drove toward the police department. Along the way, JR made a prediction. "When this all comes out," he said, "this is going to be the biggest story ever to hit the seacoast."

The boys were placed under arrest at around a quarter to ten Monday night. Technically, they were charged with juvenile delinquency, which when charged as adults would become first-degree murder for Flynn and accomplice to first-degree murder for Randall and Lattime.

The state obviously was going to attempt to have the boys tried in the adult courts, where they could be sentenced to life in prison rather than be slapped on the wrist and held in a youth center until they were eighteen years old—nineteen at best. Given the severity of the accusations, the smart money was on the prosecution getting its way.

That evening, by a stroke of luck, Bill Spencer managed to break the story of the arrest. At around eight, the reporter said, he was at a graduation ceremony and ran into a state police officer he knew who said that word on the grapevine was that the Smart homicide was solved. Apparently, the cop said, it was three teenagers out of Seabrook. Spencer made some calls and at eleven o'clock, only a little more than an hour after the actual arrests, the story was on the news.

One of the viewers that evening was Pam Smart. Since Greg's death, hardly a night went by—if any—when Pam slept alone. And so it was on June 11, Smart had invited Terri Schnell to sleep over in Hampton, and together they learned from the news that three boys, unnamed because they were juveniles, had been arrested for Greg's murder.

Now it was show time: Pam got on the phone and called her secretary, whose husband was on the Winnacunnet school board, and asked if they knew who the teenagers were. She also called the Derry police, but was told that no one from the detective bureau was available.

The next morning, Tuesday, at around 5:30, Pam was on the phone again. But this time—mere coincidence, according to Pam—she called Elaine Flynn, who said that Billy, Pete, and JR had been arrested. "I think you better get a lawyer," Elaine said before hanging up.

Later that day, Pam called everyone who might know something about the arrests. As the widow, she later said, it was within her rights to know what was going on. And so she would contact everyone, from the AG's office to one of the victim's advocates to the police, probing for details.

Her main concern was whether the police had strong evidence. Was a gun found? Or her jewelry? Were the kids confessing?

At one point, she called Captain Jackson, seeking information and expressing concern that perhaps the families of the boys would want to harm her.

"I'm afraid," said Pam. "I know these kids. Am I in any danger?"

"No," Jackson replied flatly.

"How do you know?"

"Because I know," he said. "And so do you."

That same day, Linda Wojas showed up at the Derry police department. Over the past month and a half, Pam's mother had agonized about Greg's death. To Linda, this was the first good news in a long time. What she did not know at this point was the angst that her daughter was experiencing over the arrests.

"You can't believe how relieved we are!" said Linda as she went toward Dan Pelletier as if to embrace him. "Thank you so much!"

The detective shuffled backward, out of hugging distance. "Well, uh, you know, there's still more work to do," said Pelletier.

The media, in the meantime, saw an intriguing story and ran with it. Driven by a hard-bitten news director at channel 9, Bill Spencer dove in with an aggressiveness that knew no shame. As always, he drove the cops crazy, waving his microphone in front of the boys as they were escorted into Hampton District Court for arraignment. "Did you have anything to do with Greg Smart's murder?" he shouted.

A source gave Spencer a copy of the SAU 21 newsletter with Billy's and Cecelia's photo and Pam's article about the orange juice video. The reporter then broke the story that Pam knew at least one of the accused killers.

From there, Spencer tracked down Cecelia and got her on tape telling the concocted story about Billy and herself going to Pam's in February to tape Greg.

But the most indelible moment for WMUR's viewers had to be when Spencer banged on the door of Pam's condo in Hampton, apparently catching her at a bad time.

Smart opened the door a crack. Spencer beheld Pam wearing a robe, her hair in a wreck, and looking as if she had been crying. The cameraman only got footage of the reporter at the door, not Smart. But a microphone on the camera did pick up her refusal to be interviewed.

"Pam, what's wrong?" Spencer said. "How you doin'?"

"Nothing, but I can't comment, Bill," she said, her voice beginning to quaver. "I really can't. I'm totally devastated by this. I can't comment."

Another reporter who would hurl herself into the story was Franci Richardson of the 10,000-circulation, semi-weekly *Derry News*. Outhustling the larger staffed, better financed Manchester *Union Leader*, a statewide paper, Richardson was pounding on doors all around Seabrook. She tenaciously tracked down all kinds of sources and even got quotes from the likes of Cecelia, Raymond Fowler, and Ralph Welch.

But all of the area newspapers, from Nashua to the sea, were jumping into the fray, besieging the families of the boys, friends, neighbors, and the kids who as underclassmen were still in the middle of finals at Winnacunnet High

School. Almost all of the journalists were scoring now and then with hard-to-get quotes or new details.

Most everyone, including WMUR, agreed not to use the boys' names or pictures, as state law decrees, but the *Union Leader* ran photos of Billy, Pete, and JR and identified them, without ever facing legal challenge.

Meanwhile, the Nashua *Telegraph*, like Bill Spencer, found Pam Smart "sickened and devastated" by the arrests. "I want to be happy because they caught someone," she said. "But I don't have enough information in my own mind that they are guilty."

And the *Lawrence Eagle-Tribune* drew an equally subdued response. "If you want to say anything about how I am feeling now, you could say I am very, very shocked," said the widow. "I guess you could say they were good kids."

She added: "I can't say anything about them. I work for the school district. I could lose my job. The last thing I need right now is to lose my job."

In reality, unemployment should have been the least of Pam's worries. Much closer to the last thing Smart needed was what was actually happening while Pam was issuing her refusal-to-rush-to-judgement statements.

Cecelia Pierce was getting scared.

Chapter 7

Pam had taken a few days off from work in light of the circumstances. Still, she saw Cecelia on the Wednesday after the arrests because Pam, Cecelia, and Tracy Collins were testifying in Massachusetts in the trial of the hit-and-run driver who struck Smart's car near Salisbury Beach in March. Pam's mother also attended the proceeding.

Pam took the witness stand and when the prosecutor asked who had been in that car that day, Pam said herself, Cecelia, and Tracy. As on the accident report, she neglected to mention Billy Flynn, who now just happened to be in custody at the Adolescent Detention Center in Concord for killing her husband.

Smart and Cecelia huddled briefly that day, with Pam mostly wanting to know what people were saying about her. What rumors were going around about her connection to the boys?

Yet while Pam was looking outward, her most serious threat was right before her: Cecelia Pierce was slipping out of Pam's control.

Captain Jackson had scored a direct hit when he yelled at the girl. The major effect was simply that he frightened her, especially in the wake of the boys' arrests, into thinking that she might be taken into custody.

"Every night when I was in bed I'd get up like every five minutes when a car pulled in, seeing if it was the police coming to get me," said Cecelia.

To say the least, Cecelia was struggling with conflicting emotions. She bounced back and forth between understanding that the murder was wrong, to not wanting to betray Pam, to worrying that she herself would end up behind bars.

"I couldn't sleep at night," she said. "I kept laying there thinking, 'Oh my god, if Greg's in heaven, is he looking down at me right now? What would Greg want me to do? Does he hate me?'

"And with the boys arrested, I was afraid of what they would think. If I go forward, the boys are gonna hate me—that kind of thing."

Cecelia would later tell an interviewer from the television program *Hard Copy* that her feelings toward Pam had changed: "Her lover was in jail and she didn't care. And how was I supposed to believe that she was actually my friend? I could hang myself knowing what I know and she'd be relieved because that's one less person who could tell."

Cecelia wanted to share the information with her mother, but she could not figure out how to say it. In addition, Pam had hit on one of Cecelia's, and perhaps most teenagers', deepest fears, that the girl would disappoint and draw the wrath of her mother. Pam repeatedly warned the teenager that her parents would certainly be outraged that she had done nothing to prevent the killing.

Cecelia was at her friend Robby Fields' on the Thursday night after the boys were charged when she heard on the news that a girl might soon be arrested in the Smart homicide.

The teenager could take it no longer. Cecelia started crying hysterically, murmuring, "They're gonna arrest me, they're gonna arrest me."

Her friend's family assured her that she was being ridiculous, remembered Cecelia. "They kept saying, 'Why would they arrest you? You didn't have anything to do with it.' They treated me so innocently that I just couldn't stand it any longer.

"It's one thing to know something and have nobody bother you about it, but it's another thing to know something and have everyone tell you, 'Oh, you didn't know anything.' It makes you feel twice as bad. It makes you feel twice as guilty."

So Cecelia went home.

"Mom," she said, "can I talk to you in my bedroom?"

Her mother was busy. "In a minute, Crit," Mrs. Eaton said. "Wait a minute."

"Mom, I want to talk to you *now*!"

The two went into the girl's bedroom and sat down. Cecelia was crying. "Mom, Bill and Pam were having an affair," she said.

"You've got to be kidding me," said her mother, as if it was the craziest thing she ever heard.

"No, they *were*."

"How do you know that?" asked Mrs. Eaton.

"Well, because when I stayed there that week with Pam, Bill stayed there, too. Billy and Pam were upstairs in Pam's bedroom and they were, well, doing it. I walked in on them, so I know."

"Oh, *great*," said Mrs. Eaton, as the magnitude of her daughter's remarks began to dawn on her. "Do you know any more than that?"

"Yeah, Mom. A lot more."

Around ten o'clock, Mrs. Eaton called the Derry police, who in turn reached Loring Jackson at home. When the captain and Mrs. Eaton finally made contact, Cecelia's mother said that this was something that probably should not wait. They agreed to meet on neutral ground in Haverhill.

Mrs. Eaton, Cecelia, and an aunt of Cecelia's who was visiting, got in the family car and headed into the night for Massachusetts. Throughout the drive, Mrs. Eaton's imagination was running wild. She thought that someone was going to kill them before Cecelia managed to tell her story.

"We got in the car and there was a car that had come right behind us and followed us all the way," said Mrs. Eaton. "I was petrified. I was scared to death. And Cecelia kept laughing at me."

In Haverhill, they met with Jackson and Sergeant Byron at a Friendly restaurant. Cecelia's mother and aunt sat in one booth, while the cops sat with the teenager in another. Dressed in a Winnacunnet High School sweatshirt and sipping a cola, Cecelia began to fill in the details of what the detectives had already suspected, that Pam had pulled the strings that led to her husband's death.

They drove to the Derry police department, with Mrs. Eaton following the cops, and in the early morning, Cecelia gave a half-hour videotaped statement to Byron. When Pelletier, whom Cecelia had referred to as the "cute one" earlier in the evening, showed up to run the video camera, Cecelia perked up.

Between her lack of sleep in recent days and the late hour, Cecelia was extremely tired. Still, she revealed a gold mine of information, from how she first met Pam to having heard Pam and Billy plotting the murder. She even told the cops about how Pam tried to teach her to successfully lie on a polygraph test by recasting the questions in her mind so that her answers would be true.

Around the same time, Jackson got on the telephone, awakening Bill Lyons of the attorney general's office at home.

As a law school student at the University of Maine, Lyons had spent his summers as a special police officer in the resort community of Laconia, New Hampshire, worked his way through law school, and eventually climbed to senior assistant attorney general for the criminal division. He was just now starting to catch up on his sleep after the siege of Seabrook earlier in the week.

Jackson had been calling Lyons late at night throughout the course of the investigation and now he was back at it, apprising the senior assistant attorney general of the recent breakthrough. The captain also wanted to know about the possibilities of state approval for tape-recording some telephone conversations between the newly cooperative Cecelia and one Pamela Smart.

Lyons, who knew the case inside out, said sure. He figured that could be arranged.

When the cops spoke to Cecelia about trying to have Smart incriminate herself over the telephone, the teenager insisted it would never work. Pam was already convinced that her telephones at home and at SAU 21 were being monitored. Smart had even mentioned to the girl that she wondered whether her condo was bugged.

All the same, the detectives figured it was worth a shot.

It was Tuesday afternoon, June 19, when Jackson and Pelletier showed up at the Eaton's apartment ready to conduct what in legalese is known as "a one-party consent telephone tap."

Despite the serious nature of their mission, the detectives carried some uninspiring equipment, namely two inexpensive Panasonic microcassette recorders and a cheap tapping device that was attached to the outside of the telephone receiver with a suction-cup. They also brought along an earplug that hooked up to the recorder, so one of the detectives could monitor the call.

The Derry PD's budget was tight, but was it so sparse that they could not afford something better than a dime store tapping device?

To use such equipment in a major homicide investigation—where the detectives might only get one chance—carried the potential for disaster. Nine times out of ten, no doubt, such hardware would suffice. The danger is that Murphy's Law will eventually kick in.

And on June 19 kick in it did.

The plan was for Cecelia to call Pam at work. The girl was to tell her that the Derry police were on their way over to the Eatons' place with more questions and that she was tired of lying. She was to try to get Pam talking freely.

But first, they had to be able to *hear* Smart.

The problems started with the telephone itself. The Eatons had a Princess phone with a thick plastic housing which was difficult to record through. The family rummaged around and came up with one of their old telephones, which was not much better.

Then, the detectives noticed a strong hum on the line. So Jackson called the Seabrook police to see if they had a phone that might work better. With time ticking toward the end of Pam's workday, Jackson left for the Seabrook police station and returned with a phone, hooked it up, and found that the noise was still there.

Finally, they decided to go ahead and make the call—line disturbance and all. They would try to have the excess noise filtered out later.

At five minutes before three, Cecelia, her mother, Jackson, and Pelletier huddled around the kitchen table. Cecelia, of course, manned the phone. Pelletier listened in. And both detectives scribbled messages on a sheet of notepaper, comments and questions for the girl to raise with Smart.

From the first few seconds Pam was on the phone, though, she obviously was worried about a phone tap.

PIERCE: Hi. What are you doing?

SMART: Ordering all of the stuff for next year.

PIERCE: Oh? Listen. The Derry police department called me from the car phone. They're on their way here now to question me again.

SMART: Why?

PIERCE: They said they had more questions for me. Can you hear me?

SMART: Yeah.

PIERCE: I don't know what to do.

SMART: Answer the questions.

PIERCE: What if they ask me again about you and Bill having an affair? Do you still want me to deny it?

SMART: Well, we weren't.

PIERCE: *What*?

SMART: We weren't.

PIERCE: *What*?

SMART: We weren't.

PIERCE: No?

Cecelia poked around, looking for a soft spot, but Pam was not about to discuss her affair with Billy Flynn, the murder, or make any overt remarks suggesting that Cecelia should lie.

Instead, Pam looked for other ways to insulate the girl from the investigators.

First, Smart said that if the cops started pressuring Cecelia as Jackson had earlier, she should refuse to answer any more questions unless her mother was present.

Then, in the unlikely event that the investigators wanted Cecelia to take a lie detector test, Pam told the girl that she should refuse until she hired a lawyer, who in turn would recommend against taking one. "They're gonna try to do everything they can to make you tell the truth," Smart said.

Jackson and Pelletier, meanwhile, were jotting notes such as "I don't know what to say when I'm under oath" and "You should have just divorced him" and sliding the paper over to Cecelia. One by one, the teenager dropped bits of fresh bait. Pam, however, was not biting.

PIERCE: This whole thing is so stupid. I wish you guys could have just got divorced instead, you know.

SMART: You wish that what?

PIERCE: That you guys just got divorced instead. It would have been so easy.

SMART: Well, anyways . . . all right, uh, I'll just talk to you later I guess. . . .

PIERCE: Is Patty there or something?

SMART: No, but I don't know whether my phone is tapped, you know.

Cecelia said that she would call back after the cops left, to fill her in on how the interview went. Then they hung up. The conversation had lasted less than seven and a half minutes. Cecelia had been correct: Pam said little that was useful.

Pelletier had monitored the entire conversation, but Jackson had only heard Cecelia's end. The captain rewound the tape so he could listen.

Then, the phone rang. Caught with the first recorder unready, the detectives hurriedly connected the listening device to the backup recorder. Pam was calling back.

For whatever reason, Smart now felt more free to talk. It was not the stuff that wraps up a murder investigation, but it was obvious that Pam both overtly and subtly was trying to manipulate Cecelia into maintaining her silence.

Smart began by telling Cecelia how sorry she was that the girl was being inconvenienced, especially by the reporters calling at home. All Cecelia had to do, Smart said, was say "no comment" and they would leave her alone.

It was an ideal segue into what certainly was the true reason behind the call. The police, if Cecelia stuck to her story, would also back off.

SMART: They'll just leave you alone too. You know what I mean? They're just doing part of their job and that's just, you know if . . . I don't know what the guys are saying. I doubt, you know, according to Mrs. Flynn, like that no one is confessing, and that they're all sitting around saying they didn't do it.

    So, I mean, I'm sure that the police are saying JR and Bill said that you did it. You know what

I mean? Or whatever, you know, and trying to
get everybody to confess. But that has nothing to
do with you. You're not on trial. You know what
I mean?

PIERCE: Yeah.

SMART: They're on trial, and that's it. And so you just,
you know, answer the questions and that's it.
They're gonna try and get you to talk and to confess and you know they're gonna say, ''We know
you know'' and all that, you know, try and make
you nervous. But all you have to do is just maintain the same story.

They went on for a bit about the television report Cecelia
had seen that said a girl was soon to be arrested. The teenager
said it was frightening, but Pam reassured her. The police
had arrested Billy, Pete, and JR almost immediately after
learning of their role in the murder, Smart said, and now
days had passed since Cecelia had heard the impending
arrest story.

PIERCE: Well, obviously Bill and them must—must not
be saying anything or we would have been arrested already.

SMART: We, well, I don't know what they're saying.

PIERCE: Yeah.

SMART: That's the thing. If they're saying that we knew,
then the police can't bust us because we're saying
that we didn't know, and that's it. You know what
I mean?

PIERCE: Yeah.

SMART: You can't have proof of somebody, of someone
knowing.

PIERCE: That's right.

SMART: And that's it, you know.

PIERCE: It's all in our minds.

SMART: But what's gonna happen is people start changing
stories and getting nervous. . . .

PIERCE: I know. I've heard every possible rumor there is.

SMART: Right. So have I. So that's it. I mean, that's ridiculous. Why would I, why would a twenty-two-
year-old woman like me be having an affair with
a sixteen-year-old high school student? That's just
ridiculous and people will not believe that.

Finally, they said good-bye. Lasting six minutes and
twenty-five seconds, the second call, like the first, hinted
of Pam's role in the murder but was far from incriminating.

What it showed, however, was why Pam had been so
fiercely interested earlier in the week about what evidence
the police had on the boys. Physical evidence could be
deadly, but Pam knew that the police could not make much
of a case against her based on hearsay and accusations by
teenagers who were facing first-degree murder charges.

Proof was going to be necessary, Pam said. Proof that
she was in on the murder. Proof that she was having an
affair.

She was, of course, correct.

Just before four o'clock, Cecelia called Pam at her condo
to try one last time. Now she told Pam that the cops had
left. The only new subject raised was the love letter that
Jenny Charles had found in Flynn's denim jacket months
earlier. Apparently, Cecelia said, the cops had learned of
it.

Of the three tape-recorded conversations that day, the
final one, about fifteen minutes long, was the least audible.
Months later, it would be ruled inadmissible in court.

Not that it much mattered. When Jackson and Pelletier
left for Derry at the end of the day, it was obvious that they
were going to have to do better.

And sound quality was not their biggest problem. Content
was.

In the days that followed the arrests of Billy, Pete, and
JR, Pamela Smart walked on the high wire.

She was trying to maintain her image as the grieving
widow. The act, however, could not be pushed too far. It
would be unwise, for example, if Pam publicly lashed out
at the boys, as might be expected from the wife of the dead
man. The mere suggestion that she had abandoned them

could set off a confession or a series of confessions that could land her in a cell.

At the same time, Smart wanted to defuse the crisis. She needed to let the boys know that she had not abandoned them. Furthermore, she wanted to get the heat off their backs. After all, mere teenagers could not be expected to forever remain "stand-up guys," the Mafia's term for those who remain silent until death.

As a result, people started noticing some peculiar behavior from Pam. For one, she was telling friends and others that she wished she could visit the boys, saying that since she knew these kids she felt bad over their being in jail. Some people were bewildered: She wants to visit her husband's *murderers*?

Later, Smart would anonymously mail Elaine Flynn a cassette tape of heavy metal songs that Billy had put together for Pam. (One of those tunes, reportedly, was Van Halen's "Hot for Teacher.") Pamela included a note on a sheet of lined yellow paper. "Please give this to Bill," it read. "When he listens to it, I want him to know that his true friends think of him all the time."

But one of Pam's more brazen acts was when Dan Pelletier and Barry Charewicz came to interview her at her parent's home the day after the telephone taps.

The detectives had come, tape recorder in hand, ostensibly to ask about the boys. Since Pam knew the kids, they said, perhaps she could help the detectives as they gathered information for the upcoming hearings to get the kids certified as adults.

A better bet was that it was a "shake-up interview," one in which the cops came to get a firsthand look at Smart's reaction to the mounting pressure.

Pam did not let them down. Desperate, Smart tried to turn the tide of the entire investigation.

First, she spoke of the boys, trying to convince the detectives that they had arrested the wrong people. It was undoubtedly a hard product to sell, since Pam really knew very little about what the cops knew.

"As far as I'm concerned, I'm just gonna tell the truth, no matter what, OK?" said Pam.

"Yeah," said Pelletier.

"And the truth is that I don't think these kids did this.

That is really my truth. That's my honest, my god's honest truth.''

Next, she would steer the conversation toward Cecelia, who, of course, was the only other person outside the boys with firsthand knowledge of the day-to-day planning of the murder.

"The only concern I really have honestly is I don't know if I agree with how Cecelia, poor Cecelia, is being treated in all this," she said. "I really don't know that I agree with that. I mean, Cecelia I highly doubt has anything to do with anything about this. She's not even friends with those guys as far, with the exception of knowing them in school. I mean, she never went out on the weekends or . . .''

"Yeah," said Pelletier.

". . . anything like that. And I mean, this is way too hardcore for someone like her to be involved with, I think. And she keeps feeling like she, like she's being, you know . . . I haven't talked to her a lot, but I've talked to her a couple of times and she's, you know, being accused of all these things that she doesn't know, and now her parents are like, well, maybe you shouldn't talk to Pam, you know, until this is over, and all that. And I kinda, you know, I kinda resent that because, I mean, she's my intern.''

It was almost as if Pam could not stop herself from talking. She was trying to manipulate the detectives' thinking in the case, but what she really was doing was revealing how scared she was herself.

Wary that her remarks on the telephone the day before may have been monitored, Pam began echoing those comments, trying to cast them in the light of her supposed innocence. At the same time, she tried to convince the cops to back off from Cecelia.

"She feels like she's being accused and that she didn't do anything," said Pam. "And that, I mean, for a fifteen-or sixteen-year-old kid, I guess, you know, if you're accused of something that you didn't do, I mean, nobody, I mean, even me—I'm twenty-two—I don't want to be accused of something I didn't do.

"But for a young person, I would think that would be awful, especially if you see other people getting arrested, you know, that they are, that were around you or whatever. I mean, it's probably, it would have to be scary I would think . . .''

"Uh, huh," said Pelletier.

". . . you know, even if you're not guilty."

"Well," said Pelletier, "she's just one of probably over a hundred people we've talked to since—"

"Right. I'll tell her that," interjected Pam.

"Since May first."

"You know, I say they're just doing their job and, you know, just answer, just tell 'em the truth and that's it. You just answer the questions and whatever. And she says, 'But I tell them the truth and they tell me they think I'm lying.' And you know, and I, 'I don't know what to tell you, Cecelia, you know, I can't control the police. I'm very sorry that this has happened to you.'"

The next day, Pam gave an interview to Nancy West of the *Union Leader*, who made her pitch to Smart after trailing her car and flashing the headlights to get Pam to pull to the side of the road. The two women sat down that day in Pam's office at SAU 21.

When West's story appeared on June 22, it was obvious that Pam had done it again. As in the days after the murder, Smart was back to telling reporters what was going on in the police investigation, saying that the cops had questioned her about the boys' emotional maturity. West's page-one article even began with that revelation.

No one can say for certain why Pam kept releasing such information to the press. Some people think that Smart simply was a talker, a compulsive one, who once she got going had trouble stopping. Others contend that she was trying, both after the murder and now after the arrests, to communicate with the boys, filling them in on as much of the investigation as possible and assuring them of her allegiance.

What is certain, though, is that Pam was under intense pressure: It was obvious that she herself was a suspect. She had no one to share her fears with, save Cecelia. And rumors were spreading all over, particularly in Seabrook and in the local journalism community, that Pam had had an affair with Billy Flynn and that she'd paid the boys to kill her husband.

Now and then, a newsman would ask her about the scuttlebutt. "I hear the rumors, but if anybody prints any of those rumors, then, so help me, I'll sue the pants off them," Pam told one reporter.

The *Derry News*, meanwhile, quoted her as saying, "These rumors are being spread by fifteen-year-old kids. Those rumors don't deserve the time of day from me."

Although the media either stayed away from or finessed the gossip when reporting it, questions were unavoidable. Pam's and Greg's friends all wanted to know about her relationship with the kids and how this could have happened. Pam and her father even got into a heated exchange over it. No one knew what to think.

Judy Smart, still numb and confused over the loss of her son, was emotionally twisted and turned by Pam, who would call on the phone and play on Judy's sympathy.

Several times, Pam had said that she was afraid the police were going to arrest her. "I didn't think she was guilty of anything," recalled Judy, "and I'd say, 'Pam, why are you saying such an awful thing?' And she would say, 'I just have an idea. I dream of it at night. I dream that they're gonna come in and arrest me.'"

Judy, like most people, was baffled by a big question: Why would three teenagers from faraway Seabrook want Greg dead? Night after night, Judy told her husband that she was going to call Pam and straight out ask her daughter-in-law how it could have happened. But Bill Smart convinced her to refrain.

One night, when Judy was home alone, she could hold back no longer. While chatting with Pam on the telephone, Greg's mother finally came out with it.

"I said, 'Pam, can you tell me anything about these boys? Did you know them?' And she said, 'Yes, I knew them; they were in my orange juice commercial.'

"Then I got mad. I said, 'Pam, there has to be a reason for these boys to search out Greg, your husband, go into the house, and kill him. There has to be a reason. Do you know anything about it?' And she said, no.

"But I kept pressuring her and finally she said, 'Well, I think the boy, Bill Flynn, had a crush on me.'

"So, the next night I called her again and we started talking about the boys again. I said, 'What did you have to do with them?' And she would say, 'Nothing, nothing; they were just students of mine.'

"I kept after her just awful. Then I got angry and I said, 'Pam, you've gotta tell me something. Something's wrong here. They wouldn't just go in and kill Greg for no reason.'

Well, now, instead of 'I think he had a crush on me,' Pam said, 'I think he was in *love* with me.'

"That's when it finally hit me that this girl had something to do with it."

At least now the Smarts had a clear-cut focus for their rage. Bill now let Judy in on the police department's suspicions of Pam. And one day, the Smarts and Bill's brother and his wife climbed into Bill's Jaguar and drove to the seacoast.

Even if they could not see the boys who murdered their son, the Smarts at least wanted to view the places where the tragedy had its roots. The family was curious, and they felt that the ride might help them begin to understand the incomprehensible.

First, the Smarts drove to Winnacunnet High School, and gazed at the structure. They then went across the parking lot and looked at SAU 21, where Pam worked.

Next, they drove by Pamela's condo and decided to see where the boys lived as well. Bill Smart pulled over at a telephone booth near the Hampton police station, where they ripped the page with Flynn's address from the phone book. Off they went.

Not many Jaguars cruise the streets of South Seabrook, but there was Bill Smart and company slowly rolling down Upper Collins Street and then over toward Billy's home.

When they found what they thought was Flynn's house, the Smarts drove by staring, as if it held answers to the questions that had been pounding in their heads for weeks. Then they turned around and slowly cruised by again, speaking in hushed voices.

"Is that it?"

"Yeah, I think so."

"That's it, that's it."

Months later, Bill and Judy Smart would smile about their adventure in Seabrook. "Soon as we got to the end of the road," remembered Bill Smart, "there was an unmarked police car. They had followed us from the police station. We were a hell of a bunch of detectives."

Derry's real detectives, meanwhile, were probably thinking the same about themselves.

After their stunning success in Seabrook, with the arrests of the boys and Cecelia's decision to come forward, the investigators came back down to earth.

The sound quality of the secret telephone recordings was predictably awful. Pelletier ended up spending a day in Essex, Connecticut, with Robert Halvorson, an expert in audio enhancement. Halvorson, who contracts with the FBI and who sixteen years earlier had been called in to help transcribe Richard Nixon's Watergate tapes, filtered out much of the telephone line hum, improved the level of Pam's voice, and all in all salvaged the tapes.

Meanwhile, the cops had learned from Cecelia that Pam had been upset because the boys had dropped a glove while fleeing after the murder. When he heard about that, Paul Lussier, who was with the detectives as part of a training program for patrolmen, said he had found a glove on May 2, during the line search of the field behind the condos. The state police had thrown it away.

It was an embarrassing mistake for everyone. The state police had assumed that the glove came from a nearby dumpster. Indeed, there were medical offices in the adjacent professional building and it could have come from there.

The only problem was that a murder had just occurred, the condo appeared to have been burglarized, and other evidence had been found in the immediate vicinity. Even the rawest recruit might think that a glove was worth keeping and analyzing further. If saved, it might even have produced some fingerprints.

But that was past. Now the legwork began on getting the three teenagers certified to stand trial as adults.

The Derry cops headed back to the seacoast to interview teachers and others about the boys.

As matters stood, the kids were being held as juvenile delinquents and their cases would be under the jurisdiction of the Derry District Court. To have their cases transferred to Rockingham County Superior Court, the state would have to convince the lower court judge that this was a special matter.

At least eight criteria would have to be weighed, from the severity of the charges to the maturity of the boys. The process was not a rubber stamp, but at the same time, a premeditated murder was not going to be easy for any judge to ignore.

Less than two weeks after the arrest of the boys, Pamela Smart decided to look for some legal advice.

The police were not outwardly saying it, but it seemed obvious that Pam was a suspect. Linda Wojas, a legal secretary, suggested that her daughter at least talk to an attorney, if only to have one available should worse come to worst. Some lawyer friends recommended Paul Twomey and Mark Sisti.

Any regular reader of New Hampshire newspapers at one point or another most likely has come across the lawyers' names, often in relation to a murder case or a high-profile rape.

The two men had met years earlier when they both were practicing as New Hampshire public defenders. Together, they manned their office's newly created homicide unit and for several years worked only indigent murder cases.

Eventually, Twomey went into practice for himself. A few years later, in 1988, Sisti joined him, and their offices in Chichester and Portsmouth would provide work for as many as seven lawyers.

The pair could be hellcats in the courtroom, but they led simple personal lives. Both owned small farms, raising animals like pigs, sheep, and chickens. Both were family oriented. Twomey was married with two children; Sisti had three kids from his first marriage and two with his second wife.

They were also renowned in New Hampshire legal circles for their annual Fourth of July pig roast, which attracted hordes of friends and colleagues and their families. And every year the pig would be bestowed with the name of one of their favorite prosecutors.

Forty-one-year-old Paul Twomey had a certain unmade-bed quality. As often as not, he would show up in court with his hair sticking out and his tie askew.

Paul grew up poor in Worcester, Massachusetts. Still, he got a degree in political science from Yale, where he was something of a stranger in a strange land, and he studied law at the University of Wisconsin, before settling in the Granite State.

Twomey was the more intellectual and naturally likable of the two. Soft-spoken, sometimes to the point of a mumble, Paul had a disarming sense of humor. Once, a county attorney who was running for reelection received a Xeroxed photo of his opponent in the mail. Attached was a note from Twomey. "It said that if we could work out a deal for one of his clients, then he would agree to publicly support my opponent,'' recalled the prosecutor with a laugh.

He added: "There's an expression among trial lawyers: Never bullshit a bullshitter. You see, we're all bullshitters. Paul understands that. He doesn't let what happens in court get personal.

"He's pleasant to deal with and he doesn't take himself too seriously.

"Now, Sisti, well, Sisti is a little more cynical.''

At least that was the image that Mark Sisti cultivated. His father was an auto mechanic who later became a mechanical engineer. Growing up, Mark's family moved often, up and down the East Coast. But Buffalo, New York, was where he considered home.

Thickly built and balding, Sisti, thirty-five, seemed to relish his role as an abrasive rebel. Until recently, he wore his hair in a short ponytail, a look that, while in style, was more common among his clients than his colleagues.

Sisti was the team's attack dog, snorting and sneering at the state's witnesses. Almost invariably, he would rage through proceedings against his clients as if everything were a sham. The charges, the trial, the evidence—all of it was "garbage."

"Frankly, what amazes me,'' said one prosecutor, "is that Sisti gets away with it. He conveys the same attitude across the board, with the judges, his clients, witnesses, everyone. I think he actually intimidates some judges.''

Yet Sisti was more than bluster. What a lot of people failed to recognize, to their later dismay, was how hard he labored. He had worked his way through Canisius College in Buffalo, where he studied pre-nineteenth century literature, and later, Franklin Pierce Law Center in New Hampshire. But Sisti's side jobs did not involve checking books in and out of the college library or baby-sitting freshmen in the dormitories; he was a mechanic at a gas station, an aide at a state mental hospital, and an ironworker.

And so it was in his career. Mark Sisti wasn't Muhammad Ali; he was Smokin' Joe Frazier. He was not going to beat you with fancy talk or intellectual arguments. But when he came to work, he came prepared and was ready to pound away.

On this day in June, however, with Pamela Smart seated before him, Paul Twomey decided that his job was to keep his new client from ever having to call upon their courtroom skills.

Pam had explained that she was a victim and that the Derry police were telling her nothing about the investigation of her husband's death. She mentioned that she and Cecelia had been pulled over near Hampton Beach. She did not know what to think.

Twomey had a pretty good guess what was going on. It did not take him long to make a phone call to Bill Lyons of the attorney general's office and to follow up with a letter. Twomey told Lyons that Pam Smart was now represented by counsel. All contact with her from now on should be through him.

Pam, in the meantime, told Bill and Judy Smart that she hired the attorneys in case she decided to sue some of the local newspapers for libel. A number of them, but particularly the *Derry News*, were hinting in print that she might be involved in her husband's death, and she was not going to stand for it.

Indeed, Pam had mentioned the possibility of a libel suit that day when she spoke with Twomey.

The truth of the matter, though, was that neither of the lawyers took on many civil cases of any kind.

And when Pam wrote a five-thousand-dollar check dated June 26 to Twomey and Sisti, she was not retaining the state's foremost experts on media law. She *was* hiring some pretty fair homicide defense attorneys.

June was coming to a close and Cecelia Pierce—thanks in large part to Pamela Smart, who had let the girl practice driving in her Honda CRX—earned her driver's license.

The following Saturday, a friend of Cecelia's was to come to the apartment and they were going to go to Hampton Beach. Before her friend arrived, however, Cecelia was asleep and had a nightmare.

"I had a dream that there was somebody in a brick building in the window shooting at all my friends," said Cecelia. "And I was in front of my friends running back and forth with my arms waving, saying, 'No! Not them! Not them!' And I kept getting shot over and over again. But I wasn't dying.

"And I just knew that the person in the window was Pam. But she never showed her face.

''And then I woke up. I had the chills. I was sweaty. I was scared.

''So anyway, we went to the beach and I was telling my friend about it as we were walking along. We walked the whole beach, down to the end by all the clubs. And as we got in front of the Peacock Lounge, I saw a license on the ground. I decided not to pick it up.

''And then I decided, well, I don't know. I just paid thirty dollars for my license two days ago; it's only gonna cost me twenty-five cents to mail this person his or her license; I might as well pick it up and save them some money; you know, do something good.

''So I went back. And as I was bending down to pick it up, I freaked. It was Pam's license. I found Pam's license on Hampton Beach in front of the Peacock Lounge.

''So, anyway, I picked it up, stuffed it in my bag, and when we got to my friend's house I called my mother. I'm like, 'Mom, you're not gonna believe this.' And naturally she didn't believe me.

''Then I went to work and I hadn't seen Pam in a while. This was after school was out. And that night Pam shows up and she's telling me, 'Yeah, I was gonna go clubbing tonight, but I lost my ID.'

''Then it dawned on me. So I said, 'Wait a minute' and I came out and gave it to her. I said, 'Here, I found this on the beach.' And she's like, 'No way.' I said, 'Don't ask why me, but, yeah, I found it all right.' ''

Chapter 8

As the summer progressed, it was obvious that something extraordinary would have to happen for the Derry police to build a solid case against Pam. Twomey and Sisti, who some of the Derry cops knew from past singeings on the witness stand, were not going to make it any easier.

In July, the lawyers had been in the news when a jury failed to reach a verdict in the case of Anthony Barnaby, a Canadian Indian who had confessed, and later recanted, to taking part in a double murder. It was Barnaby's third mistrial, which was as good as an acquittal. The state dropped the charges shortly afterward.

For his dramatic closing argument, Sisti had enlarged Barnaby's confession on placards and highlighted parts of it to show the jury that his client's supposed confession was nonsense. The hung jury was a ego blow to the state as well as to Paul Maggiotto, the young prosecutor who had handled the case.

The Derry cops knew that with Twomey and Sisti anything could happen in court. If the investigators were going to make charges against Pam Smart stick, they were going to have to do better than the Nashua cops had done with Barnaby. In other words, even a confession was not rock solid.

The detectives kicked around some ideas, but Cecelia Pierce remained the detectives' ace in the hole. Smart, however, clearly was uncomfortable talking freely with the girl on the telephone. They needed a situation in which Pam felt safe.

Finally, the investigators decided on what the AG's office referred to as a "face-to-face one-party intercept." In other words, Cecelia was going to wear a body wire.

The teenager had not proven to be a master of deception when she originally lied to the Derry police. During the telephone taps, though, she had seemed fairly at ease, particularly when she got rolling and had to ad-lib. Truth be told, Cecelia seemed to enjoy center stage.

State approval for the body wire granted, the detectives wanted Cecelia to go to Pam's office at SAU 21. The two could be secluded, but it was still a public place where Cecelia would be safe.

Basically, the girl was to say that the authorities wanted to interview her yet again and that she might have to take a lie detector test. The cops, of course, wanted to see how Pam would respond. With any luck, she would implicate herself.

On Thursday, July 12, Cecelia showed up around noon at the Seabrook police department. To the puzzlement of everyone, the girl brought along her fifteen-year-old cousin, who was visiting from the Midwest with her family. The girl had pleaded to come along, so Cecelia relented. And why not? It was only a first-degree murder case.

It was close to noon and Pam was at lunch. So the cops had someone run out to McDonald's and bring in Big Macs and fries, which the kids devoured.

Then Detective Pelletier and Sergeant Byron sat with Cecelia for a few minutes and went over the subject areas they wanted raised with Pam. Next, Seabrook's Carlene Thompson, who had been there the day Vance Lattime brought in the murder weapon, helped put the body wire on Cecelia.

The equipment had been borrowed from the Salem police department. Essentially, Cecelia was outfitted with a cloth shoulder holster that carried a small transmitter. The device was taped to her side beneath her right arm. The microphone was at her shoulder. And attached to another strap was an antenna that transmitted the conversation to the detectives, who would be in the parking lot. Cecelia pulled her blue Winnacunnet High School sweatshirt over the apparatus.

It was a cloudy day. In her mother's 1987 Ford Tempo, Cecelia and her cousin drove to the high school parking lot. An unmarked police car and a surveillance van followed.

Everyone got into place. Pelletier and Byron sat in the undercover car. Barry Charewicz and Michael Raymond, who until now had been busy with undercover drug work, manned the recording equipment in the van, a tan vehicle with blacked out, one-way windows, which had been borrowed from a consortium of regional police departments.

Byron, who had once tracked a murderer on foot through twelve miles of snowy woods, was a dogged cop whose mantra may well have been "cover your ass."

The sergeant, who resembled professional-football coach Mike Ditka, had an obsession with possible equipment failure. Whenever he worked a case, he always insisted that multiple simultaneous recordings be made of everything that was taped. Extra cassettes cost relatively nothing, especially in comparison to what could be lost.

On this day, Charewicz and Raymond had two recorders running in the van—one hooked directly into the receiver and one near the speaker. Pelletier, meanwhile, held one of the Panasonic recorders next to his car scanner.

Just before one o'clock, Cecelia Pierce left her cousin in the car, entered SAU 21, and went down to Pam's office.

Smart had been anxious to see her former intern. An older kid, named Billy, an ex-boyfriend of Cecelia's, had seen Pam and her friend Tracy Collins recently and told Smart that Cecelia was spreading rumors about the murder.

SMART: He told me that you're going around telling everybody I killed Greg.

PIERCE: He did?

SMART: Yeah, I've been like fucking, I almost got hospitalized last night.

PIERCE: Why?

SMART: I couldn't believe it that you would say that, that I, that *I* actually killed him, that *I* shot him. Billy told me that.

PIERCE: I did not say that.

SMART: I thought Billy had the story fucked up.

PIERCE: He did. He told me that you came looking for me and that you said that you were leaving for Florida. This was like a month ago.

SMART: For Florida?

PIERCE: He said it . . . Where's Patty? [Pam's secretary]

SMART: She's out today.

PIERCE: Oh, good. But anyways, right he, um . . .

SMART: I was just talking about you.

PIERCE: Were you?

SMART: Yeah, I was just saying I wanted to . . . Hug me, I haven't seen you in so long. I missed you.

With that, Pam jumped up from her seat and the two embraced. Worried that Pam would detect the body wire, the teenager leaned forward so that Smart would not put her hands on it. As it was, Pam's fingers ended up only a skinny inch from one of the straps.

They chatted. Obviously, Pam had been worried about losing Cecelia. Besides the remarks from Pierce's old boyfriend that were playing in her mind, Smart had been having difficulty reaching the girl on the telephone. The last time Pam tried, Cecelia's little sister unconvincingly said she was not home.

Now, as the conversation went on, Pam's began speaking faster and faster, obviously relieved to have someone with whom to discuss all that was happening.

SMART: I'm like, why would you even say that I murdered Greg? And Tracy heard the whole thing. Tracy's like, 'Why would Cecelia do that?' She's like, 'Cecelia wouldn't do that to you.' Well, I'm like, 'What the fucking hell is going on?'

PIERCE: (laughs) Meanwhile, you're thinking, 'Yeah, she knows everything,' you know . . .

SMART: Oh, I know, but I don't want to tell, tell Tracy that, you know? So I'm like, O-o-o-oh, god, because I'm like 'What the fuck.' All I can say is I'm so glad you're here, because I want to talk to you, but I was thinking totally the—the police, not the police but my lawyer told me that someday that they're probably gonna bug you and that you'd come down and talk to me.

PIERCE: I haven't even talked to the police.

Cecelia quickly moved on to other topics. One person who they both knew *was* talking to the police was Ralph

Welch. He had also been interviewed by the press and, apparently, had repeated what he learned about the murder to others as well.

PIERCE: Ralph is telling the whole town everything.

SMART: Yeah. But Ralph doesn't know anything. That's what I mean.

PIERCE: Ralph knows what he heard.

SMART: Right. And Ralph heard, uh, 'cause—'cause Ralph, the reporter told me Ralph said that he heard that I was having an affair with Bill, but it's not enough to arrest me because Ralph heard.

PIERCE: Right.

SMART: And for all anybody knows, Bill could have been totally in love with me and told the whole Winnacunnet that . . .

PIERCE: I know.

SMART: . . . he was having an affair with me, that Bill, um, Ralph's telling the truth that he did hear that. But that doesn't mean it is the truth. But if the police believed that, I'd be arrested right now, so obviously they don't believe it.

PIERCE: Obviously they don't think you'd kill Greg.

SMART: Right. No shit.

PIERCE: (laughs)

SMART: But what they're waiting for is either Ralph, I mean JR or Bill or Pete to say that I had something to do with it.

PIERCE: Right. And you know they said they won't tell. Bill—Bill would not tell on you.

SMART: I know. Even if they did say that—right?—they won't, they don't have any evidence 'cause there is no evidence.

Next, Pam and Cecelia complained about Franci Richardson, the reporter from the *Derry News*, who by now was asking questions about Flynn's having slept over at Pam's the week before Greg's death. The reporter was an irritant, to be sure, but she was not Pam's main concern.

SMART: I'm not worried about anything except the police. I think Ralph, I mean, if Pete or JR or Bill says that I did it—

PIERCE: Right.

SMART: Right. Then they can arrest me—

PIERCE: Yeah.

SMART: I want you to know that if I'm in jail there's no way in hell I'm ever going to say anything about you ever.

PIERCE: All right.

SMART: 'Cause why would I?

PIERCE: Right.

SMART: You didn't have anything to do with anything. And even if, say they have a note from Jenny or [inaudible] one phone conversation or something . . .

PIERCE: Yeah.

SMART: . . . with me and Bill, then I'd have to admit that yes, I was having an affair with Bill; I am never going to admit the fact that I asked, that I told him, that I hired them, 'cause I never paid them money. I never hired anybody.

They digressed for a bit, talking about Raymond Fowler, then moving on to Pam's concerns about her phone being tapped and her uncertainty about what Ralph Welch might know about the murder. She also kept returning to what people around Seabrook were saying and thinking about her involvement in Greg's death.

SMART: Does your mother think that I hired them to do it?

PIERCE: She—she just doesn't want me having anything

to do with you. She hasn't—she hasn't told me.

SMART: Why? Because she thinks like I'm a murderer?

PIERCE: She—she just doesn't, she doesn't want the police to keep harassing me.

SMART: I think that's right, Cecelia, you know, I think that when school starts again you can start, you know, working here if you want.

PIERCE: Yeah.

SMART: I don't know if your mother will let you or not. But, uh, when everything blows over, you know . . . But I just want you to know—

PIERCE: Are you gonna teach your course?

SMART: No.

PIERCE: No, you're not? All right. I just want to know 'cause I want to call and change it to physiology and anatomy.

SMART: All right. I'm not going to now. I may have, it matters what happens.

PIERCE: Yeah.

SMART: You know, if they got certified as juveniles, then no one will ever know anything, and they'll all be out in a year, you know, when they turn eighteen. I don't know, you know. If they get certified as adults it matters, but right now none, I know none of them have confessed. None of them have. My lawyer talked to Bill's lawyer yesterday.

Pam would again ask Cecelia what different people thought about her. And she wondered about possible evidence the police might have, such as the love note that Jenny Charles supposedly gave to the police, which of course was a fabrication.

SMART: I wonder if everybody hates me at Winnacunnet or if they just feel sorry for me. Like, could be everybody thinks I'm guilty?

PIERCE: I don't think anybody knows what to think.

SMART: Because, like, has, does anybody feel sorry for me? Like, is anybody—like how could they have killed her husband or everybody thinks I had something to do with it? Everybody thinks I had something to do with it.

PIERCE: Yeah (laughs).

SMART: Well, see, that's okay. You know? I mean, I'd rather know the truth, you know. I mean like, there's nothing I can do, but I guess people, 'cause people keep thinking that I'm getting arrested, people will come . . .

PIERCE: I've been told five times already that you were, that you were arrested.

SMART: I, so have I. My boss was told the other day that I was arrested, but obviously I'm not, you know. The police haven't even questioned me . . . but I'm just like, what the hell? I've already got best lawyers friggin' anywhere.

PIERCE: You do?

SMART: Yeah. They're fucking wicked expensive, but what could I do?

PIERCE: Obviously you can afford it.

SMART: No. Goddamn fucking. Didn't I need them? But right now they don't have to do anything unless I'm arrested, and if I get arrested, then they have to do shit. But if I get arrested the only way I would ever confess to the, um, affair would be if they had a note from Jenny.

Then Cecelia dropped a small bomb. Bill Lyons from the attorney general's office had called, she said, and wanted to see Pierce the next day. Lyons had told her, in fact, that they had Pam's love note, a revelation that seemed to cause Smart distress. It was, after all, a piece of evidence. Her voice became quiet and she grew irritated at Cecelia's picayune concerns about not being able to pick up a copy of the orange juice video because the police had it.

SMART: All I can say is that no matter what they try and make you talk about, if I were you I didn't know a damn thing.

PIERCE: Well, all I know is that I had to come and talk to you because I—I mean, I don't know what to do. I have to go talk to the attorney general. I'm just sick of lying, you know.

SMART: Well, you know, I'm just telling you that if you tell the truth, you're gonna be an accessory to murder.

PIERCE: Right.

SMART: So that's your choice. And not only that, but what is your family going to think? I mean, they're like, 'Cecelia, you knew about this?' You know?

PIERCE: Yeah.

SMART: Everybody in town is gonna be like fucking, you know, Cecelia. So if I were you, once you say no they leave you alone.

PIERCE: Uh, huh.

SMART: Once you say yes, they never leave you alone, you know?

PIERCE: Yeah.

SMART: And that's the thing. It's too, I know, it's too late now, though, you know.

PIERCE: Did you now, seeing what had happened, wouldn't you rather have had just divorced Greg?

SMART: Well, I don't know, you know. Nothing was going wrong until fucking they told Ralph.

PIERCE: No shit.

SMART: It's their stupid-ass faults that they told Ralph, you know.

PIERCE: I can't even believe that they told him. Now they're in jail and like every time I hear Motley Crue I think of Bill.

SMART: Yeah, so do I. Tell me about it.

As the conversation moved along, Pam steered it toward the possibility that Cecelia would be given a lie detector test. Pam suggested that she refuse to take it.

SMART: I don't know anything about lie detector tests, but I know every lawyer I talked to told me no matter fucking what, don't ever in your whole entire life take a lie detector test because they can't be introduced as evidence. They can only be used against you for further questioning. Like if it shows up as you're lying, they're gonna fucking bludgeon you to death before, you know, they're gonna question you for ninety hours.

PIERCE: I know. I'll have a nervous breakdown.

SMART: Right, exactly like Anthony Barnaby did in his fucking trial the other day. They questioned him for murder for seventeen hours straight and at the end he fucking confessed.

PIERCE: The guy that just had three trials?

SMART: Yeah.

PIERCE: I can't believe he had three trials.

SMART: And got off. My lawyers represented him.

PIERCE: They did? And he's off?

SMART: Yeap.

PIERCE: After confessing he's off?

SMART: Yeap. [Inaudible.]

PIERCE: Jesus Christ.

SMART: I know. Good lawyer, huh?

PIERCE: Well, maybe if you confess you'll get off anyways.

SMART: Yeah.

With Flynn, Randall, and JR remaining closemouthed, Cecelia was the one person who could bring Pam down, and Smart knew it. Now Pam would begin to play on her friendship with Cecelia in an effort to keep the girl in her camp.

SMART: I think I've been a very good friend to you and that's the thing, even if you send me to the fucking slammer or you don't, or if anybody sends me it's gonna be you, and that's the big thing, and that's what it comes down to. . . . But what good is it gonna do if you send me to the fucking slammer? Because if you think that's going to be the end of your problems . . .

PIERCE: I'll be out a pair of sneakers on my next birthday (laughs).

SMART: Don't think it's the end of your problems if you confess. No, because it's gonna be your whole family's gonna be like, 'Fucking well, you knew about a murder, how could you have lived like that?' And the newspapers are gonna be all over you: 'How could you have known about that?' you know? All your friends are gonna be like, 'What the fuck,' you know? And you're gonna be on the witness stand a million times, you know.

Cecelia was a worry for Pam, but she no doubt figured the girl could be controlled. What was more frightening was what went on out of Smart's sphere of influence, namely behind the walls of the juvenile holding facility. JR Lattime, in Pam's mind, was the weak link of the three boys.

SMART: Well, the only thing that I think is gonna happen is that sooner or later JR is gonna turn on everybody too.

PIERCE: JR?

SMART: Yeah.

PIERCE: I feel bad for him because he really didn't do anything.

SMART: You have to remember through this whole thing that he did. . . . They're fucking old enough. You're old enough to make your own decisions.

PIERCE: Yeah.

SMART: They did this all. I did not force anybody to do anything. They made their own decisions.

PIERCE: At least you didn't pay 'em.

SMART: Yes. No, I didn't pay them. They made their own decisions, you know. Remember that throughout the whole thing. Don't feel bad even though I do too. I know it's hard not to. But remember, they made up their own minds and they would . . . I don't even know what happened in my house. I don't know who was there or who was waiting in the car.

The conversation went on for a few minutes more, mainly covering old ground. Pam told the girl to visit her after going to the attorney general's office. Smart, in the meantime, had an appointment with her newly hired psychiatrist.

Pam and Cecelia stepped outside. The teenager drove off and was to meet the detectives in the parking lot not far away. The plan fell apart, though, when Pam pulled out of the parking lot and on to the street right behind the girl.

Cecelia thought Pam was following her. Every way she turned, Pam turned. Finally, Pam went another direction. Only then did the sixteen year old head toward the rendez-vous.

Pierce was a quick thinker. That day she had kept Pam talking for close to a half hour, carrying out her part in the first-degree murder investigation with great aplomb. She glibly took a slap at her own mother, calling her a "witch," and poked Pam for seeming surprised when Cecelia first walked in. "I thought you saw Greg standing behind me or something," the girl had said. Had the conversation been secretly videotaped, Cecelia was the type who probably would have winked at the camera.

If Pierce had any failings that day, it was that she may have been a little too chatty. Perhaps she should have held back a little and let Pam, who seemed quite willing, run on for a while.

All the same, the teenager had done a fine job.

But it was not enough.

* * *

That evening, the Derry police called Cecelia and her mother. They wanted Cecelia to give it one more shot so they could hammer the case down beyond any jury's idea of reasonable doubt.

The second body wire conversation was set for the next day, Friday the thirteenth.

Cecelia was to pick up where she had left off the day before, only adding a new twist or two.

The whole operation, meanwhile, was not going over very big with Cecelia's relatives who were visiting from the Midwest. Most of the clan from Mrs. Eaton's side of the family was in town: Cecelia's grandmother, an aunt and uncle, and some cousins. A number of them were against Cecelia taking part in this; it was too dangerous, they said.

Cecelia was nervous, but now she wanted to do it and get it finished. Leaving her cousin at home this time, Cecelia pulled up into the parking lot around 12:50. She went into SAU 21, but Pam was away at lunch, so the girl went back to the maroon-colored Ford Tempo.

The cops were ready for the show. This time, Pelletier and Charewicz sat in the unmarked car and Captain Jackson, along with Mike Surette, manned the surveillance van. Surette tested the recorder three times. All was go.

The only potential problem was some men who were working not far away, using heavy machinery. But background noise was a hazard in any undercover operation.

Everyone waited. Then, at around 1:10, Pam wheeled into the parking lot, noticed Cecelia, and climbed into the Tempo.

PIERCE: What's up?

SMART: Hello. I was going to call you but, oh, I figured I'd call you some other time. Your mother answers. Have you gone yet?

PIERCE: I didn't go.

SMART: Why?

PIERCE: Because Captain Jackson called and he wants me to meet him at 3:30. I'm not going to the attorney general's today.

SMART: Do you know why? Because I talked to my lawyer

and I told him they asked you and it's 'cause they're doing an investigation.

PIERCE: Oh, are they?

SMART: They are like calling like everybody now. They have to go to like grand jury to see if they have any evidence.

PIERCE: They're gonna subpoena me, I know they are.

SMART: They are. They're gonna subpoena everyone else, too, and any friends I have [inaudible].

PIERCE: They are?

SMART: Yeah, like everybody is going at different times [inaudible] like all Bill's and JR's and Pete's teachers have to go and [inaudible], um, like everyone. They would subpoena me but I'm not going because it's a conflict of interest 'cause it's my husband.

PIERCE: Oh?

SMART: But they wouldn't subpoena me really [inaudible].

PIERCE: I hate this. What happens if I lie on the stand and they find out?

SMART: How would they find out?

PIERCE: Later on.

SMART: If they, I mean, if somebody says that I did know. I don't know.

SMART: Well, who would know? Who would say that?

PIERCE: Does JR know what I know?

SMART: Even if he did know that, it's his word against yours and they can't prove it. . . . Where are you going? The Derry police?

PIERCE: Yeah. But what I was saying is if I'm, I mean, obviously I knew about it beforehand and if I get up there and lie and if then they find out about it after, I'm gonna get in trouble.

SMART: Well, if you knew about it beforehand and then

you say you knew about it beforehand you're gonna be in trouble.

PIERCE: But I did know about it beforehand.

SMART: Yeah, but if you say that you're gonna get in trouble anyways.

PIERCE: Uh, hmm.

SMART: So you are better off just—just lying. There is no way. They wouldn't, in order to arrest you and convict you for accessory to murder, that which means you knew before it happened, they would need to have evidence that you knew, somebody saying something like that is hearsay.

Like these guys are never gonna get convicted for murder unless they have fingerprints and hair and shit and everything. You know what I mean? Like, they're never just gonna get convicted because Ralph said. They're not. You know? And right now they could give two flying shits about—about anything regarding anybody else except for, they're gonna, if they truly have a letter from Jenny, like they're gonna want to know, they're gonna want to prove in court that I was having an affair with Bill.

PIERCE: Sure.

SMART: But, I told you even if I got arrested tomorrow and they said here's a letter from Jenny and it's signed "I love you, Bill, be mine forever," or whatever—I don't know, I can't even remember—then, uh, then it's, I'm gonna have to say, "Okay, yeah, I was." But I'm not going say, I'll just say nobody knew about it besides me and Bill and whoever Bill might have told.

PIERCE: What did they do with the stuff they stole?

SMART: I don't know. I have no idea.

PIERCE: Did they really steal stuff?

SMART: Uh, yeah.

PIERCE: They did?

SMART: Yeah, things were stolen from my house. But I don't know. I would assume they threw it out.

Cecelia was now tossing out simple, declarative statements about the murder and waiting for Pam to react. The teenager went on to say she hoped Bill did not leave evidence in his bedroom and recollected the night that Bill and Raymond got lost and arrived in Derry too late to kill Greg.

PIERCE: You know what? Remember that time you let Bill use your car to go up there?

SMART: Where?

PIERCE: Up to your house?

SMART: Yeah.

PIERCE: Well, that time, if he hadn't have forgotten directions he could have killed Greg then and . . .

SMART: I know, I really . . .

PIERCE: . . . and then I wouldn't even have spent the next week with you. So if I had . . .

SMART: I know, but it's history now. We can't talk about shit that should have happened. [Inaudible] should have happened, though, you know. Um, the only thing is that . . . oh, yeah, remember, I don't know if my phone's been tapped, but if it was, there was a time when I was talking to you on the phone and you said to me, "Uh, you should have just got divorced."

PIERCE: Yeah.

SMART: Something like that, and hopefully my phone wasn't tapped when you said that, 'cause I coulda shit when you said that. But if any, if my phone is tapped and anybody asks about that I'll—I'll just say that you meant like why—why if, you couldn't understand why I would have killed Greg, 'cause I would have just gotten divorced.

Pam then talked about Jenny Charles. Smart seemed doubtful that the girl would keep a love note that wasn't hers for so many months. "If they don't have that," Pam said of the investigators, "they don't have shit." And what's more, even if they did have it, why would they want to ask Cecelia about it? Why not ask Jenny?

SMART: I mean, frigging, that's what I keep saying. Everyone asks me, like the reporters: "Well, so Ralph said this." I'm like, "Well, fuckin' ask Ralph, I guess. You know, don't ask me. Ask Ralph. I don't know. You know, I don't know what to tell you, lady. Just ask fucking Ralph."

Um, but, you know, they might tell you a detail, like "Well, we've talked to Bill and Bill said." Okay? That's bullshit, 'cause those kids have not talked to a fucking soul since they've been arrested besides their lawyers, you know, and that's *it*.

And even if—if Pete, if they say, "Well, Pete said that, that Bill told him that you knew," then all you have to say is, "Well, Bill told Pete the wrong thing. Then if Bill's the murderer, he's obviously a liar, so, you know, what the hell." That's just it. I mean, they're not going to believe Bill and Pete on the witness stand against you. I mean, come on. They're friggin' . . .

PIERCE: Yeah.

SMART: They're on trial for murder you know; they're not gonna be believing you and them. All they want to know is—is there anybody else that knew about this before it happened? Because if there is, then they can really bag 'em. You know? But that's the thing. So I don't know, you know.

I mean, I wish this wasn't the circumstances. You know, I *hate* the fact that you have to be interviewed; I hate the fact that you're scared; I hate the fact that you're probably going to have to take a lie detector test. But I don't know what to tell you. If I thought if you told the truth it was going to do you any good, that's one thing, but it's not.

If you tell the truth, you cannot change what you know. You know? You can't. And if you tell the fucking truth you are probably going to be arrested. And even if you're not arrested, you're gonna have to go and you're gonna have to send Bill, you're gonna have to send Pete, you're gonna have to send JR, and you're gonna have to send me to the fucking slammer for the rest of our entire life. And unfortunately, that's the situation you're in.

And not only that, but your parents are gonna be like "Fucking Cecelia," you know, "What the hell?" I mean, I think your parents will get over the fact that you decided you didn't want to take a lie detector test. But I don't think they will get over the fact that for the next two years you're gonna be going to trials sending everybody up, you know, to the slammer for the rest. I'm just saying . . .

By now, Captain Jackson and Surette were all smiles in the surveillance van as they listened to Pam incriminating herself left and right. "Yes!" one them would say after a particularly ruinous statement. Then they would exchange high fives. "I can't *believe* this!" they said. "I can't believe she's saying this!"

If Cecelia and Pam had looked over, they might well have seen the van rocking with all the excitement inside. Instead, the roar of the heavy machinery from the nearby work crew was distraction enough, especially for Cecelia.

PIERCE: What the hell are they doing?

SMART: That's the thing. You're gonna, I mean (laughs). I don't know. But all I have to say is I feel like totally feeling you, 'cause I'm afraid one day you're gonna come in here and you're gonna be wired by the fucking police and I'm gonna be busted.

PIERCE: All I can say is if Raymond hadn't run his mouth off . . .

SMART: I know. Give me some signal that if you ever come down to me and you're wired that you are going to give me.

PIERCE: I'll just wink.

SMART: All right. You know, go like this, or . . .

PIERCE: All I have to say is (laughs)—I thought my watch said quarter past two, I was like great—um, if Raymond hadn't run his friggin' mouth off this would have been the perfect murder . . .

SMART: Right.

PIERCE: . . . because they set everything up . . .

SMART: No shit.

PIERCE: . . . to look like a burglary just like you said.

SMART: No *shit*. So it's not my fault. I, fuckin' Raymond . . .

PIERCE: If he had not run his mouth off, everything was set up perfect.

SMART: No shit. But the thing is that—that you have to realize that no matter what, Bill's not going to drag you into it—

PIERCE: Uh, huh.

SMART: 'Cause it is just going to make it even worse for him.

PIERCE: Right.

SMART: And what good is it going to do to drag—to Pete and JR—to drag you into it?

PIERCE: Yeah.

SMART: *Nothing*. It's *nothing*. You know? Plus, Pete and JR never talked to you about the murder, right? They never said, "Oh, Cecelia, you know." Right?

PIERCE: Yeah.

SMART: So as far as they know, Bill told them you know. That doesn't really mean you knew. You know I, that's the thing . . .

PIERCE: Right.

SMART: So no one's ever, don't worry about them fuckin',

don't worry about anybody. Pretend like no one is ever going to say you're lying in twenty years or two days down the road, 'cause no one is ever gonna catch you in a lie because it's impossible to catch you in a lie, 'cause people are gonna try and catch you in a lie. If anyone, it's gonna be Pete and JR and it's just gonna be their word, their convicted-criminal-arrested-for-murder word against yours, you know . . .

PIERCE: Yeah.

SMART: I mean, and any fuckin' jury in the world is gonna, they can't even arrest you on criminal word. I mean, they know they're gonna say anything they have to get, to get, you know, off. And that's the whole thing. So you have to go there and just fucking say the same goddamn fuckin' story. You know? And don't change it and that's it.

And the only thing is I don't know what they are going to ask you. I would totally shit if they said to you, "Well, Bob Smith who lives next door to Pam said she saw Bill walking into the house on the night of the murder." But I'd be like, "The stupid bitch, she waited fucking three months to say what she saw." You know what I mean? . . .

Out in Seabrook, Cecelia's family was worried. They were waiting near Seabrook Beach, at Cecelia's great-grandmother's house. The plan was for Cecelia to meet her visiting relatives after the body wire interview with Pam. For safety's sake, the girl was going to leave with them for the Midwest until Pam was arrested.

Only now, Cecelia was an hour and a half later than expected. "An hour went by and there was still no word," remembered Mrs. Eaton. "So everybody started panicking. I was staying calm because I figured she's safe. The police said they'd be there for her. But at the same time I got scared.

"Cecelia's aunt was wailing over in the corner about how I should never have let her do this, that she couldn't believe that I actually let her go, and that Cecelia's probably never gonna come back, that Pam probably shot her and killed her. And I was like, 'God, cut it out!' "

Back in the SAU 21 parking lot, however, the only person Pam Smart was shooting was herself—in the foot.

SMART: All I know is that, uh, that pretty soon JR is probably gonna roll. He was supposedly only in the car. I don't know. I have no idea. And pretty soon he is gonna be like, "Fuck Pete and Bill, I'm not going to jail for the rest of my goddamn fuckin' life." 'Cause he's gonna turn against them. And he is gonna blame me.

PIERCE: Right.

SMART: I know he is. And *that's* when I'm gonna be in trouble. *That's* when I'm gonna get arrested. But I can probably get out of it 'cause they're not gonna have any proof. You know? But, that's when I'm gonna be arrested, 'cause JR . . .

But see, I never said the words, I never said any words like, "JR, I will pay you to kill Greg." I never said anything. JR never talked to me about the murder or anything. You know? So far as he knows, Bill coulda told them *all* I'd pay them. I don't know what Bill told them to get them to go, and then that was just a lie. You know? But that's a lie. They're not going to have any proof. There's no money. They're saying, you know, there's no . . . you know what I'm saying? Like, that, 'cause that's not true. So they can't convict me 'cause of fucking JR's sixteen-year-old's word in the slammer facing the rest of his life.

PIERCE: Well, first of all, you didn't offer to pay him, right?

SMART: No.

PIERCE: So he's not gonna say that you offered to pay him. He's going to say you knew about it before it happened, which is the truth.

SMART: Right. Well, so then I'll have to say "No I didn't" and then they're either gonna believe me or they are gonna believe JR, sixteen years old in the slammer. And then who me with a professional reputation and a course that I teach. You know, that's the thing.

PIERCE: All right.

SMART: They're going to believe me.

Cecelia ended the conversation there, agreeing to drop by Pam's condo that night, and Smart got out of the car. Seconds later, left alone, Pierce let loose a sigh of relief.

"Yeow," she said quietly.

In the meantime, the pressure was just starting to build inside the surveillance van. Captain Jackson got behind the wheel and started driving back to the Seabrook police department. Thirty-two-year-old Surette, who had operated the tape recorder, decided to play back Pam's and Cecelia's conversation.

He hit the Play button and heard his own voice: "Today's date is July 13, 1990. This is a conversation recorded between Cecelia Pierce and Pamela Smart at the Winnacunnet High School in Hampton, New Hampshire. This conversation that's being recorded was with the consent of Senior Assistant Attorney General Bill Lyons."

And then . . . nothing.

Surette looked at the machine in disbelief. Nothing?

"Oh, shit!" he said to himself. He looked up at Jackson, who was driving merrily along. "He is going to kill me!"

Surette tried the recorder again. Nothing once more. Not one nanosecond of the fourteen-minute conversation had been recorded. Surette did not know it at the time, but faulty wiring was to blame.

The detective's stomach turned. He thought he was going to be ill. "How do I tell this guy?" he said to himself as he looked at Jackson. "How do I tell Pelletier?"

We're gonna have to do it again, Surette thought. That's it. We'll have to do it again.

Finally, Surette took a deep breath.

"Hey, captain," he said. "This thing didn't record. It's blank."

There was no response. All the detective could see was the back of Jackson's head. He had no desire to see the front.

When they got back to the Seabrook police department,

the detectives regrouped. Surette said a silent prayer that all was not lost.

His petition was answered.

Pelletier, holding a microcassette recorder next to the car scanner, had captured the entire conversation. The quality was not the greatest. A second visit to audio-enhancement expert Robert Halvorson would be necessary.

But to hell with that for now. Danny Pelletier had just saved the day.

At the Seabrook PD, Cecelia dropped off the body wire equipment, said good-bye to the cops, and drove toward her great-grandmother's house to meet her family. By now, her mother was weeping, what with Cecelia being way overdue and the relatives forecasting certain doom.

Then Cecelia pulled in. She was greeted with hugs and kisses all around.

Mrs. Eaton brushed away her tears. "See!" she yelled to her sister, who had been carrying on all afternoon. "Next time just shut up!"

Cecelia's luggage was already packed in the van. She got in with her relatives, said her farewells, and westward they drove.

Obviously, Cecelia would not make it to her planned get-together with Smart that evening. "My personal opinion is that if Critter had gone to Pam's condo that night, we would not have seen nor heard from Critter again," said Mrs. Eaton. "We'd have probably found the body, but I don't think we'd have heard from her."

Most likely, Cecelia's mother has watched a few too many television mysteries. It is doubtful that Pam Smart planned to kill Cecelia that night.

But then again, who can blame Mrs. Eaton? A few months earlier, who would have believed any of it?

Chapter 9

Dan Pelletier never asked for much. He came in every day and dug in on the Gregory Smart homicide. Bum leads. Lousy hours. Tons of paperwork. And just like his bosses expected, no complaints.

None of the other detectives knew Pamela Smart better than Pelletier. He talked to her on seven or eight occasions, seeing her in supposed bereavement on the night of the murder and hearing her in panic on the afternoons of the body wire conversations. And he had met most of Pam's and Greg's friends.

Now, Pelletier had just one favor to request of Captain Jackson. When the time came, if at all possible, he wanted to be the one to arrest her.

Jackson nodded. He would see what could be done.

It was just a matter of time.

The detectives were now so cocky that someone made a photocopy of Pam's picture and a quote that had appeared in the *Union Leader* and put it up on their office bulletin board. The quote was something Pam had said to correspondent Tami Plyler a little over a week after Greg's death: "I think about what our dreams were and those things will never happen. But I'm still alive and I still have dreams. I will try to go forward and do those things."

At the end of the quote, one of the cops scrawled, "Wrong, guess again." Someone else drew bars over her face. And still another detective wrote "New Hampshire State Prison" across the top.

By this time, too, the investigators among themselves took to referring to Smart as Pammy, her family's nickname for her.

Despite the self-confidence, some work still remained. The cops were not completely happy with the sound on the body wire tapes and they were not averse to additional evidence. There was talk of using Cecelia one more time, though it was dubious that the teenager was anxious to go in wearing a body wire again. Pam, after all, had been her friend. None of this was easy for the girl.

Meanwhile, others were getting anxious.

After Cecelia failed to show up at Pam's condo the night of July 13, Smart began calling the Eaton residence time and again. She could not find her former intern. Surely it crossed Pam's mind that the end was near.

Bill and Judy Smart, meanwhile, were pained by knowing much of what the investigators knew and yet still having to behave as if they suspected nothing. They saw less of Pam now that she was living in Hampton, but they talked to her and hugged her when she was around.

Greg's father would complain to Captain Jackson, half demanding to know when she would be arrested. And the captain would take the insurance salesman aside and say reassuringly, "Bill, why don't you and Judy go away for a few days? Go out on your yacht. Go to the mountains. Just take a break. We want this thing tight and right. So just relax."

Tight and right, tight and right. To Bill Smart, that seemed to be Jackson's favorite phrase. But Greg's father was sick of talk; he wanted Pamela behind bars.

Out on the seacoast, Vance Lattime, usually a man of patience, was doing a slow boil. A month and a half had passed since he had set off the chain reaction that resulted in the arrests of his son as well as Billy and Pete. And still they were the only ones sitting in jail. What about Fowler? And Pam?

On the morning of Wednesday, August 1, Lattime told some friends that if Smart was not arrested by Friday, he was going to find her and bring her down to the station himself.

He need not have worried.

Cecelia had been brought back to Seabrook, and that Wednesday the plan called for her to attempt one more secretly recorded telephone conversation. Then would come the arrest.

The attorney general's people had talked about simply bringing the case against Pam to the Rockingham County Superior Court grand jury. If she was indicted, it would be the sheriff's deputies who would arrest her.

The Derry police objected. They had worked the case hard since May 1 and felt they deserved to make the collar. Plus, the element of surprise might well lead Pam to confess or make an incriminating statement. The cops felt they should be on hand if it happened.

Indeed, Pam had a problem with keeping her mouth closed, and she might very well have said something when she felt the steel bracelets on her wrists.

The only problem was that her impending arrest was one of the worst kept secrets in southern New Hampshire.

It is uncertain exactly where the leak began, though it seems certain that it soon came from more than one source. Reporters from all over the area knew that morning that the arrest was coming. One, in fact, called Paul Twomey and mentioned it. The lawyer, in turn, called Pam and told her to be prepared for the worst. Smart had received similar warnings before, so she did not know whether to believe it this time.

Nevertheless, she called Bill and Judy Smart. Since Greg's death, Pam had called his parents often, crying about how Greg was the only thing that was good in her life and how she didn't know what to do without him. She seldom called before noon.

Now, however, she was telling Greg's parents that she was feeling especially lonesome and despondent. Something in her voice and the way she was talking told the Smarts that Pam was aware of what was coming. The couple believed that Pam was feeling them out, searching for something in their voices or a remark that would confirm the news.

That morning, from her home in Seabrook, Cecelia called Pam at SAU 21 for the final recorded telephone talk. Pierce's job was simply to say hello and say she'd heard Pam had been looking for her. Perhaps she could get Pam going once again.

Their conversation was brief and insubstantial. Probably the most interesting exchange was when Pam told Cecelia how upset she was because that morning she had accidentally run over a rabbit on the road. Cecelia was incredulous. I can't believe that you're upset about some rabbit, she said, but yet you had your husband killed and you don't care about him. Pam sidestepped the issue.

In Derry, meanwhile, Dan Pelletier wrapped up the paperwork at Derry District Court, signing the warrant for arrest and an affidavit outlining the reasons for charging Pam.

Around one'clock, the Derry cops met with an officer from the Hampton police department at the Winnacunnet High School parking lot. Dressed in their best suits and sports coats, Pelletier led Jackson and Surette toward SAU 21. Charewicz stood near the back door, in case Pam tried to slip out.

At 1:05, they entered the building. A receptionist spoke up, but Pelletier blew right past and down the stairs to Pam's office. Jackson and Byron trailed behind.

Pam was at her desk wearing a pale green dress with a wide black belt. She had just returned from having lunch at her condo with her younger brother, Jay.

"Hi!" she said when she saw Pelletier's familiar face.

"Hi!" he said.

"What's up?"

"Well, Pam, I have some good news and I have some bad news. The good news is that we've solved the murder of your husband. The bad news is that you're under arrest."

"What for?" said Pam.

"First-degree murder," Pelletier replied. "Stand up and face the wall."

Pam's mouth dropped and her eyes opened wide.

She did what she was told.

"Put your hands behind your back," Pelletier said. Then he clamped his dull blue Smith and Wesson handcuffs onto her wrists.

Before escorting Pam outside to the car, he asked if she needed anything from her office. She said her purse.

The foursome climbed the steps to the front door.

"What's going on?" an administrator wanted to know as Pam was brought out in front of her coworkers.

"We're arresting Pammy," said one of the detectives, as if it should have been obvious.

"What for?"

"For murder."

Pelletier marched her out to the unmarked cruiser. A *Lawrence Eagle-Tribune* reporter, Hilde Hartnett, acting on a tip, had been in the parking lot and snapped some photos of the arrest, with Pam in handcuffs and Pelletier grasping her upper left arm. (The detective, who seldom was ever named in newspaper articles about his work, had his moment in the sun besmirched a bit the next day when underneath Hartnett's four-column page-one photo, he was identified as Loring Jackson.)

Pam looked "wild-eyed and shaken" when she got in the cruiser, Hartnett would write the next day.

The cops, of course, were hoping Pam would say something interesting. But Pam, no doubt following her lawyer's advice, said nothing.

Byron got behind the wheel. Pelletier climbed into the backseat next to Pam. As the car pulled away, Pelletier read her the Miranda warning.

The detectives had a tape recorder handy in case Pam became talkative, but she said little the entire ride on Route 107, which Byron preferred to Route 101.

Smart's only words, in fact, came when she asked the cops about the path they were taking: "Are we going to Derry?" she asked. The detectives told her yes. "*This* way?" she said.

Meanwhile, Pelletier and Byron started discussing their respective vacations and how nice it would be to *get away* sometime soon.

Smart had her own thoughts, which at this point were not particularly lucid: "This is crazy," is what Pam remembered thinking on the drive. "Just that this is crazy. Just unbelievable. You know what I mean? Like I can't even believe this is happening. Like, I didn't cry. It was just like shock, I guess."

In Manchester, Terri Schnell was experiencing her own version of shock—as would all of Pam's friends, her parents, and relatives.

Emotionally, Terri, twenty-three, was having one of the worst years she could remember. The breaking off of her engagement and the death of Greg, one of her dearest friends, had wreaked havoc on her. So much so that one day, about two weeks after the murder, Terri impulsively went and got a tattoo—a red heart about the size of a quarter on her thigh—during her lunch break.

Now, while at her job as a customer-service representative with an insurance agency, Terri received a phone call from Sonia Simon with the news that Pam had been arrested. Smart was to be arraigned in Derry District Court that very afternoon.

Terri could not believe it. Schnell had been closer to Greg than she ever was to Pam. But this she could not fathom. Terri could not accept that Pam would ever have engineered Greg's death. It wasn't in the Pam Smart that she knew.

"I spent the whole summer with Pam, crying at her place in Hampton and in Windham, discussing everything," said Schnell. "Believe me, I'm not the type of person who will let something go by. I had asked her a million questions to satisfy myself."

Schnell got in her Toyota Tercel and drove like mad to Derry, arriving at the court building just as Smart's arraignment was ending. As the police started to bring Pam out, Schnell, in tears, tried to hug her, and was blocked by police officers. Terri ran outside and around the building, where Smart was being brought to the car for transport to the Rockingham County Jail.

"Pam, I love you!" Schnell was shouting. "This is so wrong! I love you!"

Smart got in the backseat, put down her head, and was driven away. She sobbed quietly.

Schnell, in a suit and high heels, then broke for her car to escape all the reporters who wanted to interview her or at least get her name.

Bill Smart, meanwhile, gave reporters at the courthouse a statement. Spewing anger, he growled somewhat non-sensically, "All I've got to say is that if indeed she is guilty that they teach her a lesson and give her the maximum sentence that God and Lord above us will give her!"

In lieu of the Almighty, Judge Douglas Gray of the Rockingham County Superior Court was assigned Pam's case.

Gray, who stood six foot five, was intimidating not only because of his size, but because of his imperious nature. An appointee of former Governor John Sununu, he was said to have a dry, Down East sense of humor, but few saw it when he was sat on the bench.

More often, lawyers looked up to see Gray, then fifty-seven, scowling at any and everyone who might be wasting the court's time. If anyone would be doing any intimidating in his courtroom, it was the judge himself.

Only adding to the jurist's image was his designated nickname. In the bowels of the New Hampshire State Prison in

Concord, the men's facility, Douglas Gray was known as the Hanging Judge.

In mid August, he listened to the tapes of Pam and Cecelia so that he could better rule on the question of bail for Pam Smart.

Gray also listened to the defendant. "I have spent the last twelve days behind bars in state prison, incarcerated for a crime I didn't commit," Pam said at her bail hearing. "If this court is worried about me fleeing, I can assure you that I am going nowhere because I want to be in this courtroom to prove that I am innocent of the charges."

At least part of Pam's statement was true. She was going nowhere. Citing the tapes, Gray ordered her held without bond.

The next day, a Rockingham County Superior Court grand jury indicted her. The charges: accomplice to first-degree murder, conspiracy to commit murder, and witness tampering.

For someone who liked attention, Pamela Smart now had plenty.

Her arrest, combined with the rough sketch of her affair with Billy as well as Cecelia's secretly recorded conversations, was sensational stuff for both the mainstream and fringe elements of the news media.

The attraction was obvious: Pam had violated much of what society holds sacred—her marriage vows, the responsibilities she had to the teenagers involved, and, of course, the sanctity of human life.

Smart's arrest was big news around New Hampshire and, eventually, in Boston. Had Iraq not invaded Kuwait early the next day, Pam Smart might then have been a household name in Dubuque.

Nevertheless, her story was ideal for the supermarket tabloids. The *Weekly World News*, for instance, which has come out with such blockbusters as President Bush's secret meeting with an alien from outer space, ran a two-page spread.

Before long, and only naturally, the tale would unfold on dramatic-news television shows. *A Current Affair* dubbed its story, "A Macabre Saga—Murder 101." And *Hard Copy* opened with an announcer saying that students at Winnacunnet High School were getting more than an education: ''Some bad grown-up games were going on, games that ended in a crime of passion.''

The case was also coming up on programs like *Sally Jessy Raphael*, during a segment on ''Black Widow Murders,'' and *Geraldo* where the topic was ''Fatal Marriages.''

Bill Spencer, who says he wanted to win some recognition to boost his career, appeared on both shows. It was ill-advised. He came off looking less than objective, which would later give Pam and the Wojas family fodder to attack his reporting.

On Geraldo Rivera's program, in fact, Spencer even got into an embarrassing tiff with Pam's mother, who accused the reporter of baiting Pam.

Rivera asked Spencer if perhaps Smart was getting an unfair shake from the New Hampshire media.

''The evidence is overwhelming,'' said the reporter. ''All these teenagers, Cecelia Pierce being the key figure. But there were many other teenagers who have spoken to the police.''

''That's right,'' fired back Linda Wojas. ''They are all teenagers. My nephew, who's fifteen, his mother still has a hard time getting him to change his underwear. Fifteen years old.''

''There are other teenagers,'' Spencer said.

''What would my beautiful daughter, with her wonderful husband, that had everything to live for, both of them— very beautiful marriage, very caring people—why would my daughter look at a fifteen-year-old young man?''

For Spencer, the show was a debacle. Pam's mother had a grating side, to be sure. And as her remarks about Billy Flynn would later show, she was obviously blindly supporting Pam. But as the wounded mother of a young woman in prison, Linda Wojas was beyond reproach.

A more crucial figure in the case, Cecelia Pierce, was also tainted by the publicity. Reporters from all over were hounding the teenager, the Eaton family, and the girl's friends for interviews. Cecelia consented to talk to *A Current Affair* and *Hard Copy*, accepting three hundred dollars and a thousand dollars, respectively.

She also sold her rights to the story to a Hollywood film-making company, Once Upon a Time Productions, receiving two thousand dollars up front and a promise of one hundred thousand dollars if a movie was ever made.

Cecelia's actions were even more ill-advised than Spencer's. The reporter hurt his own credibility and perhaps even that of his television station, but Cecelia was putting the state's case in jeopardy. It was ridiculous to think that the girl had gone to the police that spring eyeing a Hollywood contract. At the same time, though, Pam's lawyers knew how to make a lot out of a little. And it only took one doubtful juror to get a hung jury.

For their part, Twomey and Sisti declined to say much to the media, unless of course one counted Sisti's predictable remarks about it all being "garbage."

Some of the glossier lawyers who offered to represent Pam most likely would have gone on a media offensive to counteract what had already occurred. Yet Twomey and Sisti failed to see what could be gained by the publicity. After all, their field of play was the New Hampshire legal system. That's where Pam's fate would be decided. That's where they wanted to engage the prosecution.

Still, Twomey agreed to appear on *Hard Copy* that fall:

"I talked to a Cecelia Pierce, who said that she saw Pam and one of these minors having sex, OK? What can you tell me about the credibility of that person? What can you tell me about whether that person has said directly contradictory things in the past? The fact that somebody said something means nothing to me. I mean, is this person reliable?

"I've heard the tapes. I've read transcripts of them. And in my reading of the transcripts and my listening of the tapes I don't come to the same conclusions. And I wouldn't say the same things about the tapes as was said in court by an agent of the state.

"Pam is innocent and she has a defense. Buy your ticket and you'll find out what it is."

The arrest of Pamela Smart was a relief to some people. It was sensational to others. And to her family and friends, it was hell on earth.

For Pam's parents and her siblings, it was always there: Greg was dead. Pam was in prison. And their world was upside down.

One of Pam's friends from high school saw Linda Wojas in a restaurant one day. The friend, who remembered Pam's mother always being so full of positive energy, was saddened to see Linda looking exhausted and angry.

And angry Linda was. At forty-nine years old, she and her husband, fifty-one, were still relatively young and healthy and had saved some money. Their kids were all grown, with only their son still in college. The couple planned to travel, to enjoy their lives.

Now everything was changed forever. Their savings took a powerful hit. What's more, Pam was behind bars. Linda blamed the Derry police, the state, and the media, for starters. "This is a nightmare that we can't wake up from," she said that fall. "I see red thinking about what's happened to all of us. Everything is so unfair and so awful."

In a futile effort, Linda would even write a two-page letter directly to Judge Gray, pleading that Pam be released in their custody. "We are alarmed and do not wish to wait until we receive a telephone call informing us that she is in the medical ward before we reach out for help," she wrote.

The mother said she was certain Pam was innocent. "There's nothing indicative—ever—in Pam's personality that would ever tell you that she could be capable of something like this," she said in an interview. "Ever, ever, ever.

"Have you ever looked at a fifteen-year-old boy? Go in a school yard and you'll know what we're talking about. Are you going to tell me that my daughter would be interested in running off into the sunset, if that's the theory that you want to adopt, with a fifteen-year-old boy?

"Give Greg more credit that that, for choosing a person that he wanted to spend the rest of his life with. Fifteen years old. That's a kid."

John Wojas, meanwhile, had taken early retirement from his job as a pilot at Delta Air Lines. He was the family's breadwinner, but less vocal than his wife. "Greg is dead," he said. "Somebody did it. And we want whoever did it to pay for it. Hey, if my daughter was involved, so be it, and she has to pay the price, just like anybody else. But until she comes to me right to my face and says, 'Dad, I was involved,' I can't believe it. I've just seen this kid do too much good all her life."

At times, John could even find his sense of humor, not surprising for a man who flew commercial jets and whose job description included keeping calm in the face of crisis. "I know one thing," he said. "You would never convince me that Pam would ever have done this for insurance money. If she wanted any money she would have took care of me. Then she would have had some money.''

The Wojases found solace in the support of their family and friends. Pam's dog, Halen, who was now in their care, was also something of a comfort. ''I play with him because every time that I look at him I think of both Pam and Greg,'' said Linda. ''And I cry when I hold him. I try to make up for whatever's been done to everybody just through this foolish dog.''

''Well,'' added John Wojas, ''that's our only grandchild. We've got a grandpuppy.''

Around the same time that fall, Bill Smart and a reporter drove out to the Forest Hills Cemetery in an old car that Greg had once owned. It was a rattletrap, but Bill Smart kept it around because it reminded him of his son.

Smart stood over his son's tombstone, the woods that surrounded the graveyard bursting with color.

''This is ridiculous,'' he said, sobbing, venting whatever thoughts ran through his mind. ''This is absolutely ridiculous. There are no words to describe what this has done to this family. I feel guilty if I even laugh. This is awful. It's just not right that you bury your child.

''Sometimes I talk just to talk. I ramble and I ramble, just to talk.

''I've been beaten down. I've been betrayed. My whole family has been betrayed.''

He walked back to his car and swept his hand left to right pointing out all the nearby headstones—a police officer, an infant, and all the others.

''I'm sure every poor person that's here has a story,'' Smart said. ''And most of them probably are tragic. But this is something that didn't have to happen, that shouldn't have happened.

''You can't explain this. In your mind you can't justify it. Even if he had a million dollars of coverage.''

The arrest would also have a deep effect on Pam's and Greg's friends. The murder had shaken them like an earthquake, and this was a massive aftershock. Many did not know what to think after prosecutor Cindy White revealed at Pam's bail hearing that secretly recorded tapes existed and that Cecelia had told authorities that she walked in on Pam and ''William F.'' while they were having sex.

Eventually, the case would cause canyonlike divisions between the group of friends and at times within couples as well. People took sides, almost as if Pam's guilt or innocence was a high-stakes sporting event. Bill and Judy Smart did not make matters any better when they began to shun some of Greg's old friends, whom the Smarts learned were visiting Pam in prison.

People like Terri Schnell and Brian Washburn, who were probably closer to Greg than anyone outside his family, were anguished to think that the dead man's parents might hate them. They too were devastated by Greg's death—Schnell had gone into hysterics when she'd learned of it, screaming "Greggles! Not Greggles!" over and over—but they could not easily accept that Pam was involved. It was too mind-boggling.

But the shockwaves went even further. They rolled out and touched relatives and coworkers and practically anyone who ever knew Pam Smart. Even a cop in one of the towns near Derry who had once done Pam a favor—making a call that took care of one of her speeding tickets—received a few sidelong glances from his colleagues.

The pain even stretched into the past, to the people who knew funny and boisterous Pam Wojas back at Pinkerton Academy.

One woman, who had been close to Pam as a teenager, was in Europe when she learned of Smart's arrest. Friends had mailed her newspaper articles that she read in stunned disbelief.

The woman, who preferred not to be named, said that for weeks Pam weighed on her mind, even though they had lost contact long ago. It was all too unreal.

"One night I had a dream," said the old friend. "Pam was sitting at my kitchen table, eating soup. She was really tiny, just bones. She was skinny and sick. And she kept saying she didn't do it and how awful it was.

"And then I had to take her back. For some reason I took her to the post office after it closed, and there I handed her over to this woman. She was going back to prison."

Chapter 10

As she awaited her trial, Pam would be housed just west of Manchester at the New Hampshire State Prison for Women in Goffstown.

This, of course, was the infamous "slammer" that Pam had talked about when trying to convince Cecelia Pierce not to tell the truth to the police. Surrounded by coil upon coil of razor wire, the brick and concrete structure had room enough for more than one hundred inmates, though at any given time its population hovered around eighty.

In certain ways, the facility resembled a college dormitory. The place was clean; the walls were painted white, the doors bright red, and the floors industrial gray. It had a small library and a workout room, among other areas used for teaching and various forms of rehabilitation. The cells had solid steel doors, not bars.

It was, however, still prison.

As such, the Goffstown facility was not always a happy place. Inmates were separated from their partners, children, friends. Frequently, they had an array of emotional and psychological disturbances as well as problems with drugs and alcohol. A history of childhood abuse was common as well. Added to the mix was the unavoidable truth that most inmates came from poverty and lacked education.

"Pam's a real sore thumb in there," said her mother. "Like she said, 'Mom, I'm the only one in here with all of my teeth.'"

Home for Pam was a cell—she would refer to it as her "room"—in what is known as D Tier, Goffstown's maximum security wing. Pam's cell, like everyone's, was ten feet long by seven feet wide, with a ten-foot-high ceiling. She had a bunk, a stainless-steel toilet, sink and a footlocker for her possessions. She also had her television and a Walkman.

Visits, according to prison rule, were limited to twice a

week. And Pam's parents, sister Beth, and friends like Sonia Simon, Terri Schnell, Tracy Collins, and Tracy's boyfriend Brian Washburn made regular pilgrimages. Smart also had clergy visits.

With few options, Pam tried to make the best of her confinement.

Smart regularly wrote and called old friends.

She penned a poem, "Good-bye My Love," for Greg and mailed copies to all of her buddies.

Now a voracious reader, Pam engulfed everything from Scott Turow's *Presumed Innocent* to Drew Barrymore's autobiography *Little Girl Lost*.

She leafed through the pages of *People* and *TV Guide*, her selections for the two magazine subscriptions that the prison allowed.

And she took active part in Bible-study classes, at one point setting aside her worries about her impending trial and joining the group in a hearty rendition of "He's Got the Whole World in His Hands."

Displeased with prison food, Pam ate less, and dropped more than ten pounds. She was put on a special weight-monitoring program, to prevent possible health problems caused by not eating. If she died at least it would be thin, she joked in a letter to a friend.

What's more, Smart would tell her visitors that she was considering suicide, which always got their attention and stoked the fires of their sympathy.

Pam would also speak of her fears that they would abandon her and simply never visit again. When her friends said that was ridiculous, Smart would hint that things were not going to look very good when everything started coming out in her trial. Her friends told her to be quiet. After all, things didn't look very good right now.

During a telephone interview with Linda Wojas about a week before Christmas 1990, I mentioned that I had started work on this book and that I hoped to interview her daughter. Mrs. Wojas did not think that was likely before Pam's trial, then scheduled to begin February 4.

Yet Linda seemed anxious for the media to finally come to know the true Pam. With Christmas coming, Linda thought that her daughter would appreciate a card, and that maybe someday, after all the madness ended, I would be able to sit down and talk with her.

So, I sent Pamela Smart a Christmas card. On the front was a picture of a happy golden retriever looking out the window of a fire-engine red pickup truck, with an evergreen in the back. Opened, the card read, "Happy Holidays are headed your way."

I wrote on the inside, introducing myself, and asking Pam if she would consider being interviewed for the book, assuring her that nothing that she told me would be printed prior to her trial.

On the evening of December 21, Pam called my home collect. Reversing the charges is the only way inmates can make contact with those on the outside.

Smart had received tons of requests from all kinds of people, she said, with everyone seeming to want a piece of her story. Interviews, movie deals, book proposals.

"I don't know why I'm calling you," she said. "I just am. I'm surprised. How can you write a book on something that hasn't even happened? I was just calling to find out what the end was, because I'm wondering myself."

She went on to say, reminiscent of her interviews shortly after Greg's death, that the main reason she called was her concern about anyone attempting to portray her dead husband in a bad light.

It was a curious comment. Hardly a negative word had ever been printed about Greg. Pam was the one who was coming across poorly in the media, a natural side effect of being charged with murder.

"I just don't want his name ruined or anything," Pam said of her late husband. "Obviously, I can't do much for myself anymore. But Greg was like the nicest person in the world and he doesn't deserve any of this adverse publicity. I would like for him to be able to rest in peace. And that's all I care about right now.

"Just all this stuff about me having a sixteen-year-old lover and all these just totally absurd things. You know, I mean, I just don't understand that. And then I've heard reports that my husband supposedly beat me. It's just ridiculous.

"My concern isn't even about me. My concern is just about Greg. And that's all I care about. I don't even care if you write that I did it. I do and everything like that. But I care more about Greg. And I just, I mean, want everybody to know that Greg was not a bad person."

Pam said that she was working at the prison as a teacher, an irony that did not escape her. After her arrest, headline writers and reporters had often erroneously said that Pam was a teacher rather than media center director for the school board. (Technically it was a mistake, but not one as egregious as many have suggested: Cecelia Pierce did receive credit for her internship with Pam, and Smart had been scheduled to teach a course that fall.) All the same, she was a teacher now. At Goffstown, Pam instructed her fellow inmates in math, spelling, English, and science.

Yet, as her mother said, prison was not a place where Pam easily fit in. Her social background was different from most of her fellow inmates. But Smart also said she had no need for any of the help programs that the prison offered.

"I go to one thing in here," Smart said. "Bible study. That's it, because I am not an alcoholic. I'm not a drug addict. I'm not an incest survivor. I'm not an abuse victim.

"I don't know if I'd consider myself above these people, but I just come from a different life."

Smart came into the prison and, as was so often the case in her life, quickly became the center of attention. All of her fellow inmates wanted to get a look at her and decide for themselves whether she was innocent or guilty.

In the process, not all of the women were diplomatic. Said Pam: "Like some girl just came up to me one day and was like, 'You're a bitch and you killed your husband and you're a murderer and dah-de-dah-de-dah-de-dah, and f-ing this and f-ing that.' I mean, the language. I'm sure you can imagine. And so I say, 'Thank you very much' and go back to my room and of course bawl my eyes out.

"I've been punched twice; I was thrown up against the wall a couple weeks ago. Some girl just threw me against the wall. She didn't like me, I guess. And of course I went and told on her. So now she's in lockup for fifteen days.

"In jail you're not supposed to tell on other people or something. But I'm not going to stand around when people punch me. And I'm the smallest person in this jail, so obviously people want to pick on me just because I'm little."

Pam's placement on the maximum-security tier was a result of the seriousness of the charges against her. Her fellow inmates on D Tier were hardly like anyone Pam knew on the outside.

"There's this one girl who sleeps while she's eating,"
Smart said. "There's one girl who screams all day long that
she's murdering us all. There's one person that spends most
of the day on the phone trying to call the White House
collect to talk to President Bush.

"And one of them comes up to me and goes, 'I'm going
to murder you.' And I said, 'Why?' And she said, 'Just
because I've murdered like two hundred people and I figure
what the hell is one more?' And I'm like, 'Okay, well,
whatever.'

"It's like one day after another. It's like all this built-up
frustration. Sometimes I wish they would put me in a car
and drive me to a field and let me get out and scream at
the top of my lungs and drive me back. Then I'll be at peace
for a while."

Pam spoke of her unhappiness in prison and of the pain
she felt at being falsely accused. It tore her apart, she said,
to see her mother in tears and Greg's parents turned against
her, not to mention having five months of her life taken
from her. Furthermore, Pam said, she had not even had
time to properly grieve for Greg.

"I just feel like my life was like a piggy bank and someone
just picked it up and just threw it on the ground and it's in
like a million pieces right now," she said. "And I'm walking around trying to pick it up. And even if I find all the
pieces when I glue it back together it just won't ever be the
same. That's how I feel. I have to deal with it. What else
can I do? I can die. Or I can deal with it. And that's it.

"The other day I just had—my god, I don't know what
to call it—a breakdown or something, when sometimes
when I'm crying so hard I feel like I can't even breathe.

"And there's nights when I pray to god that I'll just die
in my sleep because I want to be with Greg and I just pray
that god will just kill me. But there are times that I've sat
in here and wondered if I slit my wrists or if I hung myself
which way I would die faster.

"Sometimes I wish I wasn't such a wimp, you know?
That I would just kill myself. I just can't because it's like
everyone would just be so sad. And I know, I just see what
death does to people."

We talked about many things. Her high school days,
career aspirations, the night she became engaged, her marriage.

Pam was concerned about how Greg would be portrayed, so I asked her to talk about him, tossing her a softball of a question: What did you and Greg have in common?

"I don't know," Pam said. "We're both like, I don't know. That's a good question. I never really thought about that.

"Well, one thing I remember that we used to do a lot is that we both liked just being around each other, and we're both like real cuddly people and we liked sitting around just being together and stuff.

"But as far as doing things, I don't even really know because like Greg loves the winter and I hate it. I love summer and the sun and beach and I think I've been to the beach once or twice with Greg, both times dragged. And he used to go on the weekends dirt bike riding and I would go to the beach. Or he likes to go skiing. And I hate skiing.

"So we did have a lot of differences. But I think one of the things that made us have a good relationship is that we never set standards for each other. We just accepted the things that were different about each other. I never, ever once said to Greg and he never once said to me, 'You can't go out with your friends,' or 'You can't do that.' "

What's more, she said, the couple seldom had disputes. When they did, everything was usually resolved quickly. "Our life was so good that we didn't even really have any problems," Pam said.

Eventually, we moved on to discuss the charges against her. To Pam, the accusations were ludicrous and surely the public must see it the same way. She talked about how immediately after the murder people were saying what a wonderful marriage the couple had, but now that she had been arrested they had completely new versions.

"I can only speculate, but if somebody was going to murder somebody, I would think that there would be signs," Pam said. "You know, the relationship would be bad; they'd be getting into fights or something; there'd be like abuse of some sort; people would be noticing these things.

"And then they would try and get separated or try and get divorced and then go through counseling. I mean, none of these things happened.

"The first step is not just that you murder somebody. I mean, I don't think that's any step. It's not a resolution.

"When I hear about somebody murdering their spouse,

it's usually like a cycle of abuse or something, like an escalating situation. It's not like one day they got in a fight and the next day they were murdered."

What motive could she possibly have? Pam asked. Her marriage was happy. Financially she was fine. To suggest that she killed Greg for $140,000 in life insurance was outlandish.

"I had every single thing that I wanted," she said. "There's not a single thing that I didn't have that I wanted. Not only that, but it's like a notion that you could just kill somebody that you married, that you loved, that you planned to spend the rest of your life with, for money is just crazy to me.

"Money only lasts so long. If I'm so frigging money mad, why would I be going out with a sixteen-year-old person that doesn't even have a job? To me it would make sense if I had like a forty-year-old lover that's like some millionaire or something."

So who did it and why? Pam said that she was reluctant to say that the arrested teenagers were involved. Just like herself, perhaps they are being falsely accused.

"I always have this picture in my mind of the killer," Pam said. "You know, this drug-addict scum with like long greasy hair, this like big man with this big green jacket. This is what I pictured the killer to be. Not this little kid who is standing in front of me. That's why I'm just so baffled by the whole thing. Because for me, I almost want the killer to be some scum that fits in my mind of someone who would have done this.

"I feel like that when I found out who the killer was that I was going to find out that this was going to make some psychotic sense. Not that any reason would ever make sense for murdering Greg. But that the person was going to be like on drugs or whacked out or something crazy like that. They were going to have been like someone who escaped from the mental institution and was nuts. It wasn't going to be someone that went to school the next day."

But as matters stood, that was whom the state of New Hampshire was accusing. School kids, among them a boy named Billy Flynn, whom Pam insisted she never knew intimately.

In a retrospective article, months later, Nancy West, the reporter from the *Union Leader* who interviewed Smart on

June 21, would write that she had been struck by how Pam rarely mentioned Greg in the course of her interview, and yet Billy's name "seemed to come easy to her lips."

So it was during my interview with the widow. When discussing Greg, it was often in the terms one sees on greeting cards. She spoke of his "unconditional love" for her, but she never could easily articulate the reasons she loved him.

Nancy West hit it right on the head. Flynn simply seemed easier for Pam to discuss, even though she was not admitting to her relationship with the boy.

"The way I remember him is like, if you were walking around and you were carrying something that was wicked heavy or something, Bill would say, 'Do you want some help with that?' He was just, like, kind.

"I used to think he was one of the most sensitive people I've ever known. Yeah, he was just really sensitive about things. If you would ask him something about his father, he had a hard time talking about it. But once he would, he would come out with all these really sensitive things. He would be able to go into deep feelings and stuff. But you would have to get it out of him.

"He cared about things. He cared about people and stuff. And when I would talk about things, he always seemed like he was interested in what I was talking about.

"I don't know. If he was totally in love with me and murdered my husband, then obviously that's why he was interested. But, you know, I don't know that."

We also talked about Cecelia Pierce. Pam never explained why her former intern would, as Smart said, lie to the police and destroy Smart's life. Pam simply hinted at the possibilities, which standing alone were hardly credible.

"There's speculation about Cecelia possibly having a crush on Bill or some involvement with Bill and feeling like I caused Bill to do this," Pam said. "And that if Bill's going to jail, I'm going, too. Like she's going to be Bill's savior.

"I just don't know. I can't give you reasons. The only reason that makes any sense is if she was personally involved. In some way small or large. And everybody she knows was suddenly in jail, everybody else that was involved. Maybe she thought she better do something fast or she's going to be where everybody else is.

"And you know what? I can't even tell you that I hate Cecelia. Because I feel sorry for her if her life is this bad and minimal, that she's planning to do this to ruin my entire life. Then I feel sorry for her. I do.

"This is going to sound crazy, but I pray for people like her, that their lives won't be so bad anymore. I feel sorry for every single person that's involved in this, because it's not happy for everyone."

And finally, why? If the boys did kill Greg and Pam was not involved, why would they do it?

"They could have done it for a lot of reasons," said Pam. "They could have been burglarizing my house and brought a gun because that's just how they were; they thought they were tough or whatever; and Greg came home and they freaked out; and he saw their faces—or I don't know—and they killed him.

"Or they could have drove there and wanted to kill him because—you know, I don't know—one of 'em, like they said, could have been in love with me or something and had some crazy idea.

"But then that doesn't make any sense to me because why would the other two go, or the other three?

"Nothing makes any sense to me. Even the notion that they're accusing me of this doesn't make any sense to me.

"You're going to say that—that I'm in love with some sixteen-year-old lover? Why wouldn't I just get a divorce? And if I'm so money mad that I'm murdering my husband for insurance, what is a sixteen-year-old lover to offer me?

"I mean, what was I going to do? Run off into the sunset with my sixteen-year-old lover, who's not even a junior in high school? It's stupid.

"My worst fear is that the kids are going to realize if they're guilty that they're facing life in prison and that if they jump on the bandwagon of everybody else's story, which the state wants them to, then they're going to get some kind of deal.

"And I swear, I'm going to be like a lunatic if the person who murdered my husband walks. I want whoever murdered Greg to go to jail for the rest of their life.

"But it's not me."

Chapter 11

One of the first things young prosecutors learn is never to be afraid to point at the defendant.

To point during one's opening or closing statement is a sign of strength and self-confidence.

It also sends an unequivocal message to a juror's subconscious.

And that message is: I am not afraid. I am not afraid of this person. I am not afraid to tell you that this person has committed a crime against all of us. And *you* should not be afraid to say he is guilty.

Paul Anthony Maggiotto was never afraid to point.

He had been working in the attorney general's office only eight months when he became lead prosecutor, or what is known as "first seat," for the *State of New Hampshire* v. *Pamela Smart*.

Maggiotto, who is lean, with jet-black hair and a full moustache, grew up on the west side of Buffalo, New York, a predominantly Italian section that also once was home to Mark Sisti. Four of Maggiotto's six siblings, in fact, went to Canisius College, the small Catholic school in Buffalo where Sisti did his undergraduate work.

The prosecutor himself went to the University of Buffalo, where he majored in English and sociology. He got involved in public interest work in New York, ski bummed in Vermont, and managed his father's gas station, Maggiotto's Mobil, before going to law school at Northeastern in Boston.

Maggiotto met his wife at Northeastern and they both ended up with jobs in New York. She was an assistant district attorney in Manhattan. He became a prosecutor in Brooklyn, where he started out working on misdemeanor sex crimes and moved his way up to homicides.

It was in Brooklyn that Maggiotto's fellow prosecutors took to calling him "the Finger," or as they liked to say it, passing him in the hallway with a smile, "the Fingah, the Fingah."

The nickname was derived from the movie *The Sunshine Boys*, where in one memorable scene Walter Matthau complains about George Burns always poking him in the chest with his "fingah."

What Maggiotto had done to earn the moniker was that he took to heart the advice about pointing at the defendant. In his summations, Maggiotto would point relentlessly. It wasn't long before people noticed that he was pointing maybe a bit more than necessary.

In fact, when he left the Brooklyn DA's office to enjoy the outdoors and slower pace of New Hampshire, one of his colleagues made a photocopy of a finger and presented it to him as a farewell gift.

Maggiotto, age thirty-four, took on the Pam Smart case in December 1990. The original lead prosecutor, Cynthia White, had a scheduling conflict and opted for another murder case she had been working.

Maggiotto's second seat was Diane Nicolosi, who at thirty-one years old, brought a range of experience to the Smart case that none of the lawyers on either side could match.

A psychology major at the University of New Hampshire, Nicolosi had worked with troubled youths after graduation. She was also the only woman to be working the case when it came to trial.

As a result, Nicolosi had a unique insight into the minds of the teenagers the case revolved around. For one thing, she had an ability to talk to kids, which helped her to establish a rapport with Ralph Welch, for instance. She also had the understanding of teenage girls and patience to work with Cecelia Pierce, who at times would become moody during the endless stream of questions.

Nicolosi, whose long face and prominent features were much in contrast to the defendant's, was also the only lawyer who had worked the case from day one, when Gregory Smart's body was found. As such, only Dan Pelletier knew the case better.

What Diane was lacking, though, was trial experience. She had only recently joined the AG's criminal division after two and a half years of working civil cases in transportation and construction.

Nicolosi liked the people side of her work. At the same time, though, she was remarkably reserved for someone whose job demanded that she stand in the spotlight and ask twelve people to convict murderers. Outside court, she avoided reporters and said little to them when she did talk.

As it would turn out, Nicolosi proved to fall in well as the prosecution's second seat. She could bring Maggiotto up to speed on the case. At the same time she balanced his well-developed ego and unabashed style of prosecuting.

Twomey and Sisti, meanwhile, were pushing hard for Pam Smart's trial to begin as soon as possible. February 4 could not come soon enough.

Billy Flynn, Pete Randall, and JR Lattime each had to move through the machinery of the certification hearings in district court in Salem, as well as the follow-up process in Rockingham County Superior Court before they could face trial as adults.

If the boys somehow remained in the juvenile justice system, they would undoubtedly put in their two years at the Adolescent Detention Center and never testify about their crime.

On the other hand, if they were finally certified—and it seemed inevitable that they would be—their lawyers would probably want to cut deals with the state. Tried as adults, each of the boys faced the possibility of life in prison. Surely the prosecution would be willing to cut time off their sentences in exchange for the boys' testimony against Pam.

It was the last thing Smart or her lawyers needed.

As it stood going into 1991, however, none of the kids were breaking rank. There had been discussions, according to JR's parents, that he could receive five to ten years if he would turn state's evidence against Pam and his friends, but the boy refused. None was willing to testify against the others.

One month before Pam's trial was to have started, Bill Spencer went on the air with a report that a Hillsborough County grand jury in Manchester had secretly indicted Pam for attempting to hire a hit man to have Cecelia Pierce murdered.

Early in her stay at the Goffstown prison, Pam supposedly asked Marianne Moses, an inmate doing two to four years for welfare fraud, to help her find someone to kill Cecelia.

The man who would arrange the hit, Moses said, was the first of her five husbands. Supposedly a bank robber in hiding, he told Moses that Pierce could be done in for fifteen thousand dollars. Moses would later say that Pam tried to secure the money from Linda Wojas by saying it was needed for attorneys' fees. "I told Pam they don't take credit cards," Moses later told *Manchester* magazine.

Besides the hit-man charge, Pam was accused of asking Moses' son George to testify that he overheard Cecelia Pierce saying that she fabricated the story about Pam's involvement. George, who had attended Winnacunnet High School, was now living with relatives in Massachusetts.

Officially, the grand jury charges were for criminal solicitation to commit murder, criminal solicitation to commit tampering with a witness, and tampering with a witness. Pam would come to plead not guilty to all charges.

With Spencer having reported the secret indictments, the court unsealed them and all of the newspapers jumped in. "These indictments as far as we're concerned are just garbage," Mark Sisti was quoted as saying. The defense lawyers called it a "publicity ploy" on the eve of jury selection and said the charges would self-destruct in court.

Back in December, Pam, too, complained about the impending charges: "I'm going to drop over dead if someone can get indicted on the word of an incarcerated individual," she said. "I mean, what is the justice system coming to?"

Maggiotto, meanwhile, had little to say about the new indictments except for a remark that found its way onto page one of the Nashua *Telegraph*. "Someday some of you in the press are going to pick up on the fact that Pam is not so smart," he said, trying to be funny but never expecting to be quoted.

Twomey and Sisti must have had a good laugh as well. Normally, Twomey might have picked up the phone and simply told Maggiotto to lay off. But now, irritated at the prosecutor for his attempts at preventing them from deposing Cecelia Pierce, the defense lawyers loaded the cannon and fired off a motion to the court: Maggiotto's remark, they said, might have prejudiced the case.

Obviously, the comment was not a case breaker. Judge Gray, in fact, would merely note the motion. At the same time, however, Gray told the lawyers to behave, urging both sides to be "mindful of the mandates of the code of conduct and the requirements of this noble process in which we are all involved.''

The same day that the new charges were released, Billy Flynn was certified by the Rockingham County Superior Court to stand trial as an adult. It seemed only a matter of time before JR Lattime and Pete Randall would meet a similar fate. It was more and more likely that a deal was going to made. But the kids were still sticking together. It looked as if it would have to be all or none.

The attorneys for both sides, meanwhile, continued preparing for trial. On January 17 and 18, 1991, they appeared in Gray's court for a pretrial hearing to consider a variety of motions by Pam's lawyers. Among other requests, the defense asked for a change of venue and that the secretly recorded tapes not be allowed as evidence.

Over those two days Twomey and Sisti, with Pam sitting quietly beside them, would question a range of witness, including Dan Pelletier, Cecelia Pierce, Bill Lyons, and even Bill Spencer.

There was a touch of drama when Sisti asked Cecelia about her lucrative movie contract. Anxious and near tears, the girl snapped: ''If I could choose between one hundred thousand dollars and Greg being alive, I'd choose Greg being alive.''

Then, there was a bit of embarrassment, when Mark Myrdek of the state police explained to Sisti and the court why he threw away the latex glove that had turned up the day after the murder.

And finally, there was quiet laughter among the reporters in the gallery when an obviously uncomfortable Bill Spencer got on the witness stand.

Sisti tried to learn the source of Spencer's story on the Hillsborough grand jury charges. When that failed, he asked Spencer to talk about how much coverage the case had received. ''I would say it's one of the largest murder stories we've covered,'' the reporter replied.

But perhaps the most compelling place to be during the pretrial hearing was the public waiting room, where Pam's family and friends were wearing and passing out little yellow ribbons. Never mind the American soldiers in the Middle East waiting to go to war with Iraq. These ribbons were for Smart, ''our hostage of the state of New Hampshire.''

When it was all over, the pretrial hearings had failed to

help the accused very much. Judge Gray denied virtually every motion.

Then, on January 22, 1991, the walls came down. Pete Randall agreed to cut a deal with the state. JR Lattime, who had tentatively also agreed to testify against Pam and then changed his mind, was forced to follow suit. As did Billy Flynn.

In exchange for the boys' testimony and pleas of guilty to second-degree murder, the state promised to recommend reduced sentences. Flynn and Randall would receive forty years in prison, with twelve deferred if they remained on good behavior. Lattime would get thirty years, with twelve deferred.

Once the boys began talking, all kinds of information came forth. As a result, the Derry cops would recover the black pillowcase with Pam's jewelry. Back in June, around the time of her son's arrest, Patricia Randall had hidden it in a hole in the wall, behind some insulation, in Pete's bedroom. Now, too, the Lattimes would give the police the box of ammunition that had been purchased for the killing. Diane Lattime said it had been under JR's bed when the police searched the place.

On January 28, Flynn, Randall, and Lattime pleaded guilty to second-degree murder. However, they were caught by channel 9's camera, at the courthouse, laughing, chewing gum, and slapping their hands, seemingly showing no regret whatsoever.

Greg Smart's father was outraged. He had argued with Paul Maggiotto about the plea bargain and made it clear that he wanted his son's killers to serve every day of their lives behind bars, if not worse. And now, to see their behavior, he could not restrain himself.

"What kind of people are these people?" he asked Bill Spencer on camera. "Ask yourself that. Who could do something like that and have no remorse?"

That same day, their case bolstered by statements from the boys, the Derry cops arrested Raymond Fowler in Seabrook. The charges: attempted murder, conspiracy to commit murder, and tampering with physical evidence. (In May 1991, Fowler would also be charged with accomplice to first-degree murder.)

On January 29, 1991, Fowler was to be arraigned in Derry District Court. When the Derry cops hurriedly brought him up the walk toward the front door, a small group of photographers crowded around. Bill Spencer ran over with a microphone and futilely shouted some questions at the teenager.

As reporters and cops milled around in the hallway waiting for the arraignment, a Derry detective was heard to say disgustedly, "Did Raymond answer all of Bill's questions?"

After Fowler was formally charged and bail was set at one hundred thousand dollars, Paul Maggiotto stood in the hallway talking to a group of reporters.

It was obvious that the state's case against Pam, already fairly strong, was now fortified. The journalists asked Maggiotto if he felt more confident. The prosecutor sidestepped the question.

"Oh, come on," one of the reporters finally said. "You *exude* confidence."

Maggiotto smiled. "If you believe that," he said, "then the act is working."

Chapter 12

Jury duty summonses were sent to 300 citizens of Rockingham County, more than for any trial in the county's history.

Because of the boys' plea bargaining, Judge Gray had granted the defense two additional weeks to prepare its case. So it was on February 19, 1991, that the jury pool arrived at the County of Rockingham Administration and Justice Building in Exeter to begin the whittling-away process of *voir dire*.

The bulk of the original 300 prospective jurors had either moved away or died, leaving 147 people to crowd into courtroom one. By midday, the judge excused seventy-five more because they admitted to already having a notion of Pam's guilt or innocence. Such a blanket dismissal was a leniency seldom seen in jury selection. But Gray no doubt wanted to prevent any later challenge to the jury's integrity.

When they were questioned by lawyers for both sides, most of those who remained appeared ready and willing to help decide Pam's fate. One woman, who was ultimately rejected, said her only concern was whether she would have enough outfits for a lengthy trial. Paul Twomey assured her that plenty of people will have worn the same clothes a few times before the trial was out. Particularly the lawyers, he said with a smile.

A gentleman who was spending his retirement raising cattle reported that things would be fine on the farm in his absence. "My wife would have to pull some more chores and we have an exchange student who would have to carry a little more of the load," he said.

Another would-be juror, a woman, was quick to dismiss any suggestion that she had been prejudiced by the press coverage. "I don't read newspapers since I had my house burn to the ground and the paper said it was just a fire in the bedroom,'' she said.

As the lawyers for both sides probed whether Pam's youth and attractiveness might somehow cloud a prospective juror's ability to be objective, a number of the candidates commented on the defendant's comeliness. ''Yesterday was the first time I had seen Pamela Smart and she *is* beautiful,'' remarked one middle-aged lady.

And when asked if it was conceivable that a good-looking adult woman like Pam could indeed be sexually involved with a teenager, most prospective jurors were nonplussed. Time and again they replied: Anything is possible in this day and age.

One homemaker went even further. Plenty of older women are attracted to younger men these days, she said. ''Look at Mary Tyler Moore!''

The defendant seemed not to miss a word. After six and a half months in prison, Pam could now at least make the appearance of having some control in her life.

Each day she sat at the defense table, legal pad and a manila file before her, scribbling notes to herself and her counselors, often whispering to them, and having a say about almost every potential juror.

Despite the defense's doubts—Twomey and Sisti had filed two motions seeking to have the trial held out of the county because of the extensive publicity—a jury was chosen in one week. The only glitch came when seven potential jurors were dismissed for talking about the case as they sat in the waiting room before being interviewed.

By the time the process had ended, the pool of would-be jurors was stretched almost to its limit. Just three people remained to be questioned when Judge Gray peered over the top of his glasses down at the lawyers and said, ''We have fifteen jurors, counselors. That's it.''

The fifteen, of course, included three alternates. Of the twelve who would actually decide Pam's fate, seven were women and five were men. They ranged in age from a twenty-four-year-old man who had recently graduated from Harvard to a seventy-five-year-old woman with a feisty independent streak. They ranged in occupation from a software engineer to a retired bank vice president to a housewife. They were all white, with the exception of one black woman.

After the last juror had been picked, Paul Twomey stood in the hallway surrounded by reporters, and finally relaxed after the wearing, marathonlike process of asking practically the same questions to person after person. He handled each of the reporters' queries patiently—his daily fill-in-the-blanks responses to the progress of jury selection.

When it was time to escape, Twomey did an impersonation that reminded everyone of a scene that Americans had been seeing repeatedly on television over the past few days: He played the part of a Pentagon spokesman being coy about the United States' recently begun ground war in Kuwait.

"And I will make no comment on the bombings or the ground fighting—until I'm sure we win," the attorney said.

Monday, March 4 was set aside to view the crime scene and other key locales.

That morning, Pamela, the jury, the judge, the attorneys, and support staff all set off some thirty miles west from the courthouse to Derry to look at the condo where Greg Smart was slain as well as to see two nearby sites for an overview of the general vicinity.

Just ten months after the murder, Pam was returning to 4E, Misty Morning Drive, where her screams had once shaken her neighbors to the quick. In the cold drizzling rain, with residents curiously peeking out of their windows, two dozen reporters, photographers, and television cameramen descended on the complex.

Summerhill Condominiums looked as if it were under siege as the journalists positioned themselves on doorsteps, sidewalks, and all over the soggy lawn. An arsenal of cameras mounted on monopods and tripods trained on the doorway of Pam's former home, hoping to catch any trace of emotion that the widow might betray upon her arrival.

Judy Liessner, who had pulled Pam into her own condo and tried to comfort her back on May 1, 1990, had not seen her old neighbor since that night. Now she watched through a window and saw a stone-faced Smart, accompanied by a sheriff's deputy, a bailiff, and her lawyers, stride by.

Past the crowd Smart went, past the feverishly clicking and whirring cameras, past the doors she had been pounding on that spring night, and up the steps to her old unit. Unlike the evening of May 1, this time she went inside.

The new tenant had asked that the media stay out of the

condo. So while Pam and the jurors were indoors, the horde passed the time musing about good restaurants and bad editors and catching up on each other. "Have you been covering this case regularly?" one reporter asked another. "Yeah," came the reply. "As you can see I've got an exclusive."

Still, there was work to do. When the lawyers and jurors popped out of the condo onto the back porch, from where Billy Flynn and Pete Randall had made their frenzied getaway, the television crews fell over themselves scrambling to document it. And when Pam and the jurors finally left, the photographers' shutters sounded off like so many ack-ack guns.

From site to site they went—the white unmarked Crown Victoria that ferried Pam, the judge's BMW, the jury bus, and a caravan of media vehicles, which included everything from reporters' personal autos to logo-bearing company cars, half of them with all kinds of strange antennae.

Traveling at a speed of ten miles per hour, the motorcade wound from the condo to the Derry Meadows Professional Park to the Hood Memorial Junior High School. And at each stop, everyone would run around and take pictures of the serious-faced widow and her entourage while the Derry cops ordered everyone to back off.

After lunch they massed again, this time at the seacoast in the parking lot of Winnacunnet High School for a look at Pam's former workplace. Again, all eyes and cameras were on Smart. Perhaps appropriately, all things considered, she looked concerned, almost afraid, as she briskly walked around back into the SAU 21 building. Leaving, she glared at the reporters.

As the jury bus finally began to pull away, a police officer let the journalists know that it was time to leave. "OK, folks," he said. "That's a wrap."

Despite their comments to reporters, Twomey and Sisti did not have a wonderful case to defend and it did not take a Clarence Darrow to figure it out.

Before the trial, of course, few people knew what evidence was coming. But any lawyer who was aware—as Twomey and Sisti obviously were—would have blanched.

It would be a long shot, at best, to counter it all. Not only was Pam's own voice on tape implicating herself time and again, but also there was a wide range of witnesses, many the product of the kids' talking to friends about the murder and its planning, who could be called at any time. The strongest, of course, were the three boys. But others could do damage as well: Cecelia Pierce, Ralph Welch, Cindy Butt, for starters.

Given any single scenario, Twomey and Sisti probably had a chance. Most likely, they could have found a way to have Loring Jackson and Dan Pelletier tugging on their collars on the witness stand. Or they could have raised enough doubts about the teenage boys who were angling to someday get out of prison. Possibly, they could even have convinced twelve people that what they heard Pam saying on tape was not what she meant.

But all of it in one case? Why would *everyone* be trying to frame the widow? And what single story could possibly explain so many damning statements, facts, and actions that were coming from all sides?

The unpredictable nature of a jury makes an acquittal possible in any trial. But no matter what Twomey and Sisti said, that did not seem to be something the defense could realistically expect.

A hung jury, however, was more reasonable. If Twomey and Sisti could pull that off, it was a safe bet that the counselors would be clinking champagne glasses toasting everyone from Paul Maggiotto on down to the courtroom bailiff who placidly rolled his tie up and down his chest throughout the proceedings.

To get a hung jury, the defense did not need a knockout. The lawyers just needed to counterpunch and cast some doubt on the state's case. In other words, cover up when the left and right hooks came raining down and hang in there. Boxer Muhammad Ali had a name for it—the rope-a-dope.

If the defense lawyers were still standing when the final bell rang, maybe, just maybe, they could pull if off.

Tuesday, March 5 dawned gray and chilly in Exeter. With the roads still slick in places from the rain the day before, would-be spectators began wheeling into the courthouse parking lot around seven, a half hour before the doors even opened, two and a half hours before Pamela took center stage in the most publicized trial New Hampshire had ever seen.

Finally it was about to begin. All of the pretrial maneuvering was over. The opposing sides in the *State of New Hampshire* v. *Pamela Smart* 90-S-1370, 1371, and 1372 were finally facing one another in trial.

By 9:15 the second-floor hallway and waiting room outside courtroom one was jammed with 200 people—reporters, relations and friends of Pam's and Greg's, the curious, as well as the rueful others who simply had business there that day.

In the mid sixties, when the courthouse was built, its designers could never have imagined any trial attracting the media barrage of this one. By now, the twenty-five-year-old structure had become too small for even much of the court's regular business.

But with the Pamela Smart case attracting overflow crowds and a few onlookers who appeared to be unstable, it also became obvious that it was not the most secure building. "I think there is a hostage-taking situation waiting to happen," a local attorney complained to a reporter from the *Hampton Union*. "And as one of the potential hostages, I object."

That morning, red-jacketed bailiffs ran metal detectors across everyone entering Judge Gray's courtroom. Before court one day, a bomb-sniffer German shepherd would be called in as well, prompting Paul Twomey to jest, "There's Halen! Our first witness!"

Officially, the room could only seat eighty, but nearly 100 people crammed in for the opening arguments. Throughout the trial, a handful of family members of various court officials would, as a courtesy, be seated closer to the action, along the wall opposite the jury and in front of the gallery. On day one, Judge Gray's wife and her guests were among those with the equivalent of box seats.

The gallery itself consisted of only eight pewlike rows, four on either side with a pale green carpeted aisle separating them. This was the nightmarish antithesis of the Smart–Wojas nuptials of May 1989. The first row on the left was reserved for the Smart family and friends. Across from them, on the right, were the Wojases and Pam's supporters.

The thirty-five reporters and photographers settled into the three rows behind Pam's family. The three rows behind the Smarts went to the general public. So many people wanted to attend the trial that after day one, numbers would be given out each morning. Only the first thirty people, many of whom were arriving in the wee hours of the morning, had a courtroom seat for the day.

Judge Gray, a firm believer in media access to the judicial system, had also permitted two television cameras in the rear of the court—a pool camera for the Boston stations and one from Manchester's WMUR, which intended to cover portions of the trial live.

Across the hall from the courtroom, the waiting area had been partitioned into two rooms. One provided a closed-circuit TV, placed on top of the Pepsi machine, for those who were shut out of the courtroom. The other was a broadcast media center, packed with monitors and video equipment as well as a dozen or more television and radio reporters.

At 9:28, escorted by a sheriff's deputy, Pamela strode into the courtroom wearing a dark blue suit. Her hair, not colored since before her arrest in August, had recently been dyed lighter. She had also changed her hairstyle during her confinement. Earlier her hair had barely reached the base of her neck. Now it dangled onto her shoulder blades, with long curls in front touching her clavicle, the rest pulled back and secured by a black ribbon.

Pam was also thinner, so much so, a friend confided, that her mother had had to pin her skirt to fit before she came into court.

Two minutes later, the jury filed in, followed soon after by Judge Gray. The justice seated himself at the bench in front of the American and New Hampshire flags. On the wall behind him was a gold, hand-carved American eagle, wings spread, with Old Glory clutched in its claws. The judge, who found relaxation in woodwork, had crafted the bird himself.

Before him and to his right sat Gray's law clerk, Kathleen Duggan, and to his left the court stenographer, Bill Wojtkowski.

On the wall facing the jury was a near life-sized, full length portrait of the great Daniel Webster, which for some lawyers was an unsettling sight. "I always get the feeling that Webster's going to step down from there and correct me or something," a defense attorney once lamented.

The room quieted. Gray nodded his OK. And Diane Nicolosi strode to the rostrum facing the jury. She introduced herself and Paul Maggiotto.

This was only Nicolosi's third opening statement in a murder trial and she was anxious. The prosecutor spoke haltingly and stumbled over words and phrases. Still, the story that Nicolosi was unfolding was compelling enough to transcend her mild manner and verbal mishaps.

"On May 1, 1990," she said, "Gregory Smart came home from a late business meeting. . . . He opened his front door, he turned on his lights, and he called for his dog. But his dog didn't respond that night . . . ."

For a half hour Nicolosi went on, methodically laying out the state's case. She also set to undermine the defense's anticipated arguments. She explained away the problems of Cecelia having signed a movie deal by pointing out that the contract only came after the girl came forward to the police. She hammered home the point that the boys were receiving deals in exchange for their *truthful* testimony. And when all was said and done, she said, there would be the incriminating tapes.

"Ladies and gentlemen," Nicolosi concluded, "we are sure that when you hear the testimony of William Flynn, Patrick Randall, Vance Lattime, Jr., Cecelia Pierce, and all of the other witnesses that we'll present to you at this trial, that you will come to the only possible verdicts in this case. At the close of the trial, Paul Maggiotto will stand before you and he will ask that you return three verdicts of guilty."

Probably no attorney in New Hampshire was of greater contrast to Nicolosi than Mark Sisti. If Nicolosi seemed to warily dip her toe in the water before venturing forth, Sisti disdainfully jumped in with both feet, looking to splash everybody around. She was quiet; he was loud. She was humble; he was brash. Inexperienced, she seemed to recite her opening remarks. Sisti, on the other hand, ad-libbed with pleasure. And while Nicolosi never revealed if the slightest bit of outrage coursed through her veins, Sisti showed little else.

Jabbing a finger at the jury and lifting the rostrum as he spoke, Sisti dubbed the state's case "one of the most vile concoctions ever assembled in one courtroom in New Hampshire" and "one of the most toxic soups that you will have to engulf and drink." He sneered at the state's key witnesses, sarcastically calling them "poor young boys." He slashed away at the very idea of their accepting a deal "to save their hides." He branded their upcoming testimony "cock and bull stories."

Billy Flynn, Sisti said, was a teenager who was crazed by an infatuation with Pam Smart and that "thrill killers" best described Flynn and his buddies, Pete Randall and JR Lattime. "These people are sick," Sisti said. "These people are obsessed. And these people aren't innocent little manipulated boys." All the state's key witness, from the three youths to Cecelia Pierce, stood to gain or lose by implicating Pam in her husband's murder, Sisti said.

Couched in this offensive, however, Sisti was ceding ground. The jury was unaware, of course, but for the first time, the defense acknowledged that Pam had indeed been having an affair with a high school sophomore. (After months of denial, Pam herself waited until just days before the opening statements to break this news to her diehard friends.)

"But let me tell you something about this affair," Sisti said. "It was an affair wherein Pam repeatedly attempted to break it off with an obsessed, infatuated sixteen year old. It is an affair that had nothing to do with Pam's involvement in the killing.

"Did it trigger Flynn to go on his little fantasy and his little thrill kill? You bet it did. Did he think everything would be, you know, OK, if he killed this woman's husband? You bet."

As for the tapes, which at this point had been heard only by a select few, Sisti beseeched the jury to look deeper than surface appearances and to put the secret recordings in the context of a confused young widow who had been shut out of the investigation into her husband's death.

So this was it. After months of keeping the cards close to the vest, this at last would be Pam's defense—an assault on the credibility of the key witnesses, a shameful admission of marital infidelity, and an explanation that said the jury had to look deeper than the surface appearances of Pam's words on the tapes.

"Be patient," Sisti told the jury. "You promised Pam that you could give her a fair trial and we believe you. We believe each and every one of you. And if you do give her a fair trial, if you in fact give her a fair trial, you will return with not guilty verdicts.''

Early in the proceedings, Paul Twomey had approached the prosecutors with a request to be told at the end of each day whom the expected witnesses would be the following day.

All of the lawyers except Nicolosi were parents. Twomey's two year old, in fact, developed bronchitis around the beginning of the trial and would keep the attorney and his wife awake nights throughout the course of the proceedings. The Smart case had been grueling for everyone's family.

Now, none of the attorneys wished to stay awake all night preparing for a witness that the other side had no intention of calling. Maggiotto and Nicolosi agreed to reveal whom they planned to summon, but they wanted the same favor in return—including what the likelihood was of Pam's taking the stand in her own defense.

Often, the uncertainty of whether the defendant will testify gives the defense a tactical advantage. In Pam's case, however, the evidence was so heavily against her that Smart almost necessarily would have to testify. The prosecutors probably could have guessed.

The deal, which was not unusual among attorneys who were civil, was struck.

That first day, the prosecution paraded out a variety of witnesses—neighbor Paul Dacier, for instance, and Derry patrolman Gerald Scaccia—who essentially set the scene of Gregory Smart's murder.

Every good prosecutor, however, is aware of the showmanship aspect of a trial, of the need to keep the jurors interested, and to bring them into the heart of the case as soon as possible. So the last witness on day one was Pete Randall.

For the first time, the public would hear the murder of Gregory Smart described firsthand.

Randall, wearing a red and black sweater, was a tough kid—physically and apparently mentally. Some people believed he tended to compartmentalize his emotions, blocking out certain memories or thoughts, which allowed him to recount even a murder without affect.

Whatever the reasons, the only time that Pete Randall seemed remotely human that day was when he first climbed behind the witness stand. About to be sworn in, Randall nervously raised his left hand instead of his right and then sheepishly corrected himself.

For most of the afternoon, Pete delivered his testimony in a flat, some would say clinical manner that led many observers to regard him as being as cold-blooded as they come.

"Now, let me call your attention to May 1, 1990," said Paul Maggiotto. "Do you recall that day?"

"Yes, I do," said Randall, matter-of-factly.

"Did you go to school that day?"

"Yes, I did."

"Can you tell me what you did after school?"

"I went to Haverhill to pick up JR's grandmother's car in order to go to Derry to kill Gregory Smart."

Randall might as well have been listing engine components.

His manner of speaking, though, was far less revolting than what Randall had to say about the slaying. It would hit no one harder than Greg's mother, who at one point burst into tears, jumped up, and hurried from the courtroom, leading Judge Gray to grant a recess.

The next day, Mark Sisti got a shot at Randall. Pete, who over the years had made comments to his buddies about whether or not he could kill someone, was the defense's best chance to further the theory that the boys were "thrill killers."

Sisti did not even bother to acknowledge Randall's existence before he started in on him.

"Uh, Pam Smart didn't make you kill anybody, right?" the lawyer asked.

"She didn't *make* me kill anybody," Randall replied.

It went on like that for most of the cross-examination, but by the time it was over, Sisti had unintentionally brought out a softer side of Randall that the jury had not seen the day before.

At one point, Sisti got Pete talking about his mother. What came through was a kid who for better or worse was obviously protective of her.

Sisti also asked Pete why he had beaten up Ralph Welch. Rather than play the tough guy, Randall began to speak about the Lattimes' adopted son, Ryan. "Ralph had said things that I didn't like," Pete said. "I mean, he had said things that, about me being mean, and maybe hurting a kid, a little kid that I really cared for.''

All the same, no one was going to be sending Pam Smart away for life based on what Randall had to say.

Then JR Lattime took the stand. He also came off as distant and unmoved by the murder. Sisti shook him from the beginning with questions about the boys discussing the case while they were in custody. The lawyer seemed to be suggesting that the teenagers had concocted an elaborate tale that blamed Pam for the murder.

Sisti also asked JR to talk about his response to the killing. He brought up the singing of ''Shoofly Pie'' and JR's comments to investigators that on the night of the murder he had been relatively unaffected by Greg's death.

''So the first night it doesn't bother you and then over time it bothers you,'' said Sisti. ''Is that what you're saying?''

''The first night the actual fact that somebody had been killed didn't even sink in,'' said JR. ''I was, like I said, scared, nervous. We tried to get back. Like I said, we went back to Seabrook; I dropped everybody off, and I went right home and went to bed.''

''OK,'' said Sisti, ''it didn't bother you because you didn't even know the guy?''

''At first that night . . . I used to think, 'Well, I didn't know him.' It's just like, you know, if you see somebody get killed over, you know, on TV, like if you see the news and that . . . And the more and more I thought about it, the more and more it started to bother me.''

For the most part, the trial was progressing smoothly. On Friday, March 8, however, while JR was being cross-examined, Judge Gray suddenly ended the proceedings for the day and instructed the lawyers not to speak to anyone about the reason.

Bill Smart stood up in the front row of the courtroom and quietly demanded that Paul Maggiotto tell him what was going on. He was afraid that JR, who had taken the Fifth Amendment just a few minutes earlier, had somehow caused a mistrial.

The prosecutor took the Smarts into a room and explained that it had nothing to do with JR. Instead, a call had come in to the courthouse for Diane Nicolosi. On the telephone was a woman who called herself Linda Avory. It was incredible, but the woman said she had attended grammar school with Pam Smart and was holding an incriminating letter from Pam about the murder.

The woman reported that Pam had written to her before Greg's death, saying the Smarts were having problems in their marriage and that Pam planned to have Greg killed. After the murder, the woman said, Smart offered to buy the letter back for ten thousand dollars.

After much hesitancy, the woman said she was coming forward and planned to deliver the letter to the Derry police department that afternoon.

She failed to show or call, however, and the prosecutors decided that she had merely been a crank caller.

The trial resumed on Monday, and Sisti and Twomey went back to working at neutralizing the state's witnesses. For the most part, they were successful. Randall's coldness proved to be off-putting. And JR seemed less than completely honest.

The flow of the trial turned, however, when Billy Flynn took the stand. Tall, with sad brown eyes, Flynn seemed to be the least likely "triggerman," as some of the journalists would later describe him.

On his first day of testimony, Flynn recalled how he met Smart, the first time they kissed, and the first time they had sex. The details had much of the gallery fascinated yet shifting uncomfortably in their seats.

"And had you ever made love to another woman before?" Paul Maggiotto asked.

"No, I hadn't," said Flynn.

"That was your first time?"

"Yes, it was."

"Is that what you told Pam?"

"Uh, no, it wasn't."

As his testimony went on that day, Flynn would also reveal the discussions and previous attempt that led to the murder.

For the media, it was sensational stuff, an intimate look into Pam's use of sex to manipulate the boy. The evening news and the next day's newspapers jumped into the Smart trial wholeheartedly. Billy's photo was on page one in both Boston newspapers and all over New Hampshire and northern Massachusetts.

"Smart's teen killer recounts sex romp," screamed the

tabloid *Boston Herald*. "Gunman: Teacher seduced me with
striptease." Meanwhile, the *Union Leader*, as it did with
much of its trial coverage, stretched a two-line banner headline across page one in a typeface most papers reserve for
declarations of war. "Flynn: Pam Smart Said, 'If You Love
Me, You'd Do This For Me.'"

The next day, Billy's seventeenth birthday, Maggiotto
asked the teenager to recall the murder. Flynn had never
been able to talk about Greg Smart's death without becoming
emotional. In pretrial interviews, he had wept in front of
Dan Pelletier and Paul Maggiotto as well as the defense
team's lawyers.

Now, a packed courtroom and a live television audience
watched raptly.

Maggiotto, knowing that he had a witness who could not
contain his emotions, was like a conductor as he brought
the boy's story to a crescendo. First, the prosecutor had
Flynn actually kneel on the courtroom floor before the jury.
Ostensibly, the prosecutor wanted the boy to demonstrate
how Greg had been positioned. Then, he showed Flynn the
knife. And then, the gun. With each new request, Billy's
eyes would again well up.

Afterward, Twomey and Sisti would jibe the prosecutor,
bestowing him with the nickname, "the Milkman," because
Maggiotto had milked Flynn's revelations and emotions for
all they were worth.

The teenager's testimony, punctuated with sniffles and
sobs, was heart wrenching, so much so that Judy and Bill
Smart were baffled by their response. Their son's murderer
was describing Greg's death and yet they felt sorry for the
boy.

Indeed, it was hard to feel anything else.

"After you pointed the gun at his head what'd you do?"
asked Maggiotto.

"I just stood there," said Billy.

"How long was it?"

"A hundred years it seemed like. And, unh, I said, um,
god forgive me."

By now Billy was weeping, but inside Paul Maggiotto
was surely smiling.

"After you said, god forgive me, what happened?" the
prosecutor asked.

Billy waited seven long seconds. "I pulled the trigger," he said, crying.

Try as he might that afternoon, Mark Sisti could not discredit Billy Flynn. As he'd done with Randall and Lattime, Sisti came out on the attack. The lawyer asked about the day after the murder and if Flynn remembered buying Sal Parks lunch with the money from Greg's wallet.

Apparently trying to shake him, the attorney also forced the boy to look directly at Pam. Billy had said that Pam once showed him a bruise, supposedly inflicted by Greg. So Sisti asked Smart to stand and told the boy to tell where the bruise had been. Flynn kept his composure.

Ever loyal to his friends, Flynn tried to defend Pete Randall, whom Billy felt the media had unjustly criticized as cold-blooded.

"OK," said Sisti, "in order to be fair, to be treated fairly by the media, you got to show some emotion up there, do ya?"

"No," said Billy. "I don't really care what the media thinks."

"You don't care?"

"No, I care what Greg's parents think."

"So you're crying for Greg's parents today?"

"No, I'm crying because I feel bad about it and I wish I never did it."

Sisti tried to hammer away at his theme that Billy was an obsessed lover, who'd killed Pam's husband without her knowledge. But Billy hung tough.

"Greg was in your way, right?" Sisti said.

"Greg was in my way?" said Flynn.

"Yeah, I mean, as long as Pam was with Greg you couldn't have Pam, right?"

"No," Flynn said. "As long as I didn't kill Greg for Pam I couldn't be with . . . I could be with Pam, but she threatened to break up with me."

"She threatened you. So you're telling this jury that the only reason that you killed Greg is because you loved Pam. Is that what you're saying?"

"No," Flynn said. "It's because Pam told me to and I loved Pam."

"And you would do whatever Pam told you to do. Is that what you're saying to this jury?"

"Whatever Pam told me to do? Yes, I probably would back then, yes."

"It's kinda like you had no brain at all?"

"I had a brain. I just, I was in love."

Billy Flynn came off as a devastated, remorseful young man. Not a liar. And certainly not someone who killed for mere titillation.

The defense surely saw it as well. Sisti soon sounded the retreat and finished his cross-examination.

Every day that the trial continued, media coverage intensified. A crew from *Entertainment Tonight* showed up. And reporters were coming in from all over the country and in some cases from around the world. Virtually all of the new arrivals were forced to watch the proceedings on television in the congested waiting room.

Other than the sheer numbers, which would burgeon to more than 100, and occasional lapses of manners, the media for the most part was restrained. Pam's daily walks from the small conference room that served as a holding cell to the courtroom and back drew the bright lights of dozens of photographers and cameramen. Even her trips to the ladies' room were documented.

At one point, in the outer hallway, someone from CNN stuck a microphone in front of Smart's face, prompting a sheriff's deputy to shove the offender against a wall. The incident also led Judge Gray to beckon all of the journalists to a meeting in his courtroom, where he doled out a verbal spanking—just in case anyone else had ideas about causing a disruption.

Yet the media's worst moment occurred the day before Cecelia Pierce testified. Cecelia and her family had come to court on Thursday, March 14, but the girl was not called to the stand that day.

After court ended, though, television crews and photographers positioned themselves outside the little room where the Eaton family had been waiting.

In a disturbing scene, the crowd swarmed around the family, pushing and shoving, as they all moved down the stairs. Cecelia, her stepfather, and best friend Karen Crowley decided to make a break for the car. Mrs. Eaton and one of the witness advocates stopped to get their coats, then headed toward the parking lot.

"When we got to the door, we could hear all this screaming,'' recalled Mrs. Eaton. "We looked out and saw all this running. I thought, Well, Christ!

"It looked like a football game and someone had fumbled the football. The only thing was that Cecelia was the football. The first thing that hit me was, Jesus, what is going on?

"Cecelia and Karen were totally petrified, but they got to the point that instead of crying they were laughing. And they got to laughing hysterically 'cause they couldn't help it.

"They were out there running around with all of these adults chasing after them. One cameraman was going so fast backwards that he went right into a car, right up on the hood, and rolled off of it. Another cameraman dropped his microphone and stuff and just kept running, dragging it on the ground behind him while everybody just jumped over it and stepped on it. He didn't care, they were just running.''

Finally, the family found their car and made their way out of the parking lot. Before heading home, they pulled over to the side of the road, looked at each other in disbelief, and burst into laughter.

When Cecelia finally did make it to the stand, she reverted to her bored, why-are-you-wasting-my-time airs, just as she had on the day that Captain Jackson yelled at her. Cecelia was scared—so much so that she was crying beforehand—but what people saw was a kid with an attitude.

Still, she corroborated Billy's testimony. Although Cecelia put the time of the incident in late April, she told the court about watching the movie *9 1/2 Weeks* with Pam and Billy. She also remembered Smart and the boy going upstairs and Billy coming back down for some ice. And lastly, she recollected accidentally catching the lovers in the act.

"When the movie was over, I had watched parts of another and I was just getting bored,'' Cecelia said. "And so I was walking up the stairs and I,—I yelled, you know, 'I hope you guys are done.' And then I went upstairs and they weren't.''

"What did you see?'' asked Maggiotto.

"Pam and Bill naked,'' said Cecelia.

"And where were they?''

"On the floor.''

"In what room?''

"In Greg's bedroom.''

"And, what kind of position were they in?"

"Pam was on top of Bill."

At this, a reporter in the gallery whispered, "Why doesn't that surprise me?"

Cecelia was an important witness. At the same time, however, her role in the case had diminished in the last month. From the moment of Pam's arrest through most of January, Cecelia had been expected to be the state's star witness. But after the boys agreed to testify, she became less pivotal.

What's more, Billy Flynn had revealed that Cecelia knew more about the murder than she had told authorities. The state never considered it enough to charge Cecelia as one of the conspirators, but the fact that she had tried to help Billy find a weapon became a blow to her credibility.

And Mark Sisti swarmed all over it in court.

"On that same topic," the attorney said, "when you had this heart-to-heart truthful conversation with the police on June 14, 1990, did you discuss with the police that you were trying to get a firearm to kill Greg Smart?"

"I don't remember," said Cecelia uncomfortably.

"You don't remember?"

"I don't think I did."

"But that—that was the, wasn't that the day that you told Mr. Maggiotto and this jury that you were gonna tell the truth to the police?"

"Yes."

"But you didn't tell the truth to the police then."

"I told the truth as I remembered it," Cecelia said peevishly. "It was late at night. I told everything I could remember and I did tell them. As soon as I remembered about that I told them."

"Well, who did you tell so that we can check it out?"

"I'm not sure."

It was vintage Sisti, taking one crack in the witness's story and using it to cast doubt on her entire testimony. The only problem was that the lawyer was only leaving the doubt dangling in the air. Sisti never clearly showed why Cecelia would lie about Pam's involvement.

That Friday, after Cecelia Pierce and Cindy Butt testified, the prosecution rested. Over eight days of testimony, Maggiotto and Nicolosi had called twenty-seven witnesses.

They also entered a variety of items into evidence, ranging

from the secretly recorded tapes to the lyrics of a heavy metal tune—''First Love,'' by the Christian band Stryper—that Pam supposedly wrote out for Billy.

Also displayed were a series of glossies of a smiling Pam in her two-piece bathing suit. The night before his arrest, Flynn threw away the pictures that Pam had given him. But Karen Knight, who owned the one-hour photo shop where the film was developed, testified that she just happened to have saved a number of faulty copies. (After the trial, a sign outside of the Knights' small shop on Route 1, blared: THE REVEALING SMART PHOTOS WERE DONE RIGHT HERE!! GET CUSTOM PROCESSING NOW.)

On Monday, it would be the defense's turn. And as reporters left for their offices to write their stories for the next day's papers, one question lingered: Would Pamela Smart testify in her own behalf?

When Monday arrived, all indications to the uncertain public were that Pam would give her side of the story.

Citing a source ''close to the case,'' correspondent Tami Plyler had an article in that morning's *Union Leader* that said Smart was expected to take the stand.

Pam confirmed it when she walked into court wearing a conservative navy blue suit, with a frilled high-collar blouse, and a black bow in her hair. If ever there was an outfit selected for courtroom testimony this was it.

That morning, three individuals were called by the defense.

The first was a Derry police dispatcher, who was used to help introduce into evidence the tapes of the emergency calls on the night of May 1.

The second was Pam's friend Sonia Simon, who said Smart behaved irrationally after the killing. ''She was almost crazy, I want to say,'' Sonia recalled. ''She wasn't the same.'' Maggiotto, in turn, mercilessly tore into Simon, making her admit that Pam had deceived even her closest friends about the affair.

The third witness was Pamela Ann Smart.

Speaking in quiet tones, for effect, Paul Twomey conducted the direct examination. Although she appeared nervous at first, Pam settled into her role as witness.

Pam told of her marriage to Greg, culminating in his affair the previous December; Pam said she had been devastated when she learned of it. She also spoke of her job at SAU 21 and how she became involved with the teenagers. And she recounted an off-and-on love affair with Flynn.

Unlike Billy, who vaguely remembered the day being in mid February, Pam definitively said she first had sex with Billy on March 24. Perhaps not so coincidentally, Billy would have been sixteen in Pam's version—too old for the widow to be charged with felonious sexual assault—but fifteen in Billy's account.

That spring, Pam said, she repeatedly tried to break off the affair. Billy, however, was taking it hard, even mentioning the possibility of suicide. Finally, toward the end of the last week in April, Pam said, she ended the relationship for good.

"Could you describe Billy's behavior and emotions as you had this conversation at this time?" asked Twomey.

"He was crying," said Pam, "and then he stopped crying. He seemed mad at first but then all the sudden he just didn't seem mad anymore. He just asked if we could be friends."

As the questioning went on, Pam explained that Billy had indeed been at her condo the week that Greg was in Rhode Island. A few days before her final breakup with the teenager, she said, the boy had dinner at her place and had even been downstairs in the basement by himself.

The suggestion was obvious: Billy left the bulkhead open so that he could get into the condo and murder Greg.

As her testimony continued, Smart corroborated almost everything the boys and Cecelia had said. She admitted to having sex with the teenager, to letting Billy use the car one evening in April (apparently the night of the first attempt on Greg's life), to driving the boys to get JR's grandmother's car, and even to being with the boys on the Sunday that Ralph Welch went to the police.

But every admission had a twist to it. Every ending suggested that she knew nothing of the murder plot.

On and on it went, culminating in Pam's explanation of her incriminating conversations with Cecelia Pierce.

Hungry for information, locked out of the police investigation, and disbelieving that the arrested boys were involved in Greg's death, Pam said she came to believe that Cecelia had knowledge of the slaying.

"So what did you do?" asked Twomey.

"Well, I figured that if she knew more about the murde
then she would tell me if I acted like I knew more abou
it," said Pam. "And I told her, well, she had said to m
that, she had asked me, did I know about the murder be
forehand. And initially I had said no.

"And then she made a statement to me that if I knev
more about it, that as long as I told her that, that she wouldn
tell anyone and that we had to stick together.

"So in my mind I thought that I would play a game wit
her and I would say that I knew more about the murder.

"Now, when you said play a game, what's the game?
asked Twomey. "What's going on? What's the point o
this?"

"To get information," said Pam.

It was far-fetched, but a least Smart had a story, no sma
feat considering the range of evidence. Where she los
ground, however, was in her unemotional presentation.
Billy Flynn had duped her, as Pam suggested, one woul
expect a least a little outrage and tears from the widow.
did not help that she remained dry eyed when recollectin
the night of Greg's death.

Now it was Paul Maggiotto's turn.

That morning, the prosecutor had stunned almost every
one in the courtroom with the needless demolition of Soni
Simon. The woman was little more than a character witnes
for Pam, and Maggiotto, perhaps anxious to finally cross
examine someone, had reduced her to tears.

With Simon having been only an innocent bystander, on
could imagine what was in store for Pam.

Strangely enough, there had been discussions among th
prosecutors proposing that Maggiotto do practically nothing
One idea was for him to simply ask, "Are you Pamel
Smart?" After she replied that she was, the prosecuto
would then ask, "Is that your voice on those tapes?" Pan
of course, would say yes. And Maggiotto, in turn, woul
say, "Thank you very much," and sit down.

Instead, the prosecutor opted to question the defendan

Immediately, Maggiotto zeroed in on Pam's failure, eve
after Billy's arrest, to tell the police about her affair wit
the boy.

"I thought if the police knew that I had an affair wit
Bill then they would automatically conclude that I was in
volved in the murder," Pam testified.

"So rather than get what you thought was the wrong person off—you can get him out of trouble—and go and tell the police about the affair, you thought it was more important to keep quiet and keep the affair quiet, right?" asked Maggiotto.

"Yes."

"So this was a conscious decision on your part *not* to tell the police about the affair."

"Right. And also the police never asked me."

"*O-o-o-oh*, they didn't ask you," said Maggiotto sarcastically. "*O-o-o-h*, if they would have asked you, you would have told them, right?"

"I can't speculate on that. I don't know."

Maggiotto would return to the point again and again. Despite all that was happening, from the murder of her husband to the police investigation to the arrest of the boys, Pam never came forward with information about her affair to the police, even though she said she had suspicions that Billy was involved.

Next, Maggiotto asked Pam to talk about her relationship with Flynn. Pam's version was that it was a tumultuous, on-again, off-again affair.

"All right," said Maggiotto, "do you want this jury to understand that Bill Flynn decided to kill your husband because you broke up with him?"

"I want this jury to understand the truth," Pam replied.

"Is that what you're claiming the truth is?"

"I don't know why Bill Flynn killed Greg. I can just come in here and give my testimony."

"So even as you sit here today, you still have no idea why he may have done this. Is that it?"

"I didn't say I had no idea, but I don't know specifically."

"Well, I'm asking you. What do you think? Why do you think he did this?"

"Probably because he thought we could be together."

Pam had certainly covered all of her bases. She had given Billy Flynn a motive. Now all she had to do was explain her own actions, in particular her taped conversations with Cecelia Pierce.

Smart claimed that it was shortly after the boys were arrested that she began her so-called "game" to garner information from Cecelia.

As such, the comments Pam made in the secretly recorded conversations were continuations of this supposed attempt to learn more. Meanwhile, her efforts to stop Cecelia from going to the police were attempts to protect herself from being unjustly accused. By playing this game with Pierce, Pam said, she now found herself in danger of being convicted.

Maggiotto was unimpressed. First, he said, Pam was hiding her affair with the accused killer of her husband. On top of that, she now had a girl who mistakenly thought Pam was involved in the murder and was threatening to go to the authorities.

"So obviously you ran right down to the police and straightened it out, right?" Maggiotto asked.

"No," said Smart. "It's pretty confusing, isn't it?"

"Yeah, it sure is," said Maggiotto. "It's very confusing and you didn't do a *damn* thing to try and straighten it out, did you?"

With that, Gray called the afternoon recess. A fire alarm—false, it turned out—sounded during the break, and court was canceled for the rest of the day.

That day, televisions in homes and businesses all over New Hampshire had been tuned to the trial. Bill Spencer's employer, WMUR in Manchester, had originally planned to broadcast only portions of the proceedings live. But the interest had been so strong that most of the trial was aired. Some of the Boston television reporters, in fact, were laughingly calling WMUR "New Hampshire's Smart station— All Smart, all the time."

WMUR officials were smiling as well—at the skyrocketing ratings. *General Hospital* was boring compared to the real-life drama playing out in the Rockingham County Superior Court. Pam's testimony, in fact, produced ratings higher than the station had seen in its thirty-seven-year history. At one point as many as 130,000 people watched Pam on the witness stand.

By now, Pam's trial received play all over the country. Reporters were flying in from everywhere. But no media outlet ran with the story any harder than the spunky *Boston Herald*, which gave it five pages of coverage after Pam's first day of testimony. "Cold as ice," screamed the page-one headline. "Smart shows no emotion in denying murder plot."

Herald columnist Peter Gelzinis, who dubbed Pam the "ice princess," could not get enough of the story. He wrote: "Should Pam get the guillotine—as seemed to be the general consensus of the overflow crowd huddled around the Pepsi machine in the waiting room—it may well be for her complete and utter inability to work up one, solitary tear of sorrow.

"A local TV reporter, shaking his head, offered this critique of Pam's morning appearance on the stand: 'I think her lawyer should have told her to stick some onion slices down her blouse. She's gotta get those tear ducts working sometime soon, or she's had it.'"

The newspaper outdid itself, however, establishing a 900 telephone number for readers to call in—at ninety-five cents a shot—and vote for whether they thought Pam was guilty or innocent. (Five hundred and forty three callers voted thumbs-down, and 101 opted for not guilty. The newspaper donated what money it made on the poll to charity.)

On Tuesday, Pam was on the stand again, only this time neither the prosecutor nor the defendant gained much ground. Instead, it was toe-to-toe combat.

Despite thoroughly going over the taped conversations with Pam, Maggiotto could not shake her story that she was obsessed with finding Greg's killer and was playacting on the tapes to learn more about the murder.

"I wanted to solve it in my own mind, in my own life, first," Smart said.

"OK," said Maggiotto, "and then what were you gonna do? Make a citizen's arrest?"

"No, I wasn't," said Pam. "At some point obviously I would have gone to the police with it."

"So, Pam Smart, a twenty-three-year-old student-teacher was going to use her own investigation skills, do her own investigation, not tell the police what you know, talk to Cecelia Pierce, go out and talk to whoever else she knows, and then, of course, write a report and just mail it in. I mean, what were you gonna do?"

Paul Twomey objected to the question as speech making, but Judge Gray overruled.

"First of all, I'm not a teacher," said Pam. "And second of all, yes, that was my intention, to figure it out on my own. My husband was murdered. I was not thinking rationally at the time. And unless you've gone through something like this, then maybe you can't understand."

Later, when an observer noted that the face-off between Maggiotto and Smart seemed to be a battle of the two most intelligent people in the room, one courthouse veteran made a correction: "It was the two people who *thought* they were the most intelligent."

Maggiotto probably should have finished sooner. Smart's explanation itself was unconvincing, but her ability to stay with it through all the twists and turns was remarkable.

The prosecutor was getting nowhere, and Smart was beginning to pick up momentum. "If I was guilty I would have pleaded guilty and plea-bargained with the rest of them," she snapped at one point.

Finally, Maggiotto did conclude. Ironically, his last questions resembled the cross-examination he had considered beforehand and abandoned.

"Is that your voice on the tapes of July 12 and July 13?" the prosecutor asked.

"Yes, it is," said Pam.

"I have no further questions."

Twomey and Sisti had little else to offer. They called Greg's friend Brian Washburn, who said Greg had told him about his affair. He also testified that around the time of the body-wire conversations, either on July 10 or July 13, Pam had made remarks suggesting that she might act as if she knew more about the murder, to elicit information from Cecelia.

Few people put it beyond Pam to try to cover for herself by saying such a thing to her friends, particularly since her lawyers had warned her that summer that Cecelia might someday put on a body wire.

Nicolosi went in for the kill with Washburn. It was essentially a nonissue, but she scored her biggest points when she asked the young man about some of the deals he was considering with movie companies that were interested in buying his rights to the story.

"So it's OK to enter into a contract and make money off the death of your best friend, right?" Nicolosi said.

Washburn sat quietly, contemplating the question and, no doubt, his lost friend.

"Everybody else is," he finally said. "It's not . . . I don't know. No, it's not all right."

By mid afternoon, all the witnesses had been called. At 2:35 P.M. on March 19, the defense rested.

At 4:45 on Wednesday morning, the day that the closing statements were to be given, Judy Smart was awoken by a telephone call. Her heart was pounding as she went to answer it, fearing that, god forbid, someone else in the family had been hurt.

Instead, it was an individual with miraculous news.

"Mrs. Smart," said the caller, "My name's Linda Avory. I've been up all night thinking about this and I've decided that I have to tell you this."

"OK," said Judy, just beginning to clear her head. "What is it?"

"I'm the one who had the affair with Greg."

"OK," said Judy, anticipating more.

"Yes, and I also have his baby."

Judy could not believe it. This was the same woman who had called Diane Nicolosi at the court in the middle of JR Lattime's cross-examination.

The woman began to explain. She lived in Milford, Connecticut, and had met Greg through his work. Several months ago, she said, she had given birth to Greg's son.

Judy woke up her husband, who spoke to the woman as well. Bill Smart remembers a lovely, pleasant voice, but more important, she sounded sincere.

The Smarts were not easily convinced, however, and asked why Pam would ever write her a letter telling of her plans to kill Greg.

"Oh," the woman replied without missing a beat, "it's because Pam knew that Greg and I were having the affair." As she went on with her elaborate explanation, it all made sense.

The conversation ended with the woman promising to contact Greg's parents again.

The past eleven months, and the trial in particular, had been trying to the Smarts. Bill had developed a stutter after Greg's death, and both he and Judy were on medication. Mrs. Smart had even struggled to maintain her composure during jury selection. And at one point in the trial, she cut loose and yelled "Hey, bitch!" at Pam as the defendant walked by.

Now, however, the couple was ecstatic. "Oh, my god!"

Judy said joyously. "Greg's got a baby! Oh, my god! We've got a grandson! Part of him is still with us!"

Bill Smart contacted Captain Jackson, who set to work contacting authorities in Connecticut, trying to locate anyone who might know a Linda Avory who had recently had a baby.

The trial, of course, continued. That morning, Dan Pelletier and Jackson arrived at the court to hear the closing arguments.

Throughout the proceedings, the police had kept a low profile. Dan Pelletier had testified, but Twomey and Sisti never went after him very hard, and the detective's appearance on the witness stand had gone relatively smoothly.

Now, the two Derry cops were ushered into seats beyond the gallery, in front of the Smart family. Each of the lawyers, even from the defense, ambled over, cordially shook their hands, and made small talk.

All things considered, it was not surprising. This had not been a trial of rancor and bad blood. Sisti occasionally needed some quiet time to take off his game face after a few hours of attacking witnesses, but for the most part, all the players had been cooperative.

During the proceedings, of course, the prosecution and defense attorneys were at war, and on a number of occasions they had barked at one another. But for the most part, they were as they should have been—civil.

It might have been different if Pam had chosen one of the out-of-state, publicity-hungry lawyers who had sought to represent her. But Sisti, Twomey, Maggiotto, and Nicolosi were all going to be back in the New Hampshire courts on other days, long after Pamela Smart's case was over.

But as Paul Twomey stepped to the rostrum for his closing argument, the matter of Pam's innocence or guilt was not settled. Some people, in fact, believed that Pam stood a chance of being acquitted.

Twomey, wearing a gray tweed jacket, had more of the air of a college professor than of an attorney defending someone charged with first-degree murder.

He began with a slap at the media, which he said had been drawn to the trial as entertainment. "It hasn't been entertainment for Pamela Smart," Twomey said. "It hasn't been entertainment for Greg Smart's parents or his family.

TEACH ME TO KILL
TEACH ME TO KILL   277**TEACH ME TO KILL   277**

It hasn't been entertainment for Pamela's family.''

Next, he pointed out the uncertainties of some of the crime scene evidence—from the towel found near Greg's head to the forensic likelihood that an object had been placed between the gun and Greg's skull. ''Something happened there,'' Twomey said of the Smarts' condo on the night of May 1, 1990. ''They did something else. They tortured that man in some other way that they won't talk about. And they're liars about it. That's the point.''

No evidence indicated that Greg had been tortured. Afterward, Twomey told a reporter that he had meant mental torture.

But the jury, and Greg's mother, only heard what the attorney said. As Twomey continued speaking, Judy Smart began to cry and pumped her fists in front of her, not wanting to believe that her son had died in such a manner.

Twomey, meanwhile, set to discrediting the boys, pinning nicknames on each of them. Patrick ''Pete'' Randall was ''the Assassin.'' Vance Lattime, Jr., was ''Lattime the Liar.'' And William Flynn was ''Billy the Kid.''

''These boys, the three of them together, have not a shred of moral decency within 'em,'' he said. ''And you can see that when they took the stand and testified to god to tell the truth. That has absolutely no meaning to those boys. None whatsoever.''

Twomey brought up the inconsistencies in their stories. Flynn, for example, had testified that he went with Pam to withdraw money from a bank in Hampton to purchase the bullets to kill Greg. The state could find no record of the transaction.

The boys, too, failed to agree on when the bullets had been bought.

And how could any of them know prior to the killing how much insurance money Pam would receive? Even Metropolitan Life did not have that exact figure beforehand.

And, finally, Twomey tried to bolster Pam's explanation of the tapes, pointing to the anguish she must have experienced in the months after her husband was killed. ''Forget about everything else in the case,'' Twomey said. ''Just think, is there a reasonably possibility that that could cause somebody such trauma and such stress that they'd act in an irrational manner?''

Overall, it wasn't Twomey's greatest closing argument.

Perhaps it had something to do with his ill daughter keeping him awake most of the night before, but Twomey's summation was disorganized and filled with uncertain and mistaken references to the testimony. Maggiotto, in fact, objected on several occasions.

In all, Twomey spoke to the jury for about a half hour. "Do the right thing," he said before returning to his seat.

Usually, Paul Maggiotto wore his wedding suit when he gave his closing statements. The false fire alarm of Monday afternoon, however, had made it necessary for him to cross-examine Pam on into Tuesday. It was not exactly a crisis, but the prosecutor's suit rotation fell out of synch and he ended up wearing the wedding suit a day earlier.

That Wednesday morning, as a sort of compromise, Maggiotto elected to wear his wedding tie. He also had his wife, Amy Vorenberg, and her parents on hand for moral support.

Like Twomey, Maggiotto also had been awake most of the night. He had stayed in a small office at the courthouse, working on his summation until about 9:30. His wife, who worried about him driving on dangerous Route 101 when he was tired, urged him to come home to Concord. Once there, Maggiotto stayed hard at it until 4:30 in the morning. He slept less than an hour, then worked some more.

First, he wrote what he wanted to say in longhand, then jotted down key words on a separate sheet of paper. When it was time to give his closing statement, Maggiotto knew what he wanted to say, but left the specific language until the actual delivery. At least part of it would have to be a response to the defense's remarks.

Now the prosecutor was standing before the jury. As in his Brooklyn days, once he got started with his summation, Maggiotto wasted no time before he let everyone know what he thought about the defendant. When it was time to accuse, he accused. When it was time to point, he pointed. Repeatedly. And with great vigor.

The prosecutor seemed electric. He began with an appeal to the jury's common sense. This was not a confusing trial, he said. If the jury felt uncomfortable with any of the evidence or testimony, there was always someone to corroborate it. The only witness who challenged it was Pam Smart.

"Most of all," Maggiotto said, "if you apply that common sense to the defendant's preposterous testimony for the last few days, you'll also come and realize that that was nothing more than a calculated effort, a last-ditch calculated effort for *this* woman to somehow try and distract you from the inescapable conclusion of what those tapes show.

"And that inescapable conclusion is that the defendant was involved and guilty of these crimes."

Maggiotto concurred with Paul Twomey that Flynn, Randall, and Lattime were despicable human beings. The question, though, was whether they had told the truth on the witness stand.

Was Pam's teenage lover a liar? "I submit to you, ladies and gentlemen, if Bill Flynn was a liar, that was one of the greatest performances you've ever seen in modern times," Maggiotto said.

And if the boys *were* liars, he added, don't you think they would have done a better job of it? Wouldn't the boys have laid it on even thicker?

Then the prosecutor focused on Pam. This was not a murder for insurance money or furniture, he said. "But think about what a divorce would have done to this woman, who I submit to you was very, very concerned with her image and very, very concerned with her professional reputation . . .

"If she got a divorce, the affair is gonna come out. It's going to ruin her reputation professionally. She's gonna lose her job."

As he neared the end of his remarks, Maggiotto brought out huge placards bearing enlargements of Pam's conversation with Cecelia. Key remarks were highlighted in yellow. Later, Maggiotto would call it poetic justice, since Sisti had used the same tactic in getting the hung jury for Anthony Barnaby the previous summer.

Maggiotto went over a few of them. Then the prosecutor made sure he pointed out Pam's comment that a jury would believe her with her "professional reputation" and "a course that I teach" over JR any day.

"This woman has counted on from day one that if this case ever came to court, she could put herself on the stand with her background, with her intelligence, with her ability to answer questions, and pull one over on you, ladies and gentlemen," Maggiotto said.

"And I submit to you based on the evidence you've heard today, don't let her do it."

Much of what Maggiotto had to say was standard prosecutorial fare, but he articulated it so well and with such vigor that people were talking about it for days afterward.

The summations completed, Judge Gray charged the jury. That afternoon they began deliberations.

Linda Avory contacted the Smarts again after they got home from court. She said she was in Derry now, visiting friends. Fearful that Smart might somehow get off on the charges, she refused to come forward until Pam was convicted. In the meantime, though, she had dropped a letter and a photo of the baby, whom she had named Gregory, into the mail for the family.

On Thursday, deliberations continued throughout the day. Reporters, running out of people to interview, began interviewing each other for stories about the extensive media coverage. They had begun, in the words of the *Boston Herald*'s Peter Gelzinis, to eat their own flesh.

The day ended without a verdict. But with the media coverage intensifying, Judge Gray decided to finally grant one of Twomey's and Sisti's motions to sequester the jury, something that had not been done in the state since 1984.

In Derry, meanwhile, the police had put a tap on the Smarts' telephone in an effort to trace the call if Linda Avory contacted the family again.

That night, when the Smarts returned home, they found the letter Avory had mailed, along with a picture of the baby.

Despite Captain Jackson's previous insistence that they leave it sealed, so as not to destroy possible fingerprints, the Smarts could not resist.

Bill and Judy and some of Greg's friends used a pair of tweezers to open the envelope and read the letter. They also marveled over the beautiful child in the photo. The boy was five months old. And Bill Smart happily noted that he looked just like Greg.

The next day, March 22, at 12:55 P.M., a bailiff stepped into the hallway outside of courtroom one and announced, "OK, we have a verdict." The jury had been out for only thirteen hours.

The courtroom quickly filled. The Smarts, their relatives,

and friends took up the entire front row on the left. The Wojases settled into their seats on the right.

Then Pam, wearing a purple and black plaid jacket and black skirt, entered and sat down. Sisti was at her left and Twomey at her right.

The jury filed in. None looked at Pam. Then Judge Gray entered.

"Will the defendant please rise and face the jury," said Raymond Taylor, the clerk of the court.

Pam and her lawyers stood. Smart pressed her hands against the table in front of her.

"Madam forelady, will you please stand," Taylor said. "Has the jury reached a verdict on each of the three offenses charged?"

"Yes, we have," said the forelady.

One by one, Taylor asked for the verdict on each of the charges.

Conspiracy to commit murder?

Guilty.

The Smarts, their entire row holding hands, cut loose with full-hearted cheers that they tried in vain to restrain.

Accomplice to first-degree murder?

Guilty.

It was as if an electric current ran through Greg's family. Again they fought to keep their cheers from ripping wide open.

Tampering with a witness?

Guilty.

Again, the cheers. All of Greg's family and friends were smiling, but their eyes were moist as well.

Mark Sisti asked that the jury be polled. "Guilty" was pronounced thirty-six additional times.

Judge Gray thanked the jurors and sent them back to the deliberation room.

Then, he set to his duty of sentencing Pam on the accomplice to first-degree murder charge. In accordance with New Hampshire law, he was required to send her to prison for the rest of her life with no chance of parole.

"Mrs. Smart," Judge Gray said evenly, "you're in custody of the sheriff. This hearing is adjourned."

Pam, whose face revealed nothing at the moment that the verdicts were announced, was escorted to the clerk of the court's office to wait until the reporters and everyone else cleared out before being transported back to prison.

She sat down, looking stunned.

"I can't believe Billy," she said to Paul Twomey. "First he took Greg's life. Now he's taking mine."

Epilogue

A week after the verdict, the Derry police successfully traced a phone call from Linda Avory to the Smarts. The call had originated in Derry.

Captain Jackson and Dan Pelletier went to the house. The woman who lived there denied knowing anything about the call, even though a photograph sitting on the television set was a larger version of the one the Smarts had received.

The woman seemed to remember bringing a smaller copy of the photo to a bingo game not long ago. And—oh, yes—it had been stolen.

It took a while, but finally the woman admitted to creating the name Linda Avory and calling the Smarts. She explained that she had been watching the trial on television for hours on end and became captivated by it.

Afraid that Pam would be acquitted, she had called Diane Nicolosi with the fake story about the incriminating letter. She had even planned to write one, but changed her mind. And then, thinking about the Smarts' pain over the loss of Greg, she made up the story about the baby. "I guess she thought she could help Billy and me by saying that there was still something left of Greg," said Judy Smart.

Not long after the Derry police solved the mystery of Linda Avory, the New Hampshire attorney general's office dropped the other charges against Pam, including the one that said she tried to hire a hit man to kill Cecelia Pierce. "To pursue these charges in Hillsborough County would serve no useful purpose at this time," said John Arnold, the state's attorney general, in a press release.

Had the matter ever gone to trial, most likely the first breeze that came through the courthouse window would have toppled the state's case. It did not help that the charges were based entirely on the testimony of inmates at the Goffstown prison.

* * *

Pamela Smart would remain in the news around New England for months after her trial. In May during her sentencing hearing on the conspiracy to commit murder and witness tampering charges, Pam upstaged her father-in-law, who was taunting her in his victim-impact statement. She jumped up and yelled, "Your honor, I can't handle this! I don't have to listen to this anymore!" Her mother stood up as well and shouted at Greg's father, "Where does your vengeance end?"

When the theatrics were over, Judge Gray calmly sentenced Pam to maximum sentences of 7½ to 15 years on her conviction for conspiracy and 3½ to 7 years on the witness tampering charges. Already serving life without parole, Pam's additional sentences are concurrent.

Not long after, J. Albert Johnson, a Boston defense lawyer with an ear for a sound bite and an eye for the cameras, replaced Twomey and Sisti as Pam's attorney. Johnson would come to file four motions with the Rockingham County Superior Court seeking a new trial. Judge Gray rejected each of them, including one that challenged the imagination by comparing Smart's trial to that of the infamous Dr. Sam Sheppard. The 1954 conviction of Sheppard, a Cleveland, Ohio area osteopath, was overturned by a landmark U.S. Supreme Court ruling restraining the media's role in trial coverage.

The next stage for Pam is the New Hampshire Supreme Court, which will probably not consider her appeal until well into 1992.

Pam and her family, in the meantime, created a sporadically published *FRIENDS of Pamela Smart Newsletter*, that is mailed to her supposed legion of supporters. And, of course, to the media. Printed on high-quality paper, the newsletter often includes a missive from Pam. "I know that the injustice I suffer in some way imprisons all of you," she wrote in one.

But the ultimate peculiarity came during the summer of 1991, when Pam's parents threw a ten-dollar-a-head Friends of Pamela Smart Cookout. Some 300 people showed up. A singer warbled an original tune called "Pamela's Song." Someone stuck a "Pame is Innocent" button on the collar of Halen, Smart's dog. And Pam even called from prison and thanked her supporters over the loudspeaker.

* * *

Guilt or innocence, of course, had been decided by the jury. When all the television trucks and reporters had left the courthouse in Exeter, only one *real* question remained: Why?

The reasons behind the killing of a promising life insurance salesman named Gregory Smart have been debated again and again.

Some have said that he was killed purely out of selfishness, that $140,000 in insurance money and a condominium full of furniture were incentive enough for Pam to instruct Billy Flynn to commit murder. Others wondered if Greg, less than a model husband, went too far in his treatment of Pam. Some have said that she truly wanted Flynn to replace Greg. And, Paul Maggiotto, of course, told the jury that Pam was afraid the affair with Billy Flynn would become public knowledge and so, rather than divorce Greg, she had him murdered.

Perhaps every answer has a grain of the truth.

Pamela Smart, although she did see a psychiatrist briefly in the summer of 1990, appears not to have had a thorough psychological evaluation. Perhaps even years of analysis would be needed before coming to a determination of the roots of her behavior. As such, any examination of the deeper reasons for her actions is speculative.

Still, many of her personality traits and actions clearly resemble those seen in individuals commonly known as psychopaths or sociopaths.

Although people tend to think of sociopaths as mass murderers, more often they move through society without physically harming others. Traits of the sociopath can be found in business, for example, where certain individuals claw their way to the top—or toward whatever goal they seek— without a thought about who is crushed in their path. The problem is a character disorder, not a mental one.

"There are probably millions of sociopaths," said Jack Levin, a professor of sociology at Northeastern University and coauthor with James Alan Fox of the 1985 book *Mass Murder, America's Growing Menace*. "Most of them would never kill anyone. Not as long as they get what they want. You can see this in the case of Pam Smart and Charles Stuart.

"They lead ordinary lives and they love their family

members, but not necessarily for who they are but for what they'll do for the sociopath. So long as things go well and the people around them are not perceived as obstacles, then everyone is safe.

"But at that time when a sociopath's goals become unrealistic or very lofty and people are seen as in the way, then those people must go."

Fox, who teaches in the criminal justice department at Northeastern, explains that one could live with a sociopath for years before seeing their true nature revealed. "In a marriage, the sociopath can appear to be very loving," he said. "But they only love you for what you can do for them. There is no sense of altruism. And if the spouse is no longer necessary, he or she becomes expendable."

The vast majority of sociopaths, particularly those who kill, are men. And when women are involved in murders, they tend not to do so for the sake of killing in itself. More often, they are involved in murder out of what they regard as self-defense—as in the case of battered wives—or avarice.

A variety of characteristics are common to sociopaths. They are bright, often more intelligent than average, and present an image of outward warmth. They also have an ability to maintain their composure without sinking into depression or breaking into tears no matter what the stress may be.

In his 1986 book *Criminal Behavior, A Psychosocial Approach*, author Curt Bartol wrote that such individuals often appear to be affectionate and can mimic the range of emotions, but in reality "true loyalty, warmth, and compassion are foreign to them."

Levin explained that sociopaths are masters of appearances. "For them, life is a stage," he said. "Every day they play a character. And they don't care about the rules that we live by, but they know the rules and they manipulate the rules and they can use those rules against us.

"The sociopath knows exactly what other people are feeling even though he or she doesn't feel those things."

Added Fox: "Sociopaths are very needy people. Throughout their entire lives they've been practicing at manipulation, exploitation, to get what they need. That's the way they survive."

At the same time, such individuals are invariably egocentric. They crave attention, which can be manifested in sexual promiscuity among other types of behavior. ''There's a kind of sociopath called the narcissistic type, who are very much taken with themselves, who need to be the center of attention,'' said Fox. ''They get their sense of self-worth not by looking at one's self but by how others see them.

''And they like attention whether it's positive or negative. Someone like Pam Smart must very much enjoy the attention she's getting with things like the picnic. Her trial's over but not forgotten and she's not forgotten. They like to be in the limelight. And her limelight continues.''

Pam, like many sociopaths, appears to have no remorse for her role in the death of her husband. For those who have the character disorder, there is no concern for anyone but themselves. As such, neither a husband with a bullet in his skull nor the pain inflicted on countless friends and families, affects them.

Usually, sociopaths will rationalize their behavior. Consider as a possibility, Pam's comments to Cecelia that the teenage boys made their own decision to kill Greg and that it wasn't *her* fault.

''It seems to be very easy for sociopaths to justify killing when they direct the action and don't physically participate in it,'' said Levin. ''If they can hire someone else to do the dirty work, if they can get impressionable young boys to carry out the killing in the name of love, if they can find a group of followers who want to feel special, they don't feel responsible.

''*They* didn't directly kill anyone. Isn't there free will? They reason this out so beautifully. They weren't directing puppets, they say. Why should they be implicated in a crime that was committed by someone else? I think they really do not relate the cause and effect relationship between the orders that they give and the commission of the crime by others.''

Levin is not an unbiased in this matter. Had JR Lattime gone to trial, Levin was prepared to testify for the defense to perhaps explain traits that he has identified on the increase among teenagers today.

Levin said he believes there is a category of the sociopathic personality that he calls ''temporary sociopaths.'' In short, teenagers will often behave seemingly without conscience at times, but change as they grow older.

The boys, of course, are far from innocent. Few excuse their behavior or sympathize with their having to spend their young adulthood behind bars.

At the same time, most people agree that the boys who killed on the night of May 1 most likely would never have murdered anyone had Billy Flynn never met up with one Pamela Smart.

"That's the sad thing," said Levin. "*That's* why Pam Smart is so guilty. She destroyed her husband's life, yes. But she also destroyed the lives of these teenage boys, who *might* have made it through those turbulent adolescent years into adulthood without having to spend much of their lives in prison."

About the Author

STEPHEN SAWICKI is a Boston-based writer. His work has appeared in *People*, *Time*, and a variety of national and regional publications. He holds degrees from Ohio Wesleyan University and Stanford University.

Compelling True Crime Thrillers
From Avon Books

BADGE OF BETRAYAL
by Joe Cantlupe and Lisa Petrillo

76009-6/$4.99 US/$5.99 Can

THE BLUEGRASS CONSPIRACY
by Sally Denton

71441-8/$4.95 US/$5.95 Can

A KILLING IN THE FAMILY:
A TRUE STORY OF
LOVE, LIES AND MURDER
by Stephen Singular with Tim and Danielle Hill

76413-X/$4.95 US/$5.95 Can

LOSS OF INNOCENCE:
A TRUE STORY OF JUVENILE MURDER
by Eric J. Adams   75987-X/$4.95 US/$5.95 Can

RUBOUTS: MOB MURDERS IN AMERICA
by Richard Monaco and Lionel Bascom

75938-1/$4.50 US/$5.50 Can